IRELAND'S
WAR OF INDEPENDENCE
1919-21
The IRA's Guerrilla Campaign
Lorcan Collins

THE O'BRIEN PRESS
DUBLIN

First published 2019 by
The O'Brien Press Ltd,
12 Terenure Road East, Rathgar, Dublin 6, D06 HD27, Ireland.
Tel: +353 1 4923333; Fax: +353 1 4922777
E-mail: books@obrien.ie. Website: www.obrien.ie
The O'Brien Press is a member of Publishing Ireland.

ISBN: 978-1-84717-950-0

8 7 6 5 4 3 2 1
23 22 21 20 19

Printed and bound in Poland by Białostockie Zakłady Graficzne S.A.
The paper used in this book is produced using pulp from managed forests.

Picture Credits
Front cover photograph: Irish Military Archives
Aislinn Delaney: page 2; Ruan O'Donnell: page 26; Lorcan Collins: pages 31, 36 and
37; Irish Military Archives: pages 41, 56, 76, 170, 171, 207 and 235; Kilmainham Gaol
Museum: pages 44, 45, 48, 95, 126, 128 (both), 141, 142, 190, 201, 238 and 249; National
Library of Ireland: pages 70, 84, 91, 98, 99, 114, 134, 153, 180–1, 226–7, 229 (bottom) and
245; Imperial War Museum: pages 144, 145, 196 and 219; Michael Ward: page 229 (top).

Published in

DUBLIN
UNESCO
City of Literature

Lorcan Collins was born and raised in Dublin. He founded
the 1916 Walking Tour in 1996 (see 1916rising.com). He
is co-author of *The Easter Rising: A Guide to Dublin in 1916*
(O'Brien Press, 2000) and author of the biography, *James
Connolly* (O'Brien Press, 2012). He was co-editor of the
16 Lives series of books and is author of *1916: The Rising
Handbook* (O'Brien Press, 2016).

DEDICATION

For my children, Fionn and Lily May.

ACKNOWLEDGEMENTS

Special thanks to Trish Darcy for affording me the time to write, and for her constant love and motivation. My two children missed out on a good few summer days when I should have been with them instead of researching, so thanks to Fionn and Lily May for their patience and support. The following people are deserving of special gratitude: Emer Ryan for her brilliant editorial skills and suggestions, which really shaped the book. For their forbearance, Michael O'Brien, Ivan O'Brien, Eoin O'Brien, Íde Ní Laoghaire, Susan Houlden and all at O'Brien Press, including Emma, Nicola, Kunak, Helen, Bex, Elena, Aoife, Brenda, Sarah, Fionnuala, Laura, Ruth and Ruth. Dr Conor McNamara was particularly helpful and offered many great suggestions and much encouragement, and gave me access to information that I would not otherwise have found. Pádraig Óg Ó Ruairc was kind enough to read the draft and gave me guidance when I needed it most. Thanks to Liz Gillis for her speedy replies and expertise. Liam Cowley was particularly helpful, too. For encouragement and knowledge: Dr John Gibney, Dr Conor Kostick, Dr Ruan O'Donnell, Stew Reddin, Gerry Shannon, Niall Bracken, Paul O'Brien, Jim Langton, Ronnie Daly, Ruairí O'Donnell, and Cuan Ó Seireadáin. Donal Fallon and Las Fallon were both helpful and kind. Thanks to Joe Connell and Professor Mary McCay in the US. Special thanks to Glenn Dunne and Berni Metcalfe at the National Library of Ireland. Thanks to Captain Daniel Ayiotis, Hugh Beckett, Lisa Dolan, Noelle Grothier, Commandant Stephen MacEoin, Adrian Short, Linda Hickey, Sergeant Ned Kelly, Corporal Kevin Byrne, CQMS Tom Mitchell, Commandant Claire Mortimer and all at the Bureau of Military Archives. Also to all at Kilmainham Gaol, especially Aoife Torpey and Niall Bergin.

For all their constant encouragement, thanks to Mamo and Dado, Orla, Mark, Diarmuid, Eibhlis, Carmel, John, Pat, Kathleen, Barry, Maireaid, Eoin, Bernie, Aoife, Oisín, Ferdia, Roisín, Nora, Gerry, Rory, Colin, Fiona, Pedro, Denise, Liam, Ciara, Dave, Daithí, Gary, Davorka, Peter, Alex, Ci, Jack, Conor, Ruth, Rita O'Hare, Gerry Adams, Nikki Gavin, Cecelia and Boppo. Always great supporters of the 1916 Walking Tour: John Donoghue, James Donoghue, Anna, Alan, JF, Josh, Ken, Fran, Ciara, Joey, Shane, Matt and all the great people at the International Bar. Thanks to Fionntan and all the people of the Market in Belfast. To Ann, Mervyn and everyone in Glasnevin Cemetery and Museum. To Matthew at the National Botanic Gardens and all the Dublin Northside attractions. To all the lads in the GPO and at Fáilte Ireland on Suffolk Street, thanks for the constant support. Best to all the great women of Moore Street. Respect to all the men and women who fought and who fight for a better Ireland. Finally, Shane Mac Thomáis, Shane Kenna and Tom Stokes, gone but not forgotten.

CONTENTS

Introduction

This book is an overview of the period in Ireland known as the War of Independence, 1919–21. It is not a complete encyclopaedia of every battle or every person who fought or died in that conflict, but concentrates mainly on the actions that the Irish Republican Army (IRA) undertook in the guerrilla campaign against British rule in Ireland. There are some accounts within that are disturbing but there are also stories of humanity, such as that of the British soldiers who helped three IRA men escape from prison, or the members of the British Army who mutinied in India when they heard about the reprisals being carried out by the Black and Tans in Ireland.

As a nation, we are, I believe, indebted to the men and women who fought for Irish freedom. We should never forget the powerful strength of the Mayor of Cork, Terence MacSwiney, who endured a hunger strike to the death, or the composure of medical student Kevin Barry who was only eighteen years of age when he was hanged. These individuals cared nothing for material wealth or possessions and exchanged their lives for the emancipation of their fellow Irishmen and Irishwomen. They fought for an Irish Republic and were Republicans. They established the first Dáil, an Irish parliament, at a time when many of the elected representatives were in British jails. They endured beatings, shootings and torture. Their families suffered in equal measure, living in fear of British raids that saw their homes destroyed and business premises burned down.

The story of the War of Independence does not have a happy ending. The Government of Ireland Act, 1920, also known as the Fourth Home

Rule Bill, had established two separate Home Rule institutions on the island of Ireland, namely Southern Ireland and Northern Ireland. According to the terms of the Anglo-Irish Treaty of 1921, which brought the War of Independence to an end, Ireland was divided into two separate states, the twenty-six counties of a newly formed Irish Free State to the south, which was set up as a dominion of the British Commonwealth, and the six Ulster counties of Antrim, Armagh, Down, Fermanagh, Derry and Tyrone to the north. Nationalists of what came to be known as the Six Counties were left to fend for themselves in an Orange-dominated province ruled from Stormont, a Protestant Parliament for a Protestant State.

THE IRISH FREE STATE

The Irish Free State had a difficult start. The revolutionary Dáil Government and Provisional Government were replaced by an Executive Council, and a Governor-General was appointed as a representative of the King. The legislature, called the Oireachtas, comprised a lower house, Dáil Eireann, and an upper house, Seanad Éireann. Members were required to take an oath of allegiance, which declared fidelity to the British King, and this was anathema to opponents of the Treaty. A devastating civil war followed, between the newly established National Army, representing those who supported the Treaty, and the anti-Treaty IRA, who refused to recognise the new Free State and wished to continue the fight for the Republic.

Following the civil war, which was won by the National Army, the anti-Treaty political party, Sinn Féin, refused to take its seats in the Dáil. Pro-Treaty members formed Cumann na nGaedheal, a forerunner of today's Fine Gael party, and they ruled until 1932. In 1926, Éamon de Valera resigned from Sinn Féin and founded Fianna Fáil, which entered the Dáil following the 1927 general election and went on to become the governing party after the general election of 1932.

In 1931, the Statute of Westminster saw Britain relinquishing its authority to legislate for its dominions, including the Irish Free State. In 1937, under a Fianna Fáil government, the citizens of the Irish Free State voted in a referendum for an entirely new Constitution of Ireland, which saw the state taking the name 'Éire' (Ireland), and a new office of President replacing that of the Governor-General. The state was officially declared a republic in 1949. The 1937 constitution claimed jurisdiction over all of Ireland, while recognising in Articles 2 and 3 that legislation would not apply in the Six Counties (Northern Ireland). These articles were reworded following the Good Friday Agreement of 1998 to remove the claim of jurisdiction over the whole island of Ireland, replacing it with the words: 'a united Ireland shall be brought about only by peaceful means with the consent of a majority of the people, democratically expressed, in both jurisdictions in the island'.

Throughout the early twentieth century, the twenty-six-county state was dominated by an ultra-Catholic insular élite who paid homage to the 1916 Proclamation of the Republic, but avoided actuating ideals enshrined in that document, such as guaranteeing 'religious and civil liberty, equal rights and equal opportunities to all its citizens' and 'cherishing all the children of the nation equally'.

A hundred years on, the people of the island of Ireland seem to be more appreciative of the past and some are striving to make Ireland 'a beacon-light to the oppressed of every land', as imagined by socialist and republican leader James Connolly in 1897. The hundreds of thousands of people who celebrated the centenary of the 1916 Rising with pride and joy are the same people who will appreciate the story of the Irish Republicans who battled against all odds in the next phase of the fight for Irish freedom, between 1919 and 1921.

THE IRA

The Irish Republican Army is better known by the acronym IRA. The term IRA was first used when the Irish-American Fenian Brotherhood invaded Canada on three successive occasions in the 1860s, fighting under a banner with the letters IRA written on it. The Fenians in the United States also wore a tunic with brass buttons that had IRA engraved on them. In the 1880s during a bombing campaign in Britain, the Fenians regularly left a 'calling card' in bombs, a piece of metal with the message IRA emblazoned upon it.

On 24 April 1916, at the start of the Easter Rising, when the Proclamation was read by Patrick Pearse outside the General Post Office, the Irish Volunteers (Óglaigh na hÉireann), the Irish Citizen Army, Cumann na mBan (Women's Council) and the Fianna Éireann (Warriors of Ireland) all stood under the banner of the Army of the Irish Republic. For the twentieth century, this is the birth of the IRA.

After the Rising, members of the Irish Volunteers who were imprisoned often signed IRA after their names in autograph books passed amongst their fellow internees. However, when referring to themselves, members might also use the term 'Volunteers'. So sometimes when talking about a certain battle they might say either 'The Volunteers waited on the road' or 'The IRA waited on the road.'

STRUCTURE

At the beginning of the War of Independence in 1919, the IRA was made up of local Irish Volunteer companies based around parishes, which were collected into battalions over larger areas, and these in turn came under the control of county brigades. In May 1921, the IRA was restructured and the Volunteers in Ireland were divided into sixteen divisions. There were three southern divisions, called First Southern, Second Southern and Third Southern. There were four western divisions, five northern divisions, three eastern divisions and a midlands division.

Each division was split into brigades. For instance, the East Limerick Brigade was in the Second Southern Division. In Ireland there were sixty-seven brigades in July 1921. Brigades were subdivided into battalions, often named after the area they covered. For example, the Fourth (Kilmallock) Battalion, East Limerick Brigade was in the Second Southern Division.

Battalions were further made up of companies, often named after the parish area from which they drew members. There might be ten companies in a battalion, each company named after a letter of the alphabet and the local parish. For example, A Company, Dungloe, First Battalion, First Northern Division.

Companies usually had a captain and a first lieutenant and a second lieutenant. The company captain was called the Officer Commanding or O/C. For instance, Denis Mulchinock was O/C Banteer Company, Fourth Battalion, Cork IV Brigade. First Southern Division.

On 11 July 1921, the IRA had a nominal strength of 115,000. There was a Scottish Brigade with 2,500 IRA members. Liverpool had 398 IRA members and London a much smaller membership of eighty-three, followed by Manchester with fifty-one. There were also twenty-four IRA Volunteers in the United States at the time.

Although nearly 70,000 service medals were issued to IRA veterans in 1942, only 15,000 of them had a 'comrac' bar. *Comhrac* (modern spelling) is an Irish word for 'fight' or 'struggle' and these medals were intended for those members of the IRA who had engaged the British in a battle.

The IRA was very well structured along the lines of an established army, but at times General Head-Quarters (GHQ), which was in Dublin, found it difficult to control the organisation; it was, after all, an underground army, and it was usually up to local IRA officers to decide upon their individual engagements. However, as a guerrilla army, the IRA was very effective and efficient considering it took on one of the strongest empires in the world at the time.

Administrators in Dublin Castle

Ireland was administered by the following people in Dublin Castle:

Lord Lieutenant

17 February 1915	Ivor Guest, First Viscount Wimborne, known as Lord Wimborne
9 May 1918	John Denton Pinkstone French, First Earl of Ypres, known as Viscount French and Lord French
27 April 1921	Edmund Bernard FitzAlan-Howard, First Viscount FitzAlan of Derwent, known as Lord Edmund Talbot

Chief Secretary to the Lord Lieutenant

5 May 1918	Edward Shortt
10 January 1919	(James) Ian Stewart Macpherson, First Baron Strathcarron, known as Lord Strathcarron
2 April 1920 (until 19 October 1922)	Hamar Greenwood, First Viscount Greenwood, known as Sir Hamar Greenwood

Under-Secretary to the Lord Lieutenant

1918	James Macmahon (jointly with Sir John Anderson from May 1920)

1920   John Anderson, First Viscount Waverley,
                            known as Sir John Anderson (jointly with
                            Macmahon from May 1920)

Inspector General of the Royal Irish Constabulary (RIC)

1 August 1916   Brigadier General Sir Joseph Aloysius Byrne

11 March 1920   Sir Thomas James Smith

15 May 1920   Lieutenant General Sir Henry Hugh Tudor
                            (initially appointed as Police Advisor and
                            took over from Thomas Smith in November
                            1920)

Royal Irish Constabulary Special Reserve (Black and Tans)

March 1920   Under the control of the RIC Inspector
                            General

Auxiliary Division of the Royal Irish Constabulary (Auxiliaries)

3 August 1920   Frank Percy Crozier

17 February 1921   Edward Allan Wood

British Army Commander-in-Chief, Ireland

1916–1918   General Sir Bryan Thomas Mahon

1918–1920   Lieutenant General Sir Frederick Charles Shaw

April 1920   General Sir Cecil Frederick Nevil Macready

Dublin Castle Intelligence

May 1920   Brigadier General Sir Ormonde de l'Épée
                            Winter, also known as Colonel Ormonde
                            Winter as his Brigadier General rank was
                            temporary

Ulster Special Constabulary (A, B and C Specials)

November 1920	Lieutenant Colonel Sir Charles George Wickham was the commander but the force was technically under Sir Henry Hugh Tudor as Inspector General of the RIC

Timeline of the War of Independence

1916

24 April	Easter Rising.
29 April	Patrick Pearse surrenders to British.
1 May	First batch of prisoners deported to British prisons.
3–12 May	Fourteen men executed in Kilmainham Gaol and one in Cork Detention Barracks.
11 June	First Irish prisoners interned in Frongoch prisoner-of-war camp, North-West Wales.
3 August	Roger Casement hanged in Pentonville Prison.
7 December	David Lloyd George replaces Herbert Henry Asquith as British Prime Minister.
23 December	Michael Collins and IRA prisoners released from Frongoch.

1917

3 February	Count (George) Plunkett, father of Joseph Plunkett, executed signatory of Proclamation, elected in North Roscommon as an independent.
19 February	Michael Collins becomes Secretary of Irish National Aid and Volunteer Dependants' Fund, distributing welfare to prisoners and families.
9 May	Joe McGuinness elected for Sinn Féin in South Longford.
11 July	Éamon de Valera, Commandant of the Third Battalion during the Rising, elected in East Clare for Sinn Féin.

25 September	Thomas Ashe, Fifth Battalion Commandant during the Easter Rising, dies after being force-fed during his hunger strike.
25 October	Éamon de Valera elected President of Sinn Féin.
26 October	Éamon de Valera elected President of the Irish Volunteers.

1918

23–24 April	General strike against conscription in Ireland.
17 May	British arrest 150 Sinn Féin activists for alleged 'German Plot'.
11 November	War in Europe ends with defeat of Germany.
14 December	General Election in Britain and Ireland.
28 December	General Election votes counted. David Lloyd George re-elected Prime Minister and Sinn Féin wins a landslide victory in Ireland.

1919

21 January	First meeting of Dáil Éireann (Assembly of Ireland) in Dublin's Mansion House. Dáil declares Irish independence. First shots of War of Independence fired at Soloheadbeg in Tipperary, killing two members of the Royal Irish Constabulary (RIC) guarding a shipment of gelignite.
31 January	*An tÓglach*, the Volunteers' publication, states that soldiers and policemen are to be treated as members of an invading army.
3 February	Harry Boland and Michael Collins assist in the escape of Éamon de Valera from Lincoln Jail. Seán McGarry and Seán Milroy also escape.
19 March	Raid carried out on Collinstown Aerodrome by IRA members who capture seventy-five rifles and 4,000 rounds.

March	Last batch of 1916 prisoners released.
1 April	Éamon de Valera elected President of Dáil Éireann. At this, the second meeting of the First Dáil, de Valera appoints the government.
10 April	Dáil Éireann votes to boycott RIC.
15–27 April	The 'Limerick soviet' prints its own money and publishes its own newspapers in defiance of Limerick's being designated a 'Special Military Area'.
13 May	Rescue of Seán Hogan at Knocklong.
11 June	Éamon de Valera lands in US to raise money and awareness of events in Ireland.
30 July	Shooting of Detective Sergeant Patrick 'the Dog' Smyth in Drumcondra, Dublin.
20 August	IRA swears allegiance to Dáil Éireann.
7 September	Liam Lynch disarms British soldiers in the town of Fermoy, Cork.
8 September	First reprisals as British burn and loot Fermoy.
10 September	British declare Dáil illegal.
12 September	Shooting of Detective Daniel Hoey in Dublin.
19 September	The Squad 'officially' founded by Michael Collins.
30 November	Shooting of Detective John Barton in Dublin.
19 December	Attempted assassination of Lord French at Ashtown, Dublin. IRA Volunteer Martin Savage killed.

1920

15 January	Local Government elections.
21 January	The Squad shoots Detective Inspector W.C. Forbes Redmond, the new Assistant Commissioner of the Dublin Metropolitan Police (DMP).
14 February	IRA members capture Ballytrain RIC Barracks in Monaghan.

18 February	Spy Timothy Quinlisk shot dead by IRA in Cork.
2 March	The Squad shoots spy John Charles Byrnes ('Jack Jameson') dead in Dublin.
20 March	Tomás MacCurtain, Lord Mayor of Cork, shot dead by masked RIC members.
24 March	The Squad shoots spy Fergus Brian Molloy dead.
25 March	New police recruits arrive in Ireland. Known as 'Black and Tans' because of the their uniform.
26 March	The Squad shoots magistrate Alan Bell (ex RIC) dead.
12 April	New Chief Secretary for Ireland, Hamar Greenwood, appointed
14 April	The Squad shoots Detective Constable Henry Kells dead.
20 April	The Squad shoots Detective Constable Laurence Dalton dead.
27 April	IRA attacks Ballylanders RIC Barracks.
27 May	IRA attacks Kilmallock RIC Barracks.
1 June	King's Inns raid in Dublin. IRA seizes weapons from British Army.
4 June	IRA order to boycott RIC members and their immediate families.
5 June	IRA ambush on British Army at Milebush, near Midleton, Cork.
15 June	The Squad shoots RIC District Inspector Captain Percival Lea-Wilson dead in Gorey, County Wexford.
17 June	Listowel Mutiny after Lieutenant Colonel Gerald Brice Smyth speech to RIC in Kerry.
26 June	Brigadier General Lucas captured by IRA.
27 June	Connaught Rangers mutiny in India. Torture of IRA men Tom Hales and Patrick Harte in Cork.
17 July	Lieutenant Colonel Gerald Brice Smyth shot dead in Cork by IRA.

21 July	Belfast 'pogrom' begins when Loyalists attack Catholic workers in shipyards.
3 August	Frank Crozier assumes command of the new special police, the Auxiliary Division of the RIC, consisting of former British Army officers.
9 August	The Restoration of Order in Ireland Act becomes law. ROIA replaces criminal courts with courts martial and coroner's inquests with military courts of inquiry, and allows for Local Government money to be withheld as punishment.
22 August	Detective Inspector Oswald Ross Swanzy shot dead by Cork IRA.
12 September	Raid on Third Tipperary IRA Brigade council meeting, later known as the 'Blackcastle Races'.
20 September	Black and Tans sack Balbriggan town in north Dublin.
22 September	IRA's Mid-Clare Brigade ambushes an RIC lorry at Rineen, killing six officers.
28 September	IRA captures British Army Barracks in Mallow, County Cork.
4 October	IRA flying columns organised.
12 October	Dan Breen and Seán Treacy escape from safe house, 'Fernside' in Drumcondra, Dublin, during police raid.
14 October	Seán Treacy shot dead on Talbot Street, Dublin.
17 October	Michael Fitzgerald dies in jail after sixty-seven days on hunger strike.
25 October	Sinn Féin Lord Mayor of Cork Terence MacSwiney dies on hunger strike in Brixton Prison after seventy-four days. Joseph Murphy dies in Cork Gaol after seventy-nine days on hunger strike.
1 November	Kevin Barry hanged in Mountjoy Jail. Ulster Special Constabulary including 'B Specials' founded.

1–9 November Siege of Tralee, County Kerry, by Black and Tans.

2 November IRA defends Ballinalee, County Longford, against Black and Tans.

21 November Bloody Sunday. Fourteen British agents shot dead in IRA operation in Dublin. In retaliation, British forces open fire in Croke Park, killing eleven people and wounding at least sixty, three of whom die later. Three IRA suspects — Dick McKee, Peadar Clancy and Conor Clune — beaten and killed in Dublin Castle.

28 November Tom Barry leads ambush at Kilmichael in west Cork, in which seventeen Auxiliaries and three IRA men die.

10 December Martial law declared in Tipperary, Cork, Limerick and Kerry.

11 December Burning of Cork by Auxiliaries, Black and Tans and British soldiers.

23 December Government of Ireland Act replaces Home Rule Act. This provides for two separate parliaments, one for 'Northern Ireland' and one for 'Southern Ireland'. Éamon de Valera returns from the United States.

26 December IRA dance at Bruff, County Limerick, attacked by British soldiers, Auxiliaries and Black and Tans. Five Volunteers killed.

1921

5 January Martial law extended to Clare, Waterford, Kilkenny and Wexford.

28 January British troops forewarned of ambush plans launch attack on IRA at Dripsey village, near Ballincollig, County Cork.

1 February Cornelius Murphy executed by British firing squad.

3 February IRA ambush on RIC patrol at Dromkeen in County Limerick.

14 February Ernie O'Malley, Frank Teeling and Simon Donnelly escape from Kilmainham Gaol.

15 February	British troops forewarned of ambush plans launch attack on IRA at Mourne Abbey near Mallow, County Cork, killing three men and mortally wounding another. IRA ambush on train carrying British troops at Upton, County Cork. Three Volunteers and six civilian passengers killed.
19 February	General Crozier resigns over British atrocities.
20 February	Twelve Volunteers killed during ambush by British troops on a farmhouse at Clonmult, near Midleton, County Cork.
28 February	Seán Allen, Thomas O'Brien, Daniel O'Callaghan, John Lyons, Timothy McCarthy and Patrick Mahoney executed by British firing squad. Six British soldiers shot in Cork city as a reprisal.
7 March	Mayor of Limerick George Clancy shot dead by Auxiliaries.
14 March	Thomas Whelan, Patrick Moran, Patrick Doyle, Bernard Ryan, Frank Flood and Thomas Bryan hanged in Mountjoy Jail.
19 March	British troops encircle IRA during ambush at Crossbarry, County Cork. Three IRA Volunteers and ten British troops killed.
25 April	Thomas Traynor hanged in Mountjoy Jail.
28 April	Maurice Moore, Patrick O'Sullivan, Patrick Ronayne and Thomas Mulcahy executed by firing squad at British Army (now Collins) Barracks, Cork.
2 May	Patrick Casey executed by firing squad at British Army (now Collins) Barracks, Cork.
16 May	Daniel O'Brien executed by firing squad at British Army (now Collins) Barracks, Cork.
22 May	General Election in Ireland for Northern House of Commons and Southern House of Commons. Sinn Féin treats elections as being for Dáil Éireann.

25 May	Custom House in Dublin occupied and then burnt by the IRA.
4 June	Thomas Keane executed by firing squad in Limerick Prison.
7 June	Edmond Foley and Patrick Maher hanged in Mountjoy Jail.
22 June	King George V opens the Northern Ireland Parliament.
8 July	Éamon de Valera meets General Sir Nevil Macready in Mansion House, Dublin to discuss a truce.
11 July	Truce comes into force.
14 September	Five plenipotentiaries appointed by Dáil Éireann to go to London: Arthur Griffith, Michael Collins, Robert Barton, Éamonn Duggan and George Gavan Duffy.
6 December	Anglo-Irish Treaty signed by five plenipotentiaries and David Lloyd George, Lord Birkenhead (F.E. Smith), Austen Chamberlain, Winston Churchill, Sir Laming Worthington-Evans, Sir Gordon Hewart and Sir Hamar Greenwood.

1922

7 January	Dáil Éireann votes on Anglo-Irish Treaty. Result is sixty-four for and fifty-seven against. Three TDs abstain.
10 January	De Valera leaves Dáil with his supporters while remaining Dáil delegates elect Arthur Griffith as President. De Valera and supporters then return to Dáil.
14 January	Provisional Government of Irish Free State formed by pro-Treaty Dáil members. Michael Collins, Chairman of Executive Committee; Richard Mulcahy in charge of Defence; Eoin O'Duffy, Chief of Staff of the National Army.
16 January	British hand over Dublin Castle to Provisional Government of Irish Free State.
31 January	Beggars Bush Barracks handed over to Free State National Army. Civil Authorities (Special Powers) Act (Northern Ireland), 1922.

21 February	Recruitment begins for the Free State Civic Guard, newly founded as the police force to replace the RIC.
March	In Limerick – the pro-Treaty National Army and the anti-Treaty IRA stand off against each other.
2 April	RIC formally ceases to exist (process of disbandment completed in August).
9 April	Anti-Treaty IRA convention in Dublin elects an army executive and ratifies Liam Lynch as Chief of Staff.
14 April	Rory O'Connor and anti-Treaty IRA take over Four Courts in Dublin.
2–3 May	Fighting erupts between IRA and National Army in Kilkenny.
20 May	De Valera and Collins make an electoral pact to enter into a coalition.
May	Five thousand British troops remain in Dublin as troop withdrawals suspended. Special Powers Act comes into force in the Six Counties with ban on all Republican organisations implemented.
1 June	Royal Ulster Constabulary founded.
3 June	British Army parades in Dublin's Phoenix Park to mark the King's birthday.
16 June	General Election. Sinn Féin pro-Treaty (leader Michael Collins) wins 58 seats. Sinn Féin anti-Treaty (leader Éamon de Valera) wins 36 seats. Labour Party 17, Others 17.
22 June	Field Marshal Sir Henry Wilson assassinated in London by Reginald Dunne and Joseph O'Sullivan.
28 June	Free State Army borrows British artillery and begins bombardment of the Four Courts — start of the Civil War.

CHAPTER ONE

Proclaiming a Republic

Ireland has a noble history of revolutionaries who, over two centuries, attempted to overthrow British rule. However, as this chapter will show, it is also a history of failed uprisings. Beginning with the United Irishmen of Wolfe Tone in 1798 and then Robert Emmet's rising in 1803, the chapter will go on to discuss how pacifist Daniel O'Connell's success in achieving rights for Catholics came to be overshadowed by the decimation of the nation during the Great Hunger of the 1840s. The 1848 rising of William Smith O'Brien and the Young Ireland movement was followed in the next generation by the abortive Fenian rising of 1867; and the Irish Home Rule Movement, which sought to bring the Irish Parliament back from London to Dublin, was hugely popular from the 1870s but it, in turn, was surpassed by the Irish Republican Brotherhood who went on to stage an uprising in 1916. The success of that Rising is measured not by who won or lost but by the fact that it led directly to the War of Independence of 1919–21.

THE UNITED IRISHMEN

Born in 1763 into a Dublin Protestant family, Theobald Wolfe Tone studied at Trinity College Dublin and in London, and was called to the bar in 1789. However, he had little interest in practising as a lawyer and instead turned his attention to politics, founding the Society of United

Irishmen in 1791. Influenced by events in the United States and France, the United Irishmen had a vision of Ireland as an independent nation of equality, where religious beliefs were irrelevant. In 1798, the United Irishmen staged a mass uprising against British rule in Ireland. The rebellion, which lasted from May until October, was ultimately crushed by the British, with the loss of 30,000 lives. Tone, who had sought French assistance in overthrowing the British, sailed into Lough Swilly with 3,000 men. However, the French fleet was captured on 12 October, Tone was taken prisoner, tried by court martial and sentenced to death. He died in prison on the morning of his execution, apparently having cut his own throat. Some fragments of the rebel armies survived for a number of years and waged a sort of guerrilla warfare in several counties.

A perception in Britain that the rebellion had been provoked by the misrule of the Protestant Ascendancy and a fear of collusion between Irish revolutionaries and the French led to the passing of the Acts of Union of 1800, which removed the Irish Parliament from Dublin. Irish MPs were now to sit as a minority amongst the British representatives in the Westminster Parliament. On 1 January 1801, the Union flag, as we know it today, was hoisted above Dublin Castle for the first time and a new entity was created, the United Kingdom of Great Britain and Ireland.

Robert Emmet, another Dublin Protestant, became one of the leaders of the United Irishmen while a student at Trinity College. Having left Trinity rather than face an inquisition into radical students, he joined his brother Thomas in France, in 1802, where he discussed Irish independence with Napoléon and Talleyrand. Determined to organise an uprising, Emmet returned to his native Dublin and, on 23 July 1803, he decided to act. Emmet's rising was confused and ineffective and lasted no more than two hours. However, his subsequent capture, after which he was hanged and then beheaded, ensured that he was immortalised as an Irish martyr. Emmet gave a speech from the dock after sentence of death was passed,

Robert Emmet, who led a rising in 1803
and was hanged and beheaded.

the last lines of which challenged future Irish revolutionaries: 'When my country takes her place among the nations of the earth, then, and not till then, let my epitaph be written. I have done.'

DANIEL O'CONNELL

Penal Laws were a series of laws imposed in an attempt to force Catholics and Protestant dissenters, such as Presbyterians, to accept the authority of the Anglican church, which in Ireland was established as the Church of Ireland. From 1607, Catholics were barred from holding public office or serving in the army. They had to pay fines for non-attendance at Anglican services and their churches were transferred to the Church of Ireland. In 1652, Catholics were barred from membership of the Irish Parliament, and Catholic landholders had their lands confiscated. The Protestant Ascendancy ruling class passed further laws to restrict the religious, political and economic activities of Catholics and dissenters, but while many of these were repealed in the eighteenth century, the ban on Catholics sitting in parliament continued after the Act of Union, 1800, and Catholics were seriously under-represented in politics, law and the civil service.

Born in Kerry in 1775, Daniel O'Connell was educated in France where he developed a lifelong abhorrence of violence for political ends. Having returned to Ireland, where he built up a large practice as a barrister, he was confirmed in his pacifism by the violence of the 1798 rebellion

and its aftermath. In 1823, O'Connell founded the Catholic Association, whose objective was to secure Catholic rights by constitutional means. With the support of the clergy, he turned it into a mass movement, campaigning and holding rallies around the country throughout the 1820s. In 1828, O'Connell was elected to the British Parliament, but could not take his seat as he was a Catholic. The following year, the Roman Catholic Relief Act was passed; O'Connell was victorious in a by-election in Clare and 'the Liberator' was able to take his seat at Westminster. It is interesting to note that although generally referred to as 'Catholic emancipation', the Catholic Relief Act actually raised by five times, to £10 per annum, the property qualification required to vote; this meant that many of the '40 shilling freeholders', those whose rent was 40 shillings or £2 per annum, lost the right the vote.

O'Connell, who was now seen as the 'uncrowned king of Ireland', gave up his practice at the bar to devote his time wholly to politics and to campaigning in the 1830s and 1840s for repeal of the Acts of Union, which he believed could be achieved by peaceful means. British political leaders quickly closed ranks against him, bringing in a coercion act to prevent mass gatherings, but a change in government gave the repeal movement the space to gather momentum. Supported by the Young Irelanders, the Repeal Association organised 'monster meetings' throughout the country, with an estimated three-quarters of a million in attendance at one meeting at the Hill of Tara. However, the Liberal government had become alarmed by the growth of the movement and, in 1843, banned a meeting scheduled to be held in Clontarf in Dublin. O'Connell was arrested, charged with conspiracy and sentenced to a year's imprisonment and a fine of £2,000. Although he continued his repeal activities following his early release from prison, it was clear that his tactics had failed, and the Young Irelanders withdrew from the Repeal Association. Knowing that he had been unsuccessful in his goal, O'Connell left Ireland in 1847 and died in Genoa later that year.

THE GREAT HUNGER

In August 1845, the potato blight, *phytophthora infestans*, was reported in the *London Chronicle* as having affected the crops in Ireland. The potato was the staple diet of the majority of the poor tenant farmers and the poverty-stricken landless in Ireland. Instead of Westminster Parliament enacting emergency legislation to ban the export of produce from Ireland and import supplies of food, a purposeful policy of *laissez-faire* was pursued. Those who could not afford food would have to rely on the sparse charity available from the state and private sources. The Irish Famine is an anachronistic misnomer as food was exported in abundance from Ireland under the armed guard of the British Army. During what is now referred to as the Great Hunger, compassion, not food, was in short supply. The Irish people were degraded by the Great Hunger and they would not easily forget that no Anglo-Irish landlord and no man of the cloth went hungry, while children perished for the want of food.

William Smith O'Brien from Dromoland, County Clare, had served as a Conservative MP in the 1820s and 1830s. However, his views changed and by 1844 he was a convinced Repealer. He became a leading member of the Young Irelanders and, with others who had split from Daniel O'Connell, founded the Irish Confederation in 1847, urging the formation of a National Guard and an armed rising. With most of the other leaders arrested, O'Brien and the Confederates still at liberty made an attempt at an uprising in July 1848 but it was ill-prepared and the Great Hunger had left the countryside weakened. The rising was a failure and many of the leaders of the movement were banished to Van Diemen's Land (Tasmania).

Considered by many to have been a form of genocide, the Great Hunger from 1845 to 1852 led to the death by starvation of over one million people, and a further one million emigrated around the world, settling in England, Scotland, Wales, Australia, Canada and the United States.

THE FENIANS

Thousands of Irish people continued to emigrate throughout the second half of the nineteenth century, and the population of the country essentially halved within one generation. A significant number of Irish male immigrants in the US were sworn into a secret society formed in 1858, the Fenian Brotherhood. Its sister organisation in Ireland, the Irish Republican Brotherhood (IRB), staged an uprising in 1867 in the same year as the American wing of the Fenians invaded Canada. Neither event was a success, adding to the growing list of failed uprisings against British rule.

Physical force nationalism enjoyed a revival in the 1880s during the Land War when Anglo-Irish landlords were targeted by 'agrarian outrages' and the Royal Irish Constabulary earned the opprobrium of the Irish when the police acted as enforcers during evictions. Irish-Americans, under the auspices of Clan na Gael (the Irish Family), the new name for the Fenian Brotherhood since 1867, brought terror to the people of England by engaging in a bombing campaign in the 1880s. One young man arrested for his bombing activities was Thomas J. Clarke.

Born in England but raised in County Tyrone, Clarke emigrated to the US where he was influenced by Jeremiah O'Donovan Rossa. O'Donovan Rossa who was originally from Rosscarbery, County Cork, had been arrested in 1865 with other leading Fenians and sentenced to penal servitude for twenty years. Following his release in 1871 on condition that he leave Ireland, he had gone to the US where he wrote accounts of his time in prison and for a time edited the newspaper, *The United Irishman.* He was also responsible for creating a 'skirmishing fund', money to send Fenians on bombing missions, such as that for which Thomas Clarke was arrested. Clarke was sentenced to life imprisonment with hard labour but he was released after fifteen years and returned to the US where he befriended John Devoy, the head of Clan na Gael.

HOME RULE

A Protestant barrister from County Donegal, Isaac Butt was greatly influenced by the suffering he witnessed during the Great Hunger and by the idealism of the Young Irelanders. He defended many Fenians and became president of the Amnesty Association in 1869. In 1870, he founded the Irish Home Government Association, which became the Home Rule League and ultimately the Irish Parliamentary Party, the largest Irish political party of the late nineteenth century.

Charles Stewart Parnell was the son of a Wicklow landowner with nationalist sympathies. He became MP for Meath in 1875 and joined Isaac Butt's Home Rule League. Parnell, who would become another 'uncrowned king', was the dominant figure in the Irish Party after the death of Butt in 1879. He married Home Rule with the campaign for tenants' rights and even managed to earn the respect of physical force nationalists. The Liberal Party in England relied on the Home Rule MPs to keep them in government, which the Home Rule MPs did in exchange for Liberal support of their cause. However, Parnell had been having a long-running relationship with a married woman, Katharine O'Shea, and when her husband sued for divorce and scandal ensued, members of the party urged Parnell to stand down. Parnell's refusal to do so, on the grounds that his private life had nothing to do with his political life, caused a bitter split in the party. Following Parnell's sudden death in 1891, the Irish Party fell apart.

Despite decades of campaigning, two Home Rule bills introduced under Liberal Prime Minister William Gladstone, in 1886 and 1893, were defeated by the House of Lords, whose members were determined to keep the Union intact. Nevertheless, in spite of opposition from Conservatives and Unionists, the Parliament Act of 1911 was passed, thus depriving the House of Lords of its absolute power to veto bills passed by the House of Commons. Finally, in September 1914, the Home Rule Act was passed into the statue books. However, there it would remain as Britain had declared war on Germany on 4 August 1914, and Home Rule was suspended until after the war.

BACKGROUND TO THE EASTER RISING

A small minority of republicans and socialists in Ireland were not willing to wait for Home Rule and, indeed, wanted freedom beyond a parliament that would be subservient to Britain. One of those was Thomas Clarke who returned to Ireland from the US with the express intention of fomenting revolution. With his close comrade, Seán MacDiarmada, a Gaelic League member who had previously promoted the republican cause in Belfast, he revived the moribund secret organisation, the IRB, and the duo swore in a new generation of dedicated activists. These included Patrick Pearse, a Gaelic League enthusiast, poet and headmaster of St Enda's School in Rathfarnham, Dublin. Another teacher at St Enda's, Thomas MacDonagh, and his fellow poet and friend, Joseph Plunkett, also took the Fenian oath to make Ireland an independent

Members of the Irish Citizen Army outside their headquarters, Liberty Hall, October 1914.

democratic republic. A renowned uileann piper and language activist, Éamonn Ceannt, who once played a selection of Irish airs for Pope Pius X in Rome, was also in the IRB. James Connolly, a Scottish-born socialist republican, eventually swore the Fenian oath and joined these men to form the seven-member Military Council of the IRB. Connolly's inclusion was important as he commanded the militant workers' defence force, the Irish Citizen Army (ICA). The ICA had been formed in Dublin during a major industrial dispute between approximately 20,000 workers and 300 employers, which came to be known as the Lockout of 1913–14. The IRB was also heavily represented at officer level in the open militant organisation, the Irish Volunteers.

THE IRISH VOLUNTEERS

The Irish Volunteers or Óglaigh na hÉireann were founded on 25 November 1913 with the intention of securing the rights and liberties common to all the people of Ireland. In reality, they were a countermeasure to the Ulster Volunteer Force (UVF), which had been formed to defend the northeastern part of Ireland against Home Rule. The UVF, which was a serious threat to the established order, imported arms from Germany and was willing to use violence in opposition to a devolved government. However, when war broke out, the majority of UVF members joined the Thirty-Sixth Ulster Division and went to fight for Britain in Europe.

THE VOLUNTEERS SPLIT

The Irish Volunteers once numbered over 180,000 but a catastrophic split saw the majority break away as the National Volunteers, loyal to the Irish Party leader John Redmond who had led the minority after Parnell's death and had gone on to secure the introduction of the third Home Rule Bill in 1911. The split came about when Redmond encouraged Irishmen to join the British forces. The Chief of Staff of the remaining

Irish Volunteers was Eoin MacNeill, who had been one of the founders of the Gaelic League, established in 1893 with the aim of restoring the Irish language. MacNeill was not a member of the IRB, but amongst the HQ staff there were several prominent IRB members: Patrick Pearse was Director of Organisation, Thomas MacDonagh was Director of Training, Éamonn Ceannt was Director of Communications and Joseph Plunkett was Director of Military Operations. Thus the Military Council of the IRB maintained a clandestine presence within the Irish Volunteer leadership.

RADICAL WOMEN

Women in Ireland had been campaigning separately from those in Britain for the right to vote, and the Irish Women's Franchise League, founded in 1908, carried on a militant campaign despite the Irish Parliamentary Party's refusal to support universal suffrage. Inghinidhe na hÉireann (daughters of Ireland), a revolutionary women's society founded by Maud Gonne, not only promoted feminism but also called for separatism from Britain. Trade unioninst Helena Molony was a member and edited *Bean na hÉireann* (Woman of Ireland), a radical separatist and feminist newspaper. which Molony described as being 'a mixture of guns and chiffon' and 'a hotchpotch of blood and thunder, high thinking and home-made bread'.

On 2 April 1914, Cumann na mBan (the women's council) was formed as a militant women's section of the Irish Volunteers. Inghinidhe na hÉireann was amalgamated with Cumann na mBan, and some women who had campaigned for suffrage joined Cumann na mBan. However, more radical women such as Molony and Countess Constance Marki-evicz, who had founded the youth movement Fianna Éireann in 1909, were attracted to the Irish Citizen Army, which was a revolutionary organisation that treated women as equals. Cumann na mBan was also a militant army with its own weapons but its members were also trained to a high level in first-aid, in preparation for the coming revolution; they wore a metal badge with the initials 'C na mB' interwoven over a Lee Enfield rifle.

IRELAND'S OPPORTUNITY

The IRB planned an uprising against British rule in Ireland as early as September 1914; as far as the leaders were concerned, the optimum time to strike was while Britain was at war, England's difficulty being Ireland's opportunity. They were determined not to let the war in Europe pass without striking a blow against the British Empire, and believed that if Home Rule did come in after the war was over, the chance of ever rousing the spirit of republicanism in the people would be gone; this was the last time that a rising might have any chance. The cultural degradation of a people ashamed of past failures would be complete.

It should, however, be remembered that those in favour of an armed uprising in Ireland were in a very small minority. There was a lot of support for the war in Europe and many Irishmen were fighting in the trenches, some believing in the cause and encouraged by John Redmond to join up, some perhaps hoping to curry favour with the British government, but in many cases simply for the want of money. Separation allowance, paid by the British Army to the wives or dependants of British soldiers, was putting food on many tables, in urban parts of Ireland at least. Dublin had the worst infant mortality rates and the worst slums in Europe. Although there was no draft in Ireland, there was what James Connolly called 'conscription by starvation'.

THE EASTER RISING

In April 1916, despite the IRB's plans, the British intercepted a ship carrying a large quantity of arms from Germany, which had been expected to arrive in time for a countrywide uprising. The arms had been procured by Roger Casement, a Dublin man who, as a diplomat in the British colonial service, had exposed the barbarism of imperialism in African and South American rubber plantations. Having always been sympathetic to the nationalist cause, he had joined the Irish Volunteers in 1913. The captain of the *Aud* scuttled his vessel rather than let the British seize his cargo. Casement, who had been following in a submarine, was captured and brought to England to stand trial. Eoin MacNeill, Chief of Staff of the Irish Volunteers, fearing that a rising without the German weapons was doomed, countermanded IRB orders to muster on Easter Sunday. MacNeill sent messengers around Ireland to stand down the Irish Volunteers and even inserted a stop-press advertisement in a newspaper to inform his men that no 'parades' would take place. The seven members of the Military Council of the IRB met in Liberty Hall on Easter Sunday to consider their options. They decided to postpone their revolution by twenty-four hours and rise up the following day, Easter Monday.

Seriously lacking in arms and without the support of the general populace, the men and women who mustered at noon on 24 April 1916 occupied several key areas of Dublin city. Patrick Pearse read the Proclamation of the Republic outside the General Post Office (GPO) to an irreverent crowd of onlookers. Meanwhile, James Connolly directed the Irish Citizen Army (ICA) to assist the Irish Volunteers in erecting barricades and securing the GPO as rebel headquarters. The Irish Volunteers and ICA were joined in their attempt to free Ireland from the British Empire by the women of Cumann na mBan and the young boys of the Fianna Éireann. Joseph Plunkett left his sick bed to fight in the GPO alongside his young aide-de-camp, Michael Collins, who had been sworn into the IRB in London by Gaelic footballer Sam Maguire. The 'chief architect' of the Rising, Thomas Clarke, was joined in the GPO by his close friend and fellow signatory of the Proclamation, Seán MacDiarmada. Thomas MacDonagh occupied Jacob's biscuit factory on the south side of the city whilst his co-signatory of the Proclamation, Éamonn Ceannt, took over the South Dublin Union. The ICA occupied City Hall and the College of Surgeons, St Stephen's Green where Countess Markievicz fought as a lieutenant alongside Commandant Michael Mallin, a former British Army soldier who had joined the ICA on its formation in 1913. Boland's Mills and Bakery, at the Dublin docks, was taken over by Éamon de Valera, a mathematics teacher who was born in New York and raised in Bruree, County Limerick. The Four Courts and Church Street area was occupied by Edward Daly, another Limerick man and the brother-in-law of Thomas Clarke. Directly across the River Liffey, railway worker and Fianna Éireann organiser Seán Heuston and his men barricaded themselves into the Mendicity Institute, Usher's Island. The rest of the country outside Dublin failed to rise up, with the exception of Galway where Liam Mellows, a socialist, led over 500 Irish Volunteers, and Wexford where the men and women of the Irish Volunteers and Cumann na mBan occupied a few buildings in Enniscorthy. But the fiercest fighting was in Dublin.

The GPO following the British bombardment, 1916.

Looking towards Sackville Street and Eden Quay as life in Dublin resumes, 1916.

The British Army was quick to engage the Army of the Irish Republic, under the banner of which the various Irish armies fought. Using heavy artillery, the British pounded the GPO, and within a few days much of the area around the post office was in flames. After a week of fighting, the revolutionaries were left with little option but to surrender. General John Maxwell, the newly appointed Commander-in-Chief of the British Army in Ireland, who had replaced General William Lowe during the Easter Rising, instigated a series of courts martial, and fourteen of the leaders of the Rising were executed in Kilmainham Gaol, Dublin. Thomas Kent was executed in Cork for the shooting of a policeman during an attempt to arrest him and his brothers in their home. In August of 1916, Roger Casement was hanged in Pentonville Prison, London.

Initially the people of Ireland were against the Rising. As mentioned, many Irish families were directly connected to the war in Europe, having a son, brother or father who was fighting in a British Army uniform. The majority of those people felt a certain compassion for the army to which their relations belonged. However, the executions caused widespread revulsion amongst the Irish at home and abroad. Together with the destruction of the capital city and the murder of a number of its citizens by the British Army, the executions caused public opinion to begin to swing over in favour of the revolutionaries. The smouldering ruins of Dublin witnessed the temporary defeat of the Irish Volunteers, but like the symbol of Irish republicanism, the Phoenix, they would rise again from the ashes.

CHAPTER TWO

Discontent and Rebellious Intentions

The IRB had deliberately taken advantage of the fact that the British government's attention had been focused on the war in Europe. As we saw in the last chapter, all talk of Home Rule had been suspended in 1914. However, having visited Dublin soon after the Easter Rising, British Prime Minister H.H. Asquith concluded that Home Rule might provide a solution to the problems he now faced in Ireland. David Lloyd George was given the task of attempting to persuade nationalists and unionists to agree on an immediate settlement. Meanwhile, in the immediate aftermath of the 1916 Rising, a couple of thousand men and a small number of women were imprisoned in Britain, which, as we will see in this chapter, served to bolster the sense of camaraderie they already felt, having fought together as one. Combined with the secret courts martial and execution of the leaders of 1916, these internments were also instrumental in changing public opinion.

Michael Collins, who had fought in the GPO during the Rising, filled the empty space left after the Irish Republican Brotherhood leaders had been executed and de Valera and Griffith had been arrested. As will be seen, following his release from internment, he set about reorganising the IRB, whilst also rising in the hierarchy of the Volunteers. The republican women of Ireland carried on as they had before, raising money for the prisoners and their dependants, and keeping the flame of revolution alive.

Sinn Féin, the political party blamed for the Rising, began to increase in popularity as evidenced by a number of successes in by-elections, a measure of how public feeling was beginning to sway over to republicanism. Additional sympathy for the cause was generated by the death in Mountjoy Jail of Thomas Ashe whilst on hunger strike with other prisoners, demanding to be treated as prisoners of war. However, the most crucial event in swaying public feeling was the attempt to introduce British Army conscription into Ireland, which was a grievous error on the part of the British Government.

The popularity of Sinn Féin was further bolstered by the arrest of republican leaders accused of being involved with the German Empire in attempting to start an armed insurrection in Ireland, the so-called 'German Plot'. By December 1918, the party had increased its seats in the British Parliament from zero in 1916 to seventy-three. However, elected Sinn Féin members abstained from Westminster and founded their own parliament in Dublin, Dáil Éireann. On the very day when the Dáil sat for the first time, the IRA shot and killed two policemen in Tipperary, thus starting the War of Independence. Two weeks later, Éamon de Valera was rescued from an English prison by Michael Collins and Harry Boland, Member of Parliament for South Roscommon. De Valera was eventually smuggled on board a ship to the United States on a fundraising mission, leaving Collins behind to run the war. A new phase in the fight for Irish freedom had begun.

FRONGOCH PRISONER OF WAR CAMP, 'UNIVERSITY OF IRISH FREEDOM'

After the Rising, over 3,500 men and women were arrested and sent to prisons such as Knutsford, Stafford, Wandsworth, Wakefield and Lewes in England, as well as Glasgow in Scotland. Some of the prisoners were

Michael Collins (X) and other IRA prisoners at Stafford jail.

released after a couple of weeks but on 11 June 1916, 1,800 men, including GPO veteran Michael Collins, were sent to Frongoch internment camp, north Wales. Until 1916, the camp had housed German prisoners of war, but they were moved out to make place for the Irish.

In the late 1940s, the Bureau of Military History began to record the stories of the men and women who were involved in the revolutionary period. The collection of stories, known as 'witness statements', is an incredible source to historians. Joe Lawless, who fought in the Rising at Ashbourne and was initially sent to Knutsford, near Manchester, recalled in his witness statement:

> Frongoch has since then been aptly termed the university of the Irish
> revolution, and so indeed it was. No more certain way of perpetuating
> the ideals of the executed leaders, and ensuring another bigger effort

to throw off the yoke of foreign domination, could have been imagined or desired by them. The police in Ireland had done their work well in selecting throughout the country the most likely disaffected persons, most of whom were Volunteers, but not all of them. These, lodged together in a camp with the leaven of those who had had their blood baptism on the streets of Dublin and elsewhere, were bound to be touched by the longing to emulate the heroic deeds of those who fought; and there were those amongst us whose intellects grasped the possibilities of this situation, and strove to make the best use of the opportunity so unexpectedly provided by the enemy.[1]

Those interned at Frongoch were accorded the status of prisoners of war and they formed a camp council; cooking, cleaning and sanitation became the responsibility of the prisoners. 'This arrangement brought us all in very close contact, and many intimate associations were formed which strengthened in later years our comradeship and loyalty,' recalled Bill Stapleton, who had fought in Jacob's factory in 1916. He continued:

It was then I first learned of the Irish Republican Brotherhood, which shortly after being released I was allowed to join. I learned more about the Volunteer organisation background when in Frongoch than I knew up to then, and got some idea of the vision and spirit of the movement in meeting and talking with many who had been prominent in Sinn Féin, the Gaelic League and the Volunteer movement. Irish classes were held regularly and some lectures in musketry etc.[2]

Joe McCarthy from Wexford, who was arrested after the Rising but did not participate in it, was sent to Frongoch. He wrote in his witness statement that in July and August of 1916, 'all the prisoners were brought in parties of about 20 men to London to appear before an Advisory Board set up by the British Government, composed of Judge Sankey and a Mr Mooney, a member of John Redmond's Irish Party [Home Rule Party]'.[3] The Sankey Commission resulted in about half of the prisoners being sent home.

For those who remained at Frongoch, though, the food and living conditions were notoriously bad. as recalled by Joe Good who had fought in the GPO in 1916, having left England for Ireland to avoid conscription:

> The continued annoyance and publicity [about] our alleged insanitary quarters caused the camp doctor, who was a civilian, to commit suicide. The camp commandant paraded us and upbraided us for this man's death. He nearly precipitated a riot thereby, because the Volunteers broke ranks and some of them approached him and swore at him. From that day forward he never addressed us and we disobeyed every order to parade. I think the instigator of most of this annoyance was Michael Collins; he was in his element making war on something. He was conspicuous in all the tussles with our warders, but he was never disliked by them. During our stay in Frongoch we were not conscious of our leaders [being in any way different from us]. They, i.e. Dick Mulcahy, Gearóid O'Sullivan and Michael Collins, did not form a clique, but played and worked with all.[4]

Originally from Waterford, General Richard (Dick) Mulcahy had been second-in-command to Thomas Ashe in an encounter with armed police at Ashbourne, County Meath, during the Rising. He was one of those leaders interned at Frongoch, alongside Corkmen Michael Collins, who fought in the GPO as aide-de-camp (assistant) to Joseph Plunkett, and Gearóid O'Sullivan, who had been the youngest IRB officer fighting in the GPO.

While, as noted by Joe Lawless above, not all of those interned at Frongoch had been active prior to the Rising, the majority would become active IRA Volunteers once they were released. Public opinion had shifted in favour of Sinn Féin. Frank Robbins, a member of the socialist republican Irish Citizen Army, recalled his amazement at how different his release was from his arrest:

On our arrival at Westland Row I was never so amazed in all my life. The reception that was given to us by the Dublin people was beyond description. A very large force of Dublin Metropolitan Police (DMP) were around Westland Row railway station, but they were simply scattered with the surging of the throng of people ... From there up to Tara Street not one of us could pass without some man's or woman's arms around us, kissing us, hugging us, slapping us on the back, and practically carrying us through the streets.[5]

Michael Collins was freed with the rest of the internees just before Christmas 1916. Collins and his comrades from the Rising set about reforming the Volunteers with a view to striking another blow for Irish freedom. He was joined in his work by Thomas Ashe who had commanded the Fifth Battalion in 1916 in a successful fight in Ashbourne, County Meath. Another man keen to continue the fight was Cathal Brugha who had been very badly wounded in the Rising, during fighting in the South Dublin Union where he was second in command. Brugha would clash regularly with Collins, who had reorganised the secret IRB in Frongoch.

Opposite: Returning prisoners are welcomed home, Loop Line Railway Bridge, Dublin.
Above: Sixty of the 276 women who were involved in the Easter Rising, photographed in August 1916.

FINANCING THE REVOLUTION

Kathleen Clarke, a founder member of Cumann na mBan, had lost to the executioner's bullet her husband Thomas, her only brother Ned Daly and her friend Seán MacDiarmada. Determined to relieve the financial distress of families associated with the Rising, she and her Cumann na mBan comrades, Sorcha McMahon and Áine Ceannt (wife of Éamonn who was executed in 1916), set up the Irish Volunteers Dependants' Fund (IVDF). Not long after this, George Gavan Duffy, who had defended Roger Casement during his recent trial, helped to found the Irish National Aid Association (INAA). This organisation had the backing of the Catholic clergy and also some Irish Parliamentary Party supporters who were less enthusiastic about the use of physical force.[6] The INAA, having a wider appeal, managed to raise nearly ten times as much as the women's fund collected. Kathleen Clarke was reluctant to combine both funds for fear that their own ideological aims might be diluted. However, when two Irish Americans from Clan na Gael came over with £5,000 and a 'merger proposal', Clarke was left with little option but to allow the funds to combine.

The new organisation was called the Irish National Aid and Volunteer Dependants' Fund (INAVDF). Control of its £28,000 fund was ultimately left in the hands of radicals when Michael Collins was given the job of secretary, in February 1917. As his duties included paying money to Volunteers who had fought in the Rising and were imprisoned as a result, an additional bond of loyalty was created between Collins and the financial beneficiaries of the fund. He now had further access to contacts within the Irish Volunteers, now the IRA, an organisation that he would control with ruthless efficiency.[7]

SINN FÉIN

Thanks to finance received from the Irish-American organisation Clan na Gael, Arthur Griffith, an IRB activist, was able to co-found with fellow nationalist William Rooney a newspaper they called *The United Irishman*. In 1900, Griffith established Cumann na nGaedheal (Irish club) to promote a 'Buy Irish' campaign. A few years later, Griffith set up the National Council to protest against the visit of the British King Edward VII to Ireland. Meanwhile, two other IRB men, Bulmer Hobson and Denis McCullough, had set up societies all over the province of Ulster, called Dungannon Clubs, to promote separatism from Britain. In 1905, Cumann na nGaedheal, the National Council and the Dungannon Clubs amalgamated to form Sinn Féin (ourselves alone). As a political party, Sinn Féin was small before 1916. However, once the Easter Rising transformed popular opinion, everything changed and the Irish Party (Home Rule Party) went into decline while Sinn Féin, mistakenly linked to the Rising, grew significantly in popularity.

If the IRA were going to be the armed wing of the Republic, Sinn Féin was going to govern it. By late 1917, there were 1,200 Sinn Féin clubs, boasting a membership of a quarter of a million people. Following an unsuccessful attempt at winning a by-election in late 1916, Sinn Féin fielded a few victorious candidates in 1917. Count (George) Plunkett, father of Joseph Plunkett, the executed signatory of the Proclamation, was elected as an Independent with 55 percent of the votes cast in the North Roscommon by-election of 3 February 1917. Even though he was not a Sinn Féin candidate, his election was seen as a victory for the party as Plunkett received the support of the IRB and, in fact, he joined Sinn Féin later on in the year. Plunkett was the first Member of Parliament (MP) to abstain from Westminster, refusing to take his seat, a policy that Sinn Féin would adopt over the coming years.

Joe McGuinness, who was part of the Four Courts garrison in 1916 and was incarcerated in Lewes Prison in East Sussex, won, by a slim majority of 47 votes, the South Longford by-election of 9 May. This was the first official Sinn Féin election victory and is often remembered for the classic election slogan 'Put him in to get him out'. The most important by-election that year was held on 10 July 1917 in East Clare, when the Commandant of the Third Battalion during the Easter Rising, Éamon de Valera, was elected in a landslide victory. Dev, as he was affectionately known, took 71 percent of the votes for Sinn Féin. In Ballybunion, County Kerry, the RIC fired into a parade of Volunteers, fatally wounding Daniel Scallon who was out celebrating the election results with his comrades.[8] Scallon died the following morning, the first IRA casualty after the Easter Rising.

A few months after his election victory, de Valera was elected President of Sinn Féin at the party's Ard Fheis (high assembly). Michael Collins and Cathal Brugha were appointed to the National Executive of the party. Sinn Féin also adopted a Republican Constitution for the first time.

The day after the Sinn Féin Ard Fheis, 26 October 1917, the Irish Volunteers held their annual convention. De Valera was elected President of the Volunteers, Cathal Brugha became the Chief of Staff, and Michael

Collins became Director of Organisation. But what of the secret oath-bound brotherhood that had organised the Easter Rising? As far as de Valera and Brugha were concerned, the IRB was irrelevant. However, Michael Collins continued with the IRB, believing that the Fenians were the key to controlling the revolution.

HUNGER STRIKE OF THOMAS ASHE

Born in County Kerry in 1885, Thomas Ashe was a teacher, member of the Coiste Gnótha (executive committee) of the Gaelic League, Gaelic Athletic Association (GAA) player, poet, playwright and champion piper.[9]

Teaching brought him to Lusk, in Fingal, County Dublin, and as a founding member of the Volunteers he commanded the Fifth Battalion during the Easter Rising. Arrested in the aftermath of the Rising, he was tried at a court martial, his sentence of death was commuted to life imprisonment. In Lewes Prison in Sussex, Ashe was elected President of the Supreme Council of the IRB. Under the general amnesty of June 1917, he returned to Ireland but managed to stay free for only a couple of months before being arrested and

Hunger striker Thomas Ashe, who died following force-feeding, was a Gaelic League enthusiast and champion piper.

charged with 'causing disaffection among the civilian population'. He was convicted and sentenced to a year's imprisonment with hard labour.

On 20 September, Ashe and others seeking political status commenced a hunger strike in Mountjoy Jail in Dublin. The prison guards and doctors engaged in a brutal policy of force-feeding the hunger strikers through unsterilised rubber tubes forced down the prisoners' throats. On the fifth day of his hunger strike, Ashe collapsed after force-feeding and was eventually brought to the Mater Hospital where he died from heart failure and congestion of the lungs. Ashe's remains lay in state in Dublin's City Hall, surrounded by Irish Volunteers in uniform. The British Army and Dublin Metropolitan Police (DMP) were confined to their barracks and stations, public houses were closed, and 30,000 mourners marched in the procession to Glasnevin Cemetery. Shots were fired over Ashe's grave by the IRA, and Michael Collins, who had the honour of giving the oration, said: 'Nothing additional remains to be said. The volley which we have just heard is the only speech which is proper to make over the grave of a dead Fenian.'[10] Within a week, the Castle authorities had given in to the demands of the other hunger strikers in Mountjoy and they began to treat them as political prisoners.

THE FIGHT AGAINST CONSCRIPTION

As the First World War raged on in Europe, the British cabinet was under increasing pressure to introduce conscription in Ireland. In April 1918, David Lloyd George, the British Prime Minister, enacted the Military Service Bill to extend conscription. Lloyd George adopted a dual approach, promising a new Home Rule bill for Ireland alongside conscription. The Irish Parliamentary Party (IPP) under John Dillon withdrew from Parliament in protest, adopting the same abstentionist policy as Sinn Féin. This was the moment when the IPP lost much of its support in Ireland. By abstaining from the Parliament at Westminster and sharing a platform with Sinn Féin, the IPP simply became a moderate version of the more dynamic and youthful Sinn Féin. To add to the IPP's woes, one of its most popular leaders, John Redmond, had died on 6 March 1918, leaving John Dillon in charge for a few months before he was replaced by Joe Devlin from Belfast. Ultimately Sinn Féin had shown that, by linking conscription to Home Rule, the British had not remained true to their word; as a consequence the IPP, rebranded by Joe Devlin as the Nationalist Party, went into serious decline.

An Irish Anti-Conscription Committee was formed, which included representatives from trades unions, Sinn Féin and the IPP. Supporting them was the all-important Catholic hierarchy who allowed an anti-conscription pledge to be signed outside all churches on 21 April 1918, followed two days later by a countrywide strike by workers. Using the Defence of the Realm Act (DORA), Dublin Castle clamped down on anti-conscription meetings and arrested anyone denouncing the war and compulsory enlistment.

The Lord Chief Justice of Ireland, a Dubliner and a Unionist, Sir James Campbell had advised the war cabinet on 28 March 1918 that conscription could now be enforced in Ireland only at the cost of tremendous bloodshed. Two days earlier, the Galway-born British Army General Sir Bryan Thomas Mahon, Commander in Chief, Irish Command, in a memorandum to the War Cabinet suggested that the 'first thing is to get all known leaders out of the way at once'.[11] Lord French, the Lord Lieutenant for Ireland, at the cabinet meeting of 23 April 1918 said that the situation was undoubtedly menacing but he felt that they would be able to enforce conscription. However, General Mahon was 'not so sanguine as to the results'.

Bill Stapleton recalled in his witness statement that the threat of conscription caused 'a big rush on the part of young men of military age to join the Volunteers. My company was increased 100 percent, and I think the same applied to all the companies of the Battalion and to the Dublin Brigade as a whole.'[12]

Women, especially those in Cumann na mBan, the Irish Citizen Army and the Irish Women Worker's Union, were key to the anti-conscription movement. A special Lá na mBan (women's day) was held on 9 June 1918 to protest against conscription, and hundreds of thousands of women signed a pledge to defeat the draft.[13]

Michael Collins gave a 'seditious' anti-conscription speech in Longford and was arrested outside the Dublin offices of the INAVDF at 32 Bachelors Walk. Collins was remanded in Sligo Jail until he was bailed out by his comrades because he wanted to join in the campaign against conscription. He was summoned to appear in Derry for a trial but decided not to attend, preferring to go on the run. Dressed in a three-piece suit, with briefcase and umbrella, Collins was, however, a most unusual IRA fugitive, who adopted a policy of 'hiding in plain sight'.

THE 'GERMAN PLOT'

To counter the anti-conscription movement, British Field-Marshal John French was appointed as the new Lord Lieutenant. French was a poor military commander who had been responsible for huge casualties in the early days of the European War when he was Commander-in-Chief of the British Expeditionary Force, and he had been replaced in France in December 1915 by Field-Marshal General Douglas Haig. French was keen to get the Irish conscripted but the Lord Lieutenant was normally just a figurehead, so he accepted the job only on condition that his political powers were extended. On 17 May 1918, he exercised those powers by authorising the arrest of Sinn Féin activists and Volunteer leaders, accusing them of being in league with the Germans. The British forces arrested 150 activists, including Arthur Griffith, Éamon de Valera, Countess Markievicz, Kathleen Clarke, Maud Gonne MacBride and William Cosgrave, the latter of whom had served in 1916 under Éamonn Ceannt. Michael Collins and Cathal Brugha evaded arrest. Coupled with the general anti-conscription sentiment in Ireland, the arrests served to bolster Sinn Féin, and Arthur Griffith was elected in a by-election in East Cavan, gaining 60 percent of the votes cast on 20 June 1918.

On 22 September 1918, a large crowd, gathered at Foster Place in Dublin to protest against the 'German Plot' arrests, listened to speeches from Helena Molony of the Irish Citizen Army and Hannah Sheehy Skeffington, feminist and suffragist whose husband Francis had been murdered by a British Army officer during the Rising. The protesters were attacked by the Dublin Metropolitan Police, and Josie McGowan, a Cumann na mBan activist who had been stationed in Marrowbone Lane during the Rising, died a week later from the injuries she received from a police baton.

BRITISH CABINET MEETING AND GENERAL ELECTION

With the end of the First World War in November 1918, one of the topics of the British cabinet meeting of 21 November was Ireland. Lord French stated that 'any reduction of the military garrison of Ireland would be fatal. Although Ireland [was] superficially quiet, it [was] seething with discontent and rebellious intentions underneath.'[14] He also advised the Cabinet that 'Home Rule in any form [was] impossible at this moment.'

The post-war general election in Britain and Ireland was held on 14 December 1918. The election was a rout for the Irish Parliamentary Party who continued to campaign for Home Rule, a policy that was waning in popularity. Sinn Féin, on the other hand, was offering an independent Irish republic, free from Westminster's control, free from conscription into foreign wars and free from monarchy. Moreover, earlier in the year, the Representation of the People Act had given the vote to women who were over thirty years of age and who met a property qualification. Women voters, and many men, had not forgotten that the IPP had failed to support the campaign for universal suffrage.

In a historic and unprecedented result, Sinn Féin secured 73 seats out of 105 in the thirty-two counties of Ireland, Unionist candidates won 26 seats and the IPP was reduced to just six. The Irish political landscape had changed significantly. Sinn Féin, the party that represented the physical force tradition and had backed the men and women of the Easter Rising, was now the majority political voice. However, Sinn Féin was an illegal organisation and half of its elected representatives were in prison.

Those elected included a large number of 1916 veterans: Éamon de Valera, Cathal Brugha, Richard Mulcahy, Seán T. O'Kelly, W.T. Cosgrave, Desmond FitzGerald, Liam Mellows, Piaras Béaslaí, Éamonn Duggan, Michael Collins and his good friend at the time, Harry Boland, to name but a few. Some were related to people executed in the Rising: Thomas MacDonagh's brother Joseph and John MacBride's brother Joseph were both elected. Joseph Plunkett's father was re-elected, this time on a Sinn Féin ticket. The enacting of the Parliament (Qualification of Women) Act, 1918 on 21 November had given women the right to run for Parliament. Countess Markievicz, who had fought in 1916 in the uniform of the Irish Citizen Army, became the first woman to be elected to the British Parliament, with 7,835 votes, twice the combined votes of the other candidates.

NEW CHIEF SECRETARY FOR IRELAND

Edward Shortt, the Chief Secretary to the Lord Lieutenant, did not get along with Lord French; their relations were so strained that Shortt was recalled. He was replaced by Ian Macpherson, a Scottish Presbyterian who, although a Liberal MP, was conservative enough to get along with French. French needed someone who would support his policies of coercion, and Macpherson was equally satisfied to support a strong policy that would eventually involve martial law, wide-scale imprisonment and an aggressive intolerance of Sinn Féin. It also suited French that Macpherson spent most of his time in Britain, involving himself in electioneering and trying to recuperate from an illness that dogged his life. He was backed up throughout his tenure by the equally conservative Under-Secretary John Taylor, who conspired to sideline the Catholic Under-Secretary James Macmahon. French would later write that Macmahon was 'now quite estranged from all of us owing to his violently Catholic tendencies, so we have to short-circuit him and make Taylor superintend all the Castle work.'[15]

As will be seen, Macpherson's first day on the job, 21 January 1919, could not have been more eventful.

THE FIRST DÁIL ÉIREANN

As promised, the seventy-three elected Sinn Féin MPs refused to take their seats in Westminster and an Irish Assembly, Dáil Éireann, was convened in the Round Room of the Mansion House, Dublin, on 21 January 1919. An invitation to the IPP and Unionists to come to the Dáil was ignored, so the new parliament was made up entirely of Sinn Féin deputies or Teachtaí Dála (TDs). A short constitution was adopted, which provided the Dáil with full legislative powers and enacted various ministries and provided for a chairman.

A Declaration of Independence was made which included ratification of the 1916 Proclamation and demanded the removal of the 'English garrison' (the British Army). An appeal to the free nations of the world included the line:

> For these among other reasons, Ireland — resolutely and irrevocably
> determined at the dawn of the promised era of self-determination and
> liberty that she will suffer foreign dominion no longer — calls upon
> every free nation to uphold her national claim to complete independence
> as an Irish Republic against the arrogant pretensions of England founded
> in fraud and sustained only by an overwhelming military occupation....

Seán T. O'Kelly, Éamon de Valera and George Gavan Duffy were selected as delegates to attend the Paris Peace Conference in the hopes that President Wilson of the US and other world leaders would recognise the right of this particular small nation to self-determination.

As Labour had agreed not to field candidates in the election, the trades unions were represented by Thomas Johnson's Democratic Programme, which was socialist in principle and gave every citizen the right to 'an adequate share of the produce of the Nation's labour'. The Democratic Programme also provided for 'the physical, mental and spiritual well-being of the children, to secure that no child shall suffer hunger or cold from lack of food, clothing, or shelter, but that all shall be provided with the means and facilities requisite for their proper education and training as Citizens of a Free and Gaelic Ireland.'

THE ROYAL IRISH CONSTABULARY (RIC)

Dublin Castle was the seat of the British Administration in Ireland. The Lord Lieutenant acted as the viceroy or king's representative but normally left the day-to-day running of the country to the Chief Secretary, who in practice tended to rely on the Under Secretary to do the work. Since 1836, policing in Ireland had been undertaken by the Irish Constabulary which had received 'Royal' status for its role in defeating the Fenians in the 1867 Rising.

The Royal Irish Constabulary (RIC), which was based outside the capital city, provided the eyes and ears of Dublin Castle. There were 1,400 police stations, more properly known as barracks, and about 9,500 members of the force spread throughout the countryside of Ireland. They got to know everyone in the locality, and anyone with 'suspicious' political leanings was duly reported to superior officers or district inspectors, who in turn reported to Dublin Castle. Constables, unlike those of the Dublin Metropolitan Police, were armed with carbines and revolvers and their six-month training was along military lines. Religious leanings

Ballinamuck RIC Barracks, County Longford.

were irrelevant in the lower ranks as the majority of constables were of the Catholic persuasion. The majority of district inspectors were of the Protestant faith.

Sometimes the IRA attacked RIC barracks and protection huts before the War of Independence, as we know it, started. For instance, two IRA Volunteers, Richard Laide and John Browne, died after attacking Gortatlea RIC Barracks in Kerry on 14 April 1918. If Daniel Scallon was the first to be killed by the police since the Rising, Laide and Browne were the first to be killed in action.

FIRST SHOTS OF WAR, SOLOHEADBEG, COUNTY TIPPERARY

The first shots of the War of Independence were fired on the same day as Dáil Éireann sat for the first time, 21 January 1919. The Officer Commanding (O/C) of the Third Tipperary Brigade was Séamus Robinson, a Belfast man who had fought in the GPO in 1916 and was interned in Frongoch. His comrades, Seán Treacy (Vice Commandant), Dan Breen (Quartermaster), Seán Hogan and five other Volunteers waited for five days for a chance to ambush the RIC who would be guarding a consignment of explosives bound for Soloheadbeg Quarry, a few miles north of Tipperary town. As it transpired, there were only two armed RIC constables and two quarry workers walking alongside the donkey and cart loaded with explosives.[16] The IRA called for their surrender, the police levelled their weapons, and Robinson, Breen and Treacy fired on them, killing Constable James MacDonnell and Constable Patrick O'Connell.

The *Nenagh Guardian* reported that a 'thrill of horror shot through the country with the tragic death of two police constables'. However, the newspaper's opinion writer commented:

> … the public feeling of all that is true in Nationalist Ireland … our country is crushed under the heel of an iron despotism … The moral is clear and the remedy is obvious. Let the rights of the Irish people be conceded, and the country will rapidly settle down to an era of peace and content unknown for 700 years.[17]

Although Breen was not the commanding officer (Robinson was), *Hue & Cry,* the organ of the RIC, issued a poster with a reward for the capture of 'Daniel Breen (calls himself Commandant of the Third Tipperary Brigade)'. The newly appointed British Army Commander-in-Chief in Ireland, General Frederick Shaw, reacted by declaring South Tipperary a 'special military area' and banning fairs, markets and all commercial traffic of every description during the search for Breen and his comrades. Robinson and Treacy were summoned to Dublin to meet Michael Collins who presumed that they would want to be spirited off to the US. However, he was surprised to hear that the Volunteers were willing to 'fight it out'; they were now officially 'on the run' as wanted men.[18]

The ambushers were denounced from the pulpit by Reverend William Condon of Tipperary who said that they would 'bring on their country disgrace and on themselves the curse of God'. Dan Breen, however, was unrepentant. He never doubted his action, even four decades later:

> I would like to make this point clear, and I state here without any equivocation that we took this action deliberately, having thought the matter over and talked it over between us. Treacy had stated to me that the only way of starting a war was to kill someone and we wanted to start a war, so we intended to kill some of the police whom we looked upon as the foremost and most important branch of the enemy forces which were holding our country in subjection. The moral aspect of such a decision has been talked about since and we have been branded as murderers ... but ... we felt that we were merely continuing the active war for the establishment of an Irish Republic that had begun on Easter Monday 1916 ... The only regret we had, following the ambush, was that there were only two policemen in it instead of the six we expected, because we felt that six dead policemen would have impressed the country more than a mere two.[19]

The official organ of the Irish Volunteers, *An tÓglach* (the Volunteer), was produced from August 1918, and contained much useful information for members of the IRA, including training instructions and directions from IRA GHQ. The February 1919 issue stated: 'The soldiers and police of the invader are liable to be treated exactly as invading enemy soldiers would be treated by the native army of any country.'

ÉAMON DE VALERA ESCAPES FROM PRISON

One of the most famous prison escapes during the revolutionary period was that of Éamon de Valera who absconded from Lincoln Jail in England, using a key delivered in a cake. Two comrades escaped with him, Arthur Griffith's close friend, journalist Seán Milroy, and Seán McGarry, who had been an aide-de-camp to Tom Clarke during the Rising and had succeeded Thomas Ashe as President of the IRB Supreme Council. They had all been imprisoned following the 'German Plot' and were determined to hatch a breakout plan.

Seán Milroy drew a postcard with a drunken reveller trying to get a key into a latch. This postcard was sent to Seán McGarry's wife who showed it to Michael Collins who was quick to spot that the drawing of the key was in fact a sketch of the skeleton key for the jail.[20] Collins organised for a blank key baked into a fruitcake to be sent to the prisoners. Four cakes in all had to be delivered from the outside until the right type of blank key was fashioned to fit the locks. Peadar de Loughrey, an IRA prisoner who had a foundry in Ireland and was an expert with metal, undertook the meticulous filing and shaping of the blank key.

On the night of 3 February 1919, Michael Collins and Harry Boland cut through barbed-wire entanglements around the prison and waited for the escapees. The key worked for all of the internal doors but Collins broke a duplicate key in the final door. Luckily de Valera, on the inside, managed to push the broken key out, and the five men made off under cover of darkness.[21] The escape was a great publicity coup for Sinn Féin and indeed for Éamon de Valera when he was smuggled back to Dublin on 20 February.

SPANISH FLU AND THE GENERAL AMNESTY FOR IRISH PRISONERS

The Spanish Influenza pandemic of 1918–20 is estimated to have resulted in the deaths of 50 to 100 million people around the world. Pierce McCan, the Sinn Féin TD for East Tipperary, had been imprisoned in Gloucester Prison after the 'German Plot'; he died there on 6 March 1919, a victim of the flu. Almost immediately, there was a general release of the Irish political prisoners in England, the authorities fearing that more would die and be seen as martyrs. Pierce McCan's remains were sent to Dublin, accompanied by many of the released prisoners. Thousands of mourners followed the cortège from Dublin Port to Kingsbridge (Heuston) train station. McCan's coffin was taken from the hearse to the train by Michael Collins and Harry Boland and accompanied on the train to Tipperary by Collins, Boland, Richard Mulcahy, Cathal Brugha and a company of Volunteers in uniform. The funeral in Thurles was a solemn and distinguished affair, attended by, according to the *Derry Journal*, 2,500 Irish Volunteers and 1,000 Cumann na mBan members. The same newspaper reported that 330 horse-drawn vehicles and 300 cyclists followed the remains through the town. Dr John Harty, the Catholic Archbishop of Cashel, spoke at the service, expressing the feelings of many in attendance: 'During the ten long months that Pierce McCan was in prison ... trial by his peers was denied him. Now he is dead and beyond the power — the tyrannical power — of the British Government.'[22]

RAID ON COLLINSTOWN AERODROME, 19 MARCH 1919

Collinstown Aerodrome (now Dublin Airport) was a base for the British Royal Air Force. A raid was planned for 19 March 1919 by Dublin IRA Brigadier Dick McKee, with the assistance of Paddy Holohan and a few Irish Volunteers who were employed as civilian workers at Collinstown. On the day of the raid, as they left work at six o'clock, the civilian workers gave the guard dogs at the aerodrome a feed of raw meat laced with morphine, which ensured that the animals slept soundly that night. Four motorcars carrying twenty-five IRA Volunteers left Parnell Square for Collinstown at midnight. In order to avoid the sound of shots being fired, the Volunteers were supplied with knuckle-dusters and daggers. As it transpired, they did not need them, as the night was wet and the sentry guarding the entrance was warming himself beside a stove inside the guard-hut. The IRA charged into the guardroom and arrested a dozen soldiers. They captured seventy-five much-needed rifles and 15,000 rounds of ammunition. When the Volunteers were leaving, the sentry who had been caught off guard pleaded with them, 'Ah, for the love of God, don't leave me here.' To save him from getting in trouble, the Volunteers took him outside, rolled him around in the dirt and smeared his face with muck to give the appearance of a man who had been jumped upon.

SECOND SESSION OF FIRST DÁIL

On 1 April 1919, the Dáil convened for the second time in the Mansion House, Dublin. As a result of the general amnesty for Irish prisoners, there was a larger attendance. Éamon de Valera was elected Príomh-Aire (President) of Dáil Éireann, replacing Cathal Brugha, and a cabinet was selected the following day. Brugha became Minister for Defence and Michael Collins was made Minister for Finance. Countess Markievicz became the Minister for Labour, the first female minister in Ireland; it would be another sixty years before another woman was appointed as a cabinet minister. At a further meeting, on 10 April, De Valera proposed that RIC members should be ostracised in their communities. The motion was seconded by Eoin MacNeill, and thus began the boycotting and shunning of the police. Having previously operated on the ground as the eyes and ears of the British authorities, RIC members now had nothing to pass on and the authorities were starved of information.

'LIMERICK SOVIET'

In Limerick, trade unionist Robert Byrne, Adjutant of the Second Limerick City Battalion IRA, was on hunger strike. Having been arrested in January 1919 under the Defence of the Realm Act (DORA), Byrne had been imprisoned in Limerick Prison where he had led an agitation for political-prisoner status, which had ultimately led to his undertaking a hunger strike. In mid-March, illness had forced his transfer to Limerick Union hospital. On 6 April 1919, an IRA rescue party went to free him from the hospital. When the IRA charged into the ward, an RIC man who was guarding Byrne shot him; the rescue party, however, did not at first realise that he had been fatally wounded and spirited him away to a safe house.[23] Byrne died later from his wounds. Two RIC men were also badly wounded, one fatally.

Using DORA, the British reacted by declaring Limerick a 'special military area' under their control. Effectively, any persons who wished to enter or leave Limerick required a permit to do so. Obviously this affected not alone the IRA but also impinged upon citizens going about their daily business. In reaction, the workers of Limerick, under the auspices of the United Trades and Labour Council, called for a 'General Strike against British Militarism'. Committees were formed and money and newspapers were printed; the price of bread and other necessary goods was controlled. However, a lack of support from the British trades unions and the vehement opposition of the Catholic Church meant that the 'Limerick Soviet', as the newspapers called it, was short-lived. Nonetheless, a number of soviets were declared during the revolutionary period 1919–21, with some IRA members, such as trade unionist and writer Peadar O'Donnell, holding very left-wing views.

The primary aim of the majority of the IRA during the War of Independence was to establish a republic, and people like Arthur Griffith were in no way supportive of a communist revolution as envisaged by men like Peadar O'Donnell. However, in May 1920, railway workers began to refuse to transport arms, ammunition and members of the British Army. This strike forced the British to use the roads system, which was slower and prone to attacks by the IRA. The protest was not defeated until wide-scale sackings of the striking workers were completed by December 1920.

SEÁN HOGAN RESCUE

Edmond O'Brien of the Galbally IRA recalled that after Soloheadbeg, south Tipperary was a military area and raids were intensified in the search for Séamus Robinson, Seán Hogan, Seán Treacy and Dan Breen, all of whom were on the run.[24] In May 1919, the 'Big Four', as they became known, attended a secret Volunteer dance in Ballagh, County Tipperary. Seán Hogan met a girl and went off to another dance in Enfield with her. Hogan was arrested in Enfield by the RIC and word came that he was going to be transferred to Cork by train, as was the normal procedure. Breen, Treacy and Robinson decided to attempt a rescue, a venture fraught with danger. Nonetheless, a decision was made to contact the Galbally IRA and attack the train at Knocklong to rescue Hogan.

On the evening of 13 May, the IRA waited for the arrival of the seven o'clock train and for the correct signal that Hogan was on board. The signal was to be given by four Galbally IRA men, Seán Lynch, Jim Scanlon, J.J. O'Brien and Edmond Foley, who would be in one of the carriages. When the train arrived, Treacy and the Galbally IRA man, Edmond O'Brien, boarded and hastily made their way towards the carriage where Hogan was being guarded. The IRA men shouted 'hands up', but O'Brien noticed that one of the policemen was about to shoot the prisoner, so he 'blazed at him, shooting him dead'.[25] Treacy then grappled with RIC Sergeant Peter Wallace who was well-built and determined to fight. The IRA Volunteers who had already been on the train joined the fight, and the RIC sergeant was wounded. It was too much for one RIC man, who jumped head-first through the glass of the train window. Hogan was told to run, and Lynch and Scanlon tackled another RIC man, Constable O'Reilly, who was knocked into submission using the butt of his own rifle. Lynch and Scanlon then made their escape. Meanwhile, Breen and Robinson, who had been guarding the gate to the station, ran to the fight, but Breen took a bullet from Constable O'Reilly who had recovered sufficiently from his beating to commence firing at the IRA as they left the carriage.[26] The IRA had rescued Hogan, but Seán Treacy had a bullet in his neck from which he was bleeding profusely, and Dan Breen was badly injured.

Constable Michael Enright had been killed in the ambush and Sergeant Peter Wallace died of his injuries the following day. A number of men were arrested on suspicion of being involved with the rescue of Hogan, including Patrick Maher and Edmond Foley. Two trials failed to reach a verdict but in February 1921, a military court martial sentenced Edmond Foley and Patrick Maher to death. Foley had been part of the rescue team but Maher was an innocent man. Both men were hanged in Mountjoy Jail on 7 June 1921.[27] Before they were executed, Foley and Maher released a joint statement which read: 'Our souls go to God at 7.00 in the morning, and our bodies when Ireland is free, shall go to Galbally.'

CHAPTER THREE

True Faith and Allegiance

One of the most important aspects of any conflict is propaganda. As we have seen, Sinn Féin, aided by the ineptitude and brutality of British policy in Ireland, had succeeded in winning support at home. They now needed to win the hearts, minds and wallets of their emigrant cousins in the United States. The US was, and perhaps still is, the dominant nation amongst all the nations of the world, and it was crucial that Ireland should be seen as a cause to champion. President Woodrow Wilson understood that Irish-Americans were a loyal constituency of his Democratic Party; however, he viewed the situation in Ireland as an internal matter to be resolved by the British Government, and he had held firmly to this view throughout the First World War. Following the Armistice, Wilson once again faced the appeals of Irish-Americans to recognise Ireland as one of what he had called the 'small states' that deserved 'self-determination'.

While Éamon de Valera spent eighteen months in the US, raising funds and making sure to keep Ireland in the news headlines, Michael Collins, now a key figure in both the political and the armed struggle, continued his intelligence war in Dublin. Collins brought the campaign against the police to a new level with the development of a highly dedicated group of hit men, the Squad, whose first target was the three detectives who had pointed out to the British who the ring-leaders of the 1916 Rising were. An attempt was made to bring the IRA in every county under the control of Dublin, and Volunteers took an oath to Dáil Éireann in August 1919. The following month, Liam Lynch and members of the IRA managed to disarm a patrol of British soldiers at Fermoy, which was a propaganda coup for the republican cause in Cork.

David Lloyd George had succeeded H.H. Asquith as British Prime Minister at the end of 1916 but the British Government remained slow to react to the changing tide of events in Ireland, reluctant even to admit that what was taking place in Ireland was a war. Eight months after its establishment, Dáil Éireann was finally banned, succeeding only in increasing support for the Volunteers. Despite the ban, Collins was confident enough to advertise the launch of the Dáil Loan scheme, established to raise money from nationalist subscribers for the republican government. Just before Christmas 1919, the IRA ambushed the Lord Lieutenant, Lord French, at Ashtown, Dublin. Although the ambush failed, it was clear that the fight was set to continue.

THE AMERICAN COMMISSION ON IRISH INDEPENDENCE

The Irish Race Convention gathered in Philadelphia on 22 and 23 February 1919. Five thousand delegates representing various strands of Irish-America came together and sent a message of support to Sinn Féin and in particular to Éamon de Valera. They also made demands for Irish independence and set up the Irish Victory Fund. The following month, a resolution was passed in the House of Representatives in favour of Irish 'self-determination':

> That it is the earnest hope of the Congress of the United States of America that the Peace Conference now sitting at Paris and passing upon the rights of various peoples will favourably consider the claims of Ireland to self-determination.

The 1919 St Patrick's Day Parade in New York was miles long. One banner held by clergy bore the words, 'We stand for a Free and Independent Ireland' and another, carried by women and girls, said, 'England, damn your concessions! We want our country'.[1]

The Paris Peace Conference, also known as the Versailles Peace Conference, was the meeting held at the end of the First World War to set the peace terms for the defeated countries. It had begun in January 1919 and involved diplomats from thirty-two countries and nationalities. In addition to the creation of the League of Nations and the signing of five peace treaties with the defeated states, the Conference also involved itself in setting new national boundaries. Irish Republicans felt that their interests should be represented there.

An enormously influential group of Irish-Americans representing the Irish Race Convention, including Judge John Goff, Judge Daniel Cohalan, Eugene Kinkhead, Frank Walsh, Edward Dunne, Michael Ryan and another nineteen individuals, persuaded President Woodrow Wilson's private secretary, Joseph Tumulty, to set up a meeting in New York with Wilson before he sailed for Paris for the Peace Conference. Judge Cohalan had to pull out of the meeting as Wilson considered him a disloyal American (he had dealt with Germany concerning the 1916 Rising). At what turned out to be a disagreeable and fractious meeting in the Metropolitan Opera House, Wilson reiterated to the delegation his view that the Irish question was a domestic problem for the British. However, he did send a government official, George Creel, to Ireland; Creel met Michael Collins and Harry Boland and reported back to the American President that 'sentiment in Ireland and America will harden in favour of an Irish Republic' unless the British at least introduced dominion status.[2]

A sub-committee of the Irish Race Convention was sent to Paris, comprising prominent Irish-Americans Frank P. Walsh, Edward F. Dunne and Michael J. Ryan, collectively known as the American

Commission on Irish Independence (ACII). In Paris, the Commission members were welcomed by Seán T. O'Kelly, Ceann Comhairle of the First Dáil, who had been sent to Paris in an endeavour to secure international recognition for Dáil Éireann. Walsh, Dunne and Ryan met President Wilson on 17 April. In the course of their meeting, Wilson said that once peace (with Germany) had been resolved, he would advise British Prime Minister Lloyd George that unless the Irish question were settled, American–British relations would be seriously affected.

Two potential meetings between Lloyd George and the ACII were cancelled, but Walsh, Dunne and Ryan decided to visit Ireland and, in fact, received the blessing of the British Prime Minister for the visit. They arrived on 3 May and were met by Éamon de Valera, W.T. Cosgrave and Joe McGuinness. The delegation was also received by the Lord Mayor of Dublin, Laurence O'Neill. The ACII men visited various parts of Ireland, including Mountjoy Jail, but controversially they also addressed the third session of the First Dáil, on 9 May, where they congratulated the Irish people for voting to create an Irish Republic. The Commission was given a display of British rule in Ireland when armed British troops surrounded the Mansion House for hours in a show of strength, searching unsuccessfully for Michael Collins and Robert Barton, TD for West Wicklow. Pro-British newspapers were hysterical about the visitors and one paper printed the headline: 'Impudent Yanks Flaunting "Irish Republic" Before Our Eyes'.

The original aim of the American Commission's visit had been to secure a safe passage to France for Éamon de Valera to meet with Wilson. Now the delegation's speeches in Ireland had incensed the British so much that Lloyd George would never agree to such a measure. Wilson maintained that he had been 'well on the way to getting Mr de Valera and his associates' over to Paris but that the Commission had 'kicked over the apple cart' with its actions in Ireland. The Commission returned to Paris but had no luck in securing a further meeting with Wilson; the hopes of obtaining a hearing in Versailles for an Irish delegation came to nothing. The Commission did, however, release a report on conditions in Ireland, outlining the brutal conditions in the jails for political prisoners, and the poverty, hunger and destitution being endured in Dublin. The *Manchester Guardian* reported on the Commission's findings:

> It cannot be denied that women and men have been arrested and detained for long periods without trial, that the imprisonment fatally broke the health of a few of them and destroyed the reason of others, that scores of other political prisoners sentenced by court martial have been in conflict with the prison authorities, that police truncheons, firemen's hoses, handcuffing behind back for several days (including days of solitary confinement in punishment cells) have been used to reduce them to subjection, that the conflict still goes on and the end is not in sight….[3]

ÉAMON DE VALERA IN THE USA

On 11 June 1919, Príomh Aire (President) of Dáil Éireann Éamon de Valera landed in New York. Britain had a new ally in the US, President Wilson, but if he could not be won over to the cause of Irish freedom, perhaps de Valera could win over the American people instead. A trip to the US by one of the surviving commandants from the Rising would also be useful in raising finances for the fledgling Irish Republic. Irish contacts in the US told de Valera that if he wanted a loan raised there, he would need to go there personally. The British suspected that de Valera might be intending a trip and, at the request of the American Embassy in London, the State Department put his name on a 'passport refusal list'. However, the State Department did not reckon on the Liverpool IRB who smuggled de Valera on board the *Lapland*.

Harry Boland, who had been on a fundraising mission in the US since May 1919, was tasked with looking after de Valera in the US. Boland's IRB comrade and personal friend Michael Collins now had a fairly free hand to run the war without any interference from de Valera.

Éamon de Valera, Michael Collins and Harry Boland enjoy a lighter moment in Dublin.

Significantly, de Valera would be absent from Ireland during some of the worst months of the war; as a consequence, Michael Collins assumed a leadership role in the eyes of the Irish people.

THE DUBLIN METROPOLITAN POLICE

The Irish Parliament passed the Dublin Police Act in 1786, establishing a small police force in Dublin. The Act divided Dublin into four districts, each under a chief constable with ten constables, who were backed up by night watchmen, and all under the control of a High Constable in Dublin Castle. However, less than ten years later, the Dublin Police were replaced by a civic guard, which came under the control of Dublin Corporation.

In 1814, when Robert Peel was Chief Secretary for Ireland, he helped pass an act through the British Parliament providing for a peace preservation force of resident magistrates and fifty constables who could be temporarily deployed in areas of unrest. They garnered the nickname 'Peelers' and were also under the direct control of Dublin Castle. In 1829, Peel as Home Secretary in Britain, masterminded the act which led to the establishment of the London Metropolitan Police, whose members were nicknamed 'Bobbies' (from Robert). The Irish Constabulary was established in 1836, as an armed police force for the Irish countryside (the Royal was added in 1867 after the force defeated the Fenians). At the same time, the Dublin Metropolitan Police (DMP) was also founded, specifically for the capital city. However, the force earned a poor reputation, especially during the 1913–14 Lockout when its members killed a number of strikers. The DMP was divided into sections A to F, with the detective branch being G-Division. Detectives were known as G-men, a phrase that was exported to the US in the 1920s and used to describe FBI agents; it has mistakenly been etymologised as Government-men.

SHOOTING OF DETECTIVE SMYTH

Mick McDonnell was a Wicklow man who had fought in Jacob's factory in 1916 and was interned in Frongoch. In the prison camp he came into close contact with other IRB men, including Michael Collins. On his release, McDonnell was made Quartermaster of the Second Battalion IRA Dublin Brigade. Dick McKee, the Brigadier of the Dublin Brigade of the IRA, asked McDonnell, on behalf of Michael Collins, to shoot the detectives, or G-men, who were responsible for identifying the executed 1916 leaders and who were still watching the Volunteers.[4]

The first G-man that McDonnell targeted was Detective Sergeant Patrick 'the Dog' Smyth (often misspelled as Smith). Smyth was responsible for numerous raids on the premises of the *Gaelic Press* printer, Joe Stanley; he 'was not only an obnoxious detective officer, but he also had strong anti-Sinn Féin prejudices.'[5] Smyth may also have known what Collins looked like, as he had raided 44 Parnell Square, and finding another Volunteer, Fionán Lynch, in the bed Collins normally used, had told his colleagues that it was not Collins.[6] Seán Kennedy, who had fought alongside Lynch in the Four Courts in 1916, recalled the prisoners being scrutinised by G-men in Richmond Barracks after the Rising. 'Among the Detective Officers concerned I noticed Smyth, Hoey, Gaffney, Barton, all of whom, with the exception of Gaffney, were subsequently executed by our forces during the Tan War.'[7]

Mick McDonnell asked Tom Keogh, his half-brother who had fought alongside him in Jacob's in 1916, and two more Second Battalion IRA Dublin Brigade men, Jim Slattery and Tom Ennis, to shoot Smyth. An IRA Intelligence Officer, Mick Kennedy, who knew Smyth by sight, was also present as they waited around Drumcondra Bridge in north Dublin. Their target always travelled home by tram from the city centre, and the plan was to shoot him as he alighted from a tram.

After many nights of waiting, they eventually shot Smyth on 30 July using .38 revolvers. This calibre was too small, and Smyth was able to run from his assailants. Keogh and Slattery continued to fire as the wounded detective made it into his home at 51 Millmount Avenue. Smyth died of his wounds six weeks later. McDonnell, having been very concerned that the G-man might recover and identify him, resolved never to use .38s again. As Jim Slattery later recalled, 'we used .45 guns after that lesson.'[8] The men who carried out the shooting of Detective Smyth formed the nucleus of the famous Squad.

IRA OATH TO DÁIL ÉIREANN

Richard Mulcahy had set up a General Head-Quarters (GHQ) of the IRA in March 1918. Mulcahy was Chief of Staff of the IRA but he was also in the oath-bound IRB, as was the IRA's Director of Organisation, Michael Collins. In fact, the majority of the IRA's GHQ staff were IRB members too. In reality, the GHQ staff exerted little real control over the IRA outside of Dublin but they did provide education and propaganda through their newspaper *An tÓglách* (the Volunteer), which carried the tagline 'The Official Organ of the Irish Volunteer'. *An tÓglách* contributors were mainly sworn members of the IRB.

In an effort to undermine the supreme authority of the Brotherhood and in order to keep Michael Collins in check, Cathal Brugha, the Minister for Defence, made a good attempt at getting the IRA under control. At a meeting of the Dáil, Brugha, moved that:

> Every person and every one of those bodies undermentioned must swear allegiance to the Irish Republic and to the Dáil:
> 1. The Deputies.
> 2. The Irish Volunteers.
> 3. The officers and Clerks to the Dáil
> 4. Any other body or individual who in the opinion of the Dáil should take the same Oath.

The suggested oath was as follows:

> I, A.B., do solemnly swear (or affirm) that I do not and shall not yield a voluntary support to any pretended Government, authority or power within Ireland, hostile and inimical thereto, and I do further swear (or affirm) that to the best of my knowledge and ability I will support and defend the Irish Republic and the Government of the Irish Republic, which is Dáil Éireann, against all enemies, foreign and domestic, and I will bear true faith and allegiance to the same, and that I take this obligation freely without any mental reservation or purpose of evasion, so help me God.[9]

Cathal Brugha's motion was carried, with thirty for and five against, and IRA Volunteers all over Ireland swore the oath.

LIAM LYNCH DISARMS BRITISH SOLDIERS AT FERMOY

While working in Mitchelstown as an apprentice at the hardware trade, Liam Lynch, originally from Barnagurraha near Anglesboro in County Limerick, immersed himself in reading and joined the Gaelic League. In 1916, as an employee of Barry's Hardware in Fermoy, Lynch witnessed the Kent brothers crossing Fermoy Bridge under arrest. The subsequent execution of Thomas Kent encouraged him to dedicate his life to the cause of Irish freedom, and he joined the Irish Volunteers. On 6 January, when Cork IRA was divided into seven battalions, Lynch was elected Officer Commanding (O/C) of Cork Number 2 Brigade. As his area contained 4,300 British military and 490 police, he badly needed weapons.[10]

Lynch's comrade in the Cork IRA, Michael Fitzgerald from Fermoy, had raided Araglin RIC Barracks on Easter Sunday, 20 April 1919 and successfully secured some rifles. Lynch decided to try to obtain weapons from the British in a similar fashion. On 7 September 1919, Lynch, Dan Hegarty (Brigade Vice O/C), Owen Harold (O/C Mallow Company), Edward Waters and Brian Kelly were being driven in a car by Leo O'Callaghan when they overtook a party of British soldiers from the Shropshire Light Infantry on the way to the Wesleyan church in Fermoy. The IRA car came to a halt in front of the British soldiers and beside a number of other IRA Volunteers who had been casually waiting in the vicinity. Lynch blew a whistle and the occupants of the car and the other IRA Volunteers pounced on the British and quickly snapped the rifles from their grasp. One of the soldiers, Private William Jones, a Welshman, 'who proved more aggressive' than the others, was fired on and died later that day.[11] The captured weapons were loaded into two cars,

O'Callaghan's and another driven by Jack Mulvey. A mile from Fermoy the Volunteers stopped and cut the ropes on a couple of trees that they had sawn through earlier, thus blocking the approach of any British in pursuit.[12]

On the night after the ambush, the British forces stationed in Fermoy ran riot, angered by the shooting of Private Jones. The *Freeman's Journal* published this report:

> About 9 o'clock, a party of soldiers, said to belong to the Shropshire
> Light Infantry, to which regiment the party attacked on Sunday belonged,
> accompanied by a number of artillery men, proceeded to break windows
> in the Square, Bank Street and Patrick Street ... Between 20 and 30 shops
> were looted in about an hour and a half ... The attack by the soldiers on
> the shops was obviously an organised one ... and was led by a soldier
> with a whistle which he blew at intervals to rally his followers and direct
> their movements.[13]

The Wesleyan Ambush is of particular importance for two reasons. Firstly, the British Army had not been engaged by the IRA since 1916, and this time the troops lost. Secondly, it resulted in the first large-scale example of a policy of reprisals by the British on the civilian population.

A number of IRA Volunteers were arrested because of what came to be known as the Wesleyan Ambush; most were released but Dan Hegarty, John Joe Hogan and Michael Fitzgerald were committed to Cork Gaol. As will be discussed further in Chapter Eight, Fitzgerald died on hunger strike on 17 October 1920.

DÁIL ÉIREANN: LOAN SCHEME AND PARLIAMENT BANNED

In September 1919, Michael Collins, as Minister for Finance, launched a spectacular and provocative Dáil Éireann Loan scheme, whereby bonds were issued to raise funds to finance the Dáil. The hope was to raise

£250,000 in Ireland and the same amount in the US. These bonds would be repaid with 5 percent interest after the withdrawal of the British military forces. By July 1920, the Loan had collected £370,000 in Ireland alone, symbolic of the hope and trust in the Dáil that the people had at the time. The launch of the scheme coincided with the banning of the Dáil, and any newspapers which published the prospectus were suppressed.

DÁIL ÉIREANN BANNED

On 10 September 1919, the British tried to silence democracy in Ireland by banning Dáil Éireann, the assembly of elected representatives who refused to take their seats at Westminster. The ban was reinforced by raids on Sinn Féin offices around Ireland. On 12 September, at Sinn Féin headquarters at 6 Harcourt Street, Ernest Blythe and Patrick O'Keeffe, two members of Dáil Éireann, were arrested by forty British soldiers and ten members of G-Division of the DMP under Detective Daniel Hoey.

Raid by British military forces on Sinn Féin headquarters, Harcourt Street, Dublin, 12 September 1919.

The police seized documents relating to the Dáil Éireann Loan scheme but missed an opportunity to capture Michael Collins who was actually there in one of the offices. A large cheering crowd gathered on Harcourt Street and the British soldiers were forced to attempt to restore order at bayonet point. Someone shouted, 'Up the Republic', and the soldiers tried to capture him but the crowd prevented them from carrying out an arrest. Raids were carried out around Ireland in Cork, Belfast, Derry, Waterford and Kilkenny. The homes of Count Plunkett and W.T. Cosgrave were also raided.

THE SQUAD

The Squad was formed officially on 19 September 1919. Before that, as we have seen, as early as 1 May 1919, there had existed another squad. The principal mover in the original squad had been the 1916 veteran, Mick McDonnell. McDonnell recalled that following his release from Frongoch he 'was appointed Captain Quartermaster in the Second Battalion to take the place of Michael O'Hanrahan who was executed in 1916. I remained with the Second Battalion until I took over the Squad early in 1919.'[14]

This first Squad had shot Detective Smyth on 30 July and Detective Hoey on 12 September 1919. As well as having been directly involved in the ambush of Smyth and Hoey, Mick McDonnell also gave the orders and was involved in at least four more shootings between September (when the Squad was officially formed) and the following April 1920. He mainly used himself, Tom Keogh and Jim Slattery for those six shootings. A sworn member of the IRB, he was in close contact with Michael Collins.

Vinny Byrne, who had fought in Jacob's in 1916 and was a member of the Second Battalion IRA Dublin Brigade, reckoned that the first-time Squad was made up of himself, Mick McDonnell, Tom Keogh, Jim Slattery, Paddy Daly, Joe Leonard and Ben Barrett. He recalled that the first full-time paid Squad was made up of the aforementioned seven men who were joined by Seán Doyle, Paddy Griffin, Eddie Byrne, Mick Reilly and Jimmy Conroy. Those men were called the Twelve Apostles, and Byrne was emphatic that they were commanded by Mick McDonnell.[15]

However, another IRB man, Paddy Daly, said that Mick McDonnell was not in the Squad, which is highly unlikely. Paddy Daly recalled the first meeting when Dick McKee told him to report to 46 Parnell Square, the meeting place of the Keating Branch of the Gaelic League. When he went to the meeting, on 19 September 1919, he saw Joe Leonard, Ben Barrett, Seán Doyle, Tom Keogh, Jim Slattery, Vinny Byrne and Mick McDonnell. 'We met Michael Collins and Dick Mulcahy at the meeting and they told us that it was proposed to form a Squad.' Daly recalled that of all the men there that day only four were picked as full-time Squad members: Joe Leonard, Seán Doyle, Ben Barrett and himself in charge. Later in the same statement, he says: 'Mick McDonnell was one of the best men in Dublin, but he had one fault. He was always butting in, and on account of that he often did damage because he was too eager. He was not a member of the Squad.'[16]

Backing Daly up in his assertion that he was the Squad leader, William Stapleton recalled in his witness statement that he had been selected by GHQ with some others to bring the Squad up to twelve. 'I understood at the time, and confirmed it at a later date, that the senior members of the Squad were — Paddy Daly in charge, Tom Keogh and Jim Slattery.' Stapleton recalled meeting the full Squad at 100 Seville Place: Tom Keogh, Jim Slattery, Frank Bolster, Mick Kennedy, Eddie Byrne, Vinny Byrne, Joe Leonard, Ben Byrne, James Conroy and Paddy Griffin. Stapleton excluded Mick McDonnell in his list.

It is clear that there were two sections of the Squad, one very much led by Mick McDonnell, which operated with part-time members who were working at jobs. The other section was under the control of Paddy Daly and those men received a wage. An interesting incident occurred on 30 November 1919 when John Barton was shot dead. As will be seen below, both sections of the Squad went to ambush him, one under McDonnell and the other under Daly.

Of course, the 'Big Four' from Tipperary, Séamus Robinson, Seán Treacy, Seán Hogan and Dan Breen, were also on hand in Dublin and acted as extra guns when the Squad needed them. Owen Cullen acted as a driver for a short time and two Clare men, Paddy Kelly and Mick Brennan, were employed occasionally.

THE INTELLIGENCE DEPARTMENT

The Squad did not shoot random policemen in Dublin. All potential targets were researched and decided upon after much deliberation. The Squad received direct instructions through the GHQ Intelligence Department, and Michael Collins was the Director of Intelligence or DI.[17] Liam Tobin was Director of Intelligence under Michael Collins. Tom Cullen was Assistant Director of Intelligence and underneath Cullen was Frank Thornton, Deputy Assistant Director of Intelligence. GHQ Intelligence staff were numerous and included Joe Dolan, Frank Saurin, Ned Kelleher, Joe Guilfoyle, Paddy Caldwell, Paddy Kennedy, Charlie Dalton, Dan McDonnell and Charlie Byrne who were all Intelligence officers.[18] The Department of Intelligence was based at 3 Crow Street in Temple Bar but Collins was not a frequent visitor to this office.[19] Charlie Dalton, who worked closely with Collins, recalled:

> During the daytime Michael Collins worked from an office of his own, and at no time did he visit the Crow St. or Brunswick St. offices. Inter-communication was maintained by his special messenger, Joe O'Reilly. In the evening time Michael Collins used to meet Liam Tobin and Tom Cullen at one of his numerous rendezvous in the Parnell Square area — these were Jim Kirwan's, Vaughan's Hotel and Liam Devlin's.[20]

Liam Devlin's pub was at 68 Parnell Street and was 'Joint No. 2', a well-known meeting place for Collins and the IRA. Paddy Daly of the Squad lived next door. Kirwan's pub was popular with the Tipperary IRA men and was at 49 Parnell Street. Vaughan's was on Parnell Square, so all three meeting places were within a stone's throw of each other on the northside of Dublin city.

Dalton recalled:

> Michael Collins used as his personal office Miss Hoey's in Mespil Road; also Mary St., and finally Harcourt Terrace ... which was an ordinary dwelling house, and in the front bedroom the DI had his papers. These were concealed in a secret cupboard on the landing, in which he himself could take refuge should the house be raided while he was in occupation.[21]

Collins used the Intelligence operatives and the Squad with tremendous success to retaliate against the British; he became the most successful Director of Intelligence of the IRA in the history of the movement. According to some of those closest to him, though, he was also extremely demanding, bossy and prone to bullying. He had a reputation for being a womaniser and a heavy drinker and prone to bouts of depression. However, he carried a huge burden on his shoulders; he was responsible for ordering killings and for the safety of his activists. The future of the Irish nation was in his hands and, without doubt, there are few Irish leaders who elicited such loyalty and devotion from the populace.

DETECTIVES WORKING FOR COLLINS

Michael Collins had a number of operatives who worked for him in Dublin Castle. Ned Broy, a G-man, came over to the side of the IRA, and it was thanks to him that Collins and Seán Nunan managed to get into Great Brunswick Street (Pearse Street) Dublin Metropolitan Police

Station, on 7 April 1919, to read all the files they had on republicans. Broy reported daily to Collins and proved to be an invaluable source of up-to-date information, until he was arrested in 1921. Joseph Kavanagh spied for the IRA and Collins until he died in 1919. Knowing that he was terminally ill, he made sure to draft a colleague in Dublin Castle, James McNamara, to act as a spy after his death.

David Nelligan wrote a memoir, *The Spy in the Castle,* concerning the tremendous amount of work he did on behalf of the IRA. Nelligan actually resigned his position as his brother Maurice was in the IRA, but Collins convinced him to ask for his job back. Nelligan was recruited into MI5 in 1921, and after the arrest of Broy was an invaluable asset to Collins.

Lily Merrin worked as a typist in the British military intelligence offices in Ship Street Barracks, attached to Dublin Castle, and always made sure that an extra carbon copy was inserted into her typewriter to pass on to Collins. Most serendipitously of all, Nancy O'Brien, who was specifically employed by Sir James Macmahon, the Under-Secretary, to decode secret British messages, passed them to her second cousin, Michael Collins.

SHOOTING OF DETECTIVE DANIEL HOEY

Piaras Beaslaí described the police detectives from G-Division swooping on the 1916 prisoners as a 'flock of carrion crows' picking out victims for the firing squad. 'Anybody who had seen that sight may be pardoned if he felt little compunction at the subsequent shooting of these same "G" men.' One of the G-men who had picked out Seán MacDiarmada from amongst the rank and file was Daniel Hoey. Austin Stack was arrested by Hoey for wearing a Volunteer uniform, for which 'crime' he received two years in prison. Hoey was also in charge of the raid on the Sinn Féin office at 6 Harcourt Street on 12 September, and was getting close to Michael Collins. During that raid, as Detective

Hoey was looking at a tray of papers, an IRA Volunteer warned him that the last man who had picked up that tray was Detective Smyth (who had been shot dead on 30 July). That evening, Mick McDonnell told Jim Slattery that they 'very nearly got the man we want to guard. They nearly got him today.' He was referring to Collins.[22] McDonnell, Slattery and Tom Ennis shot Detective Daniel Hoey dead on Townsend Street, beside Great Brunswick Street DMP Station (now Pearse Street Garda Station) on 12 September 1919.

THE *IRISH BULLETIN*

The underground Irish Government found a way of disseminating information to foreign and Irish journalists through the production of a daily report called the *Irish Bulletin*. Edited by Desmond FitzGerald from 11 November 1919, it became very reliable for the accuracy of its reporting, although obviously it leaned towards support of the Republican cause. Cathleen Napoli-McKenna used a mimeograph, a type of printer, to produce every issue during the war in Ireland. 'The *Bulletin* was sent to the London correspondents of the European and World press with whom Desmond FitzGerald had made friends on visits to London. The result was soon seen in an increase of news items and articles about Ireland in foreign papers.'[23]

Robert Brennan of Sinn Féin's publicity department recalled that the *Irish Bulletin* was delivered to hundreds of addresses abroad: 'This publication was doing such damage to England's presentation of the Irish case that, in time, its attempted suppression became one of the major objectives of the British Military Government.'[24] Besides Sundays and bank holidays, not one issue of the *Irish Bulletin* was missed between November 1919 and July 1921. Even when FitzGerald was arrested in February 1921, Erskine Childers took over the production of the *Bulletin* without a hitch.

SHOOTING OF DETECTIVE JOHN BARTON

Another of the G-men who had picked MacDiarmada for court martial was John Barton who had remarked to him, 'Sorry Seán but you can't get away that easy.'[25] That is not to say that the G-Division detectives who were targeted by the Squad were shot simply for their actions after the Easter Rising. They had all been warned on a number of occasions to cease interfering in the political situation but all had continued their harassment of Sinn Féin and the Volunteers.

According to David Nelligan, the IRA agent working in Dublin Castle, Barton was not long in G-Division when he discovered 'a little arms dump' and the Castle was jubilant. Nelligan said that Barton was easily the best detective in these islands, had plenty of touts working for him and was known to be well off financially.[26] Mick McDonnell, Tom Keogh, Joe Leonard, Vinny Byrne and Jim Slattery went in search of the detective on 30 November 1919. On College Street, they heard a couple of shots and saw Barton on the ground. Slattery said later that Detective Barton had been shot by Paddy Daly's section of the Squad.[27] This is backed up by Joe Leonard who was on the same mission that night and was shocked to experience a heavy fusillade of firing from an unexpected place.[28] This firing clearly came from Paddy Daly's section. Vinny Byrne said that Barton 'got as far as the Crampton Monument … when fire was opened on him … He went down on his side … and raised himself a little on his right knee and said "Oh, God, what did I do to deserve this?" With that, he pulled his gun and fired up College Street.'[29] It was the last thing he did before he died.

AMBUSH ON LORD LIEUTENANT FRENCH AT ASHTOWN

The Squad next undertook to execute John French, Lord Lieutenant of Ireland, and after a number of attempts the men finally received good intelligence that their target would be returning by train to Dublin from his country seat at Drumdoe House in Roscommon. French was expected to arrive, on 19 December, at Ashtown Station in Dublin, from where he would be driven to the Viceregal Lodge in the Phoenix Park. The full-time paid Squad of Paddy Daly, Joe Leonard, Ben Barrett and Seán Doyle were joined by Mick McDonnell, Jim Slattery, Tom Keogh and Vinny Byrne. Martin Savage, who had fought in the Easter Rising when he was seventeen years of age, insisted on coming along. The 'Big Four', Séamus Robinson, Dan Breen, Seán Treacy and Seán Hogan, were also invited by McDonnell. As there was a taxi drivers' strike over petrol permits, the IRA men made their way to Ashtown on bicycles. They awaited the arrival of their quarry in Kelly's public house where they consumed soft drinks.

When the signal came that French's train had arrived in the station, the Volunteers all left the pub, and Breen, Keogh and Savage attempted to push a large farm-cart onto the road to block the convoy as planned.[30]

A British sergeant points to a bullet hole in Lord French's car following an ambush at Ashtown in December 1919.

However, the cart proved too heavy and a policeman on point duty was interfering with their progress. This delay allowed the first car, which contained French, to pass before the men had managed to get the cart into the road. The Squad members, expecting French to be in the second car, launched a grenade attack and fired their guns at it. In the deadly exchange of fire, Martin Savage was mortally wounded and died in Breen's arms. Breen himself was badly wounded in the leg. After the British retreated, the IRA succeeded in capturing the second car, which had nothing in it but luggage. The driver, Corporal Applesby, was in fear of his life after he surrendered, but one of the IRA men let him know that they didn't shoot prisoners.

Savage's corpse was left in the yard of Kelly's pub as the proprietor would not open the door, and the ambushers made their way back to the city.[31] Breen was eventually brought to the Malone home at 13 Grantham Street, where he spent three months convalescing. He later married one of the women who had looked after him there, Brighid Malone, whose brother Mick Malone had been killed during the Battle of Mount Street Bridge in 1916. Breen maintained that the ambush had been worth the risk for the potential sensation of shooting a 'Field-Marshal of the British Army, head of the Irish Government' in the capital city of the country he was supposed to rule, and all 'within a stone's throw of half a dozen of Britain's military garrisons'.[32]

CHAPTER FOUR

Low-Down Lot
of Scoundrels

The War of Independence continued into 1920. As the year opened, Sinn Féin maintained its electoral success when the party dominated the polls and took over town councils in the Local Government elections. Later that month, the Squad shot a high-ranking district inspector of the RIC who had come to Dublin to take over police Intelligence. Another significant incident was the capture in February of Ballytrain RIC Barracks in Monaghan by Ernie O'Malley and the IRA. The following month, police with blackened faces shot the Lord Mayor of Cork, Tomás MacCurtain; a jury at his inquest accused Prime Minister Lloyd George of wilful murder. Three men found to have been spying for the British, were unmasked and shot by the IRA. The reign of terror for the people of Ireland had only just begun when the Black and Tans arrived in March. Meanwhile, Alan Bell, who had been tasked with discovering the hundreds of thousands of pounds that the Irish Government had at its disposal, was shot by the Squad.

In an attempt to take control of the situation, the British undertook a shake-up of the administration of Dublin Castle. Warren Fisher, the Head of the British Civil Service, made certain recommendations, including the appointment of a new chief secretary, a new general officer commander of the British Army, a new special police advisor, and a new joint under-secretary; this chapter discusses the men who were appointed to these roles. Ultimately, though, British policy in Ireland was incoherent and failing, while support for Sinn Féin was continuing to grow, bolstered by widespread revulsion at British brutality.

LOCAL GOVERNMENT ELECTIONS, 1920

The last thirty-two-county all-Ireland local elections were held in January and June 1920. For the first time, *all over* Ireland, proportional representation (PR) with a single transferrable vote (STV) was used. Sligo Corporation elections had used the system in 1919 and the University of Dublin (Trinity College) had done so the previous year. The introduction of PR and the STV throughout Ireland had required an Act of Parliament, the Local Government (Ireland) Act, 1919. It is interesting to note that although Britain considered Ireland to be part of a 'united' kingdom, both islands used different electoral systems. Clearly the Act was designed to undermine Sinn Féin following its resounding victory in the General Election of 1918.

However, Westminster failed to hinder Sinn Féin's growing popularity. The urban area elections in January gave Sinn Féin control of nine of the eleven corporations. When the rural elections were held in June, Sinn Féin made even greater gains and took control of twenty-nine out of thirty-three councils.[1]

Arthur Griffith was reported in the *Fermanagh Herald* as having said:

Sinn Féin had to face this election with its political organisation suppressed by the English Government, its election literature interdicted, its transit arrangements deliberately obstructed by the Motor Permits Order, its secretary, Ald. Kelly, seized and imprisoned without charges, and its Press stifled. And in spite of it all, it has swept the country … [The people] have repeated — if possible more emphatically in 1920 — the verdict of 1918. That is their answer to the brutal and dastardly regime of coercion to which they have been subjected, and which, as these elections show, has intensified their determination to be masters in their own land. Let us see whether the English Coalitition Government will now apply Proportional Representation to its own land. England is an oligarchy and the oligarchs don't like PR.

Proportional representation was also credited by the *Fermanagh Herald* with 'helping the minorities'. 'Women are much in evidence. Mrs. Tom Clarke won the aldermanship for two Dublin areas, and the ladies in the city council now number six — all Sinn Feiners.'[2]

Kevin O'Higgins, who had replaced W.T. Cosgrave as Minister for Local Government after Cosgrave's arrest in 1920, succeeded in persuading the councils to give their allegiance to Dáil Éireann. Dublin Castle stopped all payments to corporations and councils in July 1920.

RIC DISTRICT INSPECTOR WILLIAM REDMOND SHOT BY THE SQUAD

Frank Thornton, who was Deputy Assistant Director of Intelligence during the War of Independence, recalled his part in the shooting of the new Assistant Commissioner of the Dublin Metropolitan Police, William C. Forbes Redmond, in Harcourt Street in January 1920. Redmond 'had been transferred from Belfast to take over the organisation of Intelligence … in Dublin City.'[3] Thornton went up to Belfast where a contact in the RIC, a Sergeant McCarthy from Kerry, sneaked him into a police barracks where he stole a photograph of Redmond and passed it to the Squad.

Around this time, according to Paddy Daly, the Squad was increased by four to make eight. Daly, Joe Leonard, Ben Barrett and Seán Doyle were now joined as full-time paid members by Tom Keogh, Jim Slattery, Vinny Byrne and Mick Reilly. After Redmond's arrival in Dublin, the detectives became very active and the G-men were given orders to find Michael Collins.

Tom Cullen, Assistant Director of Intelligence, booked a room in the Standard Hotel on Harcourt Street to keep an eye on his fellow guest, Redmond, whose apartments in Dublin Castle were not ready. Joe Dolan, who was a member of IRA GHQ Intelligence, said that Detective James McNamara 'who was working with our Intelligence, gave us information about Redmond.'[4]

That information was that Redmond was attending a meeting in Dublin Castle on 21 January. A few Squad members were placed at the Castle gates, some on George's Street, and a group at each end of Grafton Street. Joe Leonard, Seán Doyle and Paddy Daly were told by Collins to wait on Harcourt Street. Daly was annoyed that he would not get a chance to shoot Redmond as the other Squad members would probably encounter the target first. Collins replied that the goalkeeper often gets as much of the ball as any of the team.

As it transpired, Collins was right. Daly remembered seeing 'Tom Keogh and another man crossing the road to the railings side of the Green'. Daly turned to Joe Leonard to let him know that Keogh was coming. The 'other man' was Redmond. Daly fired when the new Assistant Commissioner was two yards from him, 'and he fell mortally wounded, shot through the head'.[5] Daly said that he was the only one who shot Redmond but Joe Dolan remembered it slightly differently, recalling that just as Redmond 'came as far as Montague Street, Paddy Daly pulled out his revolver and shot him under the ear and Tom Keogh pulled out his revolver and shot him in the back.'[6] In any case, Redmond had been shot dead.

According to Joe Leonard, Redmond was 'a knight in shining armour — concealed beneath his coat', which was a reference to the fact that the detective inspector wore a bulletproof jacket. Leonard explained that the 'knight' should also have worn a helmet, 'but one day he forgot to don his vizor and fell a victim, in Harcourt Street, to his own neglect.'[7]

ATTACK ON BALLYTRAIN (SHANTONAGH) RIC BARRACKS, MONAGHAN

Born in Castlebar, County Mayo, and raised in Dublin, Ernie O'Malley had given up his medical studies to become a full-time activist with the IRA. In early January 1920, he was sent to County Monaghan 'as a GHQ organiser, travelling from one company area to another, drilling, lecturing and training the Volunteers'.

It was in that capacity that O'Malley was present during a meeting held at the home of two Rockcorry Company IRA men, John and Edward McGahey; also present were Eoin O'Duffy, O/C Monaghan Brigade, and other local IRA Volunteers. At the meeting, a plan was agreed and arrangements made to attack Ballytrain RIC Barracks. Philip Marron recalled in his witness statement that an extensive plan of road blocking was ordered all over County Monaghan to prevent the arrival of British reinforcements.

On the night of 14 February 1920, about thirty IRA Volunteers made their way to the RIC Barracks situated at a crossroads in a village called Shantonagh, about a mile and a half from Ballytrain. They occupied the adjoining premises and a shop in front of the two-storey police station, with Ernie O'Malley and a few other men guarding the rear position. Two men, Paddy McCabe and Thomas Donnelly, experts in explosives, were instructed to use a mine to blow a hole in the gable wall of the barracks.[7] Eoin O'Duffy occupied a nearby post office, which was used as a command post.

When the shooting commenced, the police were asked to surrender but they refused. The fight had lasted in all about four hours when the police were advised to move to the end of the building. The mine was detonated, and the explosion caused the gable wall to fall in. 'We found the police constables huddled in a corner against the opposite gable,' said Philip Marron who later joined the Garda Síochána.[8] All of the garrison's rifles, revolvers and ammunition were seized.

Ballytrain RIC Barracks following an attack by the Monaghan Brigade of the IRA.

O'Malley recalled an exchange he had with Michael Collins in which the latter asked him what he thought of Eoin O'Duffy. 'Well, I liked his typing best of what I have seen,' said O'Malley.[9] O'Duffy shot off one of his own fingers during the War of Independence, by accident, and later tried to claim the Black and Tans did it. He went on to lead the fascist Army Comrades Association or Blueshirts in the 1930s.

QUINLISK THE SPY

Dick Walsh, Mayo IRA Brigade Adjutant, was often in Dublin for Volunteer business. While there, he got to know Timothy Quinlisk, a Wexford man introduced to him by Michael Collins in the Munster Hotel, a safe boarding house at 44 Mountjoy Street. A former British Army corporal who had been captured in France during the First World War, Quinlisk had become Brigade Quartermaster Sergeant in Roger Casement's

Irish Brigade whilst a prisoner of war.[10] Walsh did not trust the heavy-drinking Quinlisk but had to share a room with him a few nights each month from late 1918 through to 1919. Quinlisk's rent was being paid by Collins, who was getting some Intelligence information from him but suspected that he was working for Dublin Castle. Collins lacked proof, though, and told Walsh to keep an eye on him.

According to Walsh, Collins was tiring of Quinlisk and, wanting to be rid of him, gave him £100 on the understanding that he would go to Germany. However, Quinlisk promptly spent it all at the Galway Races and returned to Dublin penniless.[11] Seán Ó Muirthile, who would later become Quartermaster General of the Free State's National Army, set a trap for Quinlisk, who was badgering everyone to get a meeting with Collins. Ó Muirthile told Quinlisk that the 'Big Fella' was going to Cork and would meet him at a certain hotel. In fact, Collins had no intention of going to Cork, but it was a test to see if Quinlisk would pass on the information to the British. Ó Muirthile and Liam Archer, another Intelligence agent working for Collins, decoded a cipher from the Inspector General of the RIC to the County Inspector in Cork, detailing the lie that Collins would be in Cork the following day. This proved that Quinlisk was a spy. On being shown the decoded letter at a meeting of the Keating Branch of the Gaelic League, Collins responded by saying of Quinlisk, 'That … has signed his death warrant.'[12]

However, it would appear that some in the Cork IRA were already on to Quinlisk; Michael Murphy, Commandant of the Second Battalion Cork Number 1 Brigade, remembered being called to Wren's Hotel as a man named 'Quinn' was talking loudly about wanting to contact Michael Collins. 'Quinn' arrived a few nights later at the Thomas Ashe Sinn Féin Club at Father Mathew Quay in Cork and warned everyone that the club was about to be raided by the British. However, Quinlisk had apparently arranged the raid in order to ingratiate himself with the Cork IRA. Murphy later told him that Collins was in Clonakilty (at a time when

Murphy knew him to be in Dublin) and that they needed a man who could assemble a Hotchkiss machine gun. He said that if Quinlisk could do it, he would earn £10. On 18 February 1920, Michael Murphy and two other IRA men, Frank Mahony and Jimmy Walsh, brought Quinlisk to a field on the outskirts of Cork city and shot him. They found on his person a letter written by him and addressed to the RIC, saying that Collins was in Clonakilty.[13] Timothy Quinlisk was one of 196 suspected spies killed by the IRA during the War of Independence.

JOHN CHARLES BYRNES, ALIAS JACK JAMESON

Speaker's Corner at Hyde Park in London has long had the reputation for being a place where the police take a relaxed attitude to people who want to espouse their political or religious beliefs on a public platform. The Irish Self-Determination League regularly held court there during the war in Ireland. Beside them there was a communist group who befriended the League's President, Art O'Brien, and the General Secretary, Seán McGrath. The communists ingratiated themselves with O'Brien and McGrath by giving them arms and ammunition for the IRA in Ireland. One of the communists, who called himself Jack Jameson, impressed O'Brien and McGrath with a plan to create a mutiny in the British Army in Ireland, and they agreed to organise a meeting for him with Michael Collins in Dublin. The meeting with Collins went ahead, and Jameson promised to procure more arms.

However, most of the men in the Squad were unimpressed by Jameson and not entirely convinced of his authenticity. Jameson, in the company of Liam Tobin, the Deputy Director of Intelligence under Michael Collins, delivered a bag of revolvers to Frank Thornton, the Deputy Assistant Director of Intelligence, in the doorway of Kapp and Peterson's tobacco shop at the intersection of Bachelors Walk and Sackville Street (O'Connell Street) in Dublin. Thornton pretended to go down to the basement of the building but when

Jameson and Tobin had left, he gave the revolvers to Tom Cullen who was waiting at 32 Bachelors Walk, an office used by the INAVDF and by the IRA. Meanwhile, James McNamara, a police detective who was working for the IRA, was asked to report any potential raids that day. Around midday, McNamara contacted Thornton and said that there was a raid due at 3pm on the New Ireland Assurance Society's premises, right above Kapp and Peterson's. The premises were indeed raided, and although the police ransacked the place, they could not find the revolvers. According to Thornton, 'following other incidents which happened it was finally decided that Jameson was a spy and would have to be shot.'[15]

Joe Dolan from IRA GHQ Intelligence and Paddy Daly cycled out into the countryside to find somewhere to shoot the spy. They went as far as the then village of Ballymun and chose a place in Lovers' Lane. A couple of days later, having been told that he was going to meet Collins, Jameson was brought by tram to Ballymun by Paddy Daly. Instead of Collins, he found Ben Barrett, Tom Kilcoyne and Joe Dolan waiting for him. They searched him and found incriminating documents. Dolan recalled that as he cocked his revolver, Jameson said: 'If you shoot me, you shoot one of your best boys.'[16] John Charles Byrnes, alias Jack Jameson, a British spy posing as a communist, succeeded in getting closer to Michael Collins than any other agent; he was shot dead by the Squad on 2 March 1920.

Britain's First Lord of the Admiralty, Walter Long, later informed the British Cabinet that Byrnes was 'the best Secret Service man we had.'[17] Apparently the man known to the IRA as 'Jack Jameson' had previously infiltrated the Soldiers', Sailors' and Airmen's Union in London as an undercover agent of the secretive British military A2 Branch, whose aim was to combat Bolshevik agitation in the armed forces.

TOMÁS MacCURTAIN SHOT BY RIC

Tomás MacCurtain was born on 20 March 1884 in Ballyknockane, County Cork. A dedicated member of the Gaelic League and a founding member of the Irish Volunteers, he was imprisoned in Frongoch after the Rising. As Brigadier of the First Cork Brigade, he reorganised the Volunteers in Cork city and county, with the assistance of his second-in-command, Terence MacSwiney. In the Local Elections of 1920, Mac-Curtain was elected as a Sinn Féin councillor and on 30 January, he was elected Lord Mayor of Cork.

At 2am on 20 March 1920, a party of RIC under District Inspector Swanzy left King Street Barracks with faces blackened. When they reached Thomas Davis Street, they knocked at MacCurtain's door, which was answered by his wife Eibhlís who was pushed aside as two

Crowds gather outside the home of Tomás Mac-Curtain, where he was shot dead in the early hours of the morning of 20 March 1920.

RIC men ran up the stairs. They shouted for MacCurtain to come out and when he did, in a half-dressed state, they shot the Lord Mayor dead. MacCurtain's brother-in-law, James Walsh, who was in the house at the time, narrowly escaped with his life as the RIC aimed a number of shots in his direction. The five MacCurtain children, the youngest of whom was only ten months old, were also in the house when their father was killed.

As the funeral cortege went from MacCurtain's Blackpool home to the Cathedral of Saints Mary and Anne, the two city battalions of the IRA marched company by company in military formation behind the bier. The Dáil was fully represented and even Cathal Brugha and Michael Collins marched in the procession. There was no oration for MacCurtain in St Finbarr's Cemetery but three volleys were fired over his grave.

At the inquest into his death, the jury returned a damning verdict:

> We find that Alderman Tomás MacCurtain, Lord Mayor of Cork, died from shock and haemorrhage, caused by bullet wounds, and that he was wilfully wounded under circumstances of the most callous brutality, and that the murder was organised and carried out by the Royal Irish Constabulary officially directed by the British Government.
>
> We return a verdict of wilful murder against David Lloyd George, Prime Minister of England; Lord French, Lord Lieutenant of Ireland; Ian McPherson, late Chief Secretary of Ireland; Acting Inspector General Smith of the Royal Irish Constabulary; Divisional Inspector Clayton of the Royal Irish Constabulary; District Inspector Swanzy and some unknown members of the Royal Irish Constabulary.[18]

As will be seen in Chapter Six, the IRA later took their revenge on District Inspector Swanzy, one of the men who had shot MacCurtain dead on the morning of his thirty-sixth birthday.

DOUBLE-AGENT BRIAN MOLLOY

Brian Fergus Molloy was a sergeant in the British Army. He was supposed to be double-crossing the British and working for the IRA but was, in fact, working for the British and double-crossing the IRA. Vinny Byrne from the Squad recalled that on 23 March 1920, he met Frank Saurin and Molloy in the Café Cairo, one of the many stylish coffee houses on Grafton Street in Dublin in the 1920s. Saurin, an IRA Intelligence Officer at GHQ, introduced Molloy to Byrne saying, 'Our friend is very anxious to meet Liam Tobin and I am sure you could arrange it.' Liam Tobin was the Director of Intelligence under Michael Collins. Vinny Byrne agreed to arrange a meeting for the following evening at 5.30pm and said that they should meet on Grafton Street. However, knowing that Molloy was a spy, the Squad decided to shoot him instead of introducing him to Liam Tobin.

Byrne recalled that the Squad assembled near the appointed meeting place the following day, 24 March 1920. Instead of meeting him, they kept an eye on their quarry. Molloy 'waited about three-quarters of an hour and then moved off down Grafton St. We made several attempts to get him, but, owing to the large number of people in the street, it was very difficult. He turned into Wicklow St. We opened fire and he fell dead.'[19] According to Paddy Caldwell, Molloy was shot 'in the vicinity of the International Bar' on the corner of Wicklow Street and St Andrew's Street.[20] Civilians in the area started to shout and made attempts to capture the IRA men, who quickly dispersed.

Analysing this the following day, Vinny Byrne and the others came to the conclusion that the crowd had believed the IRA to be police dressed in civilian clothes, and were concerned that the action was similar to the shooting of Tomás MacCurtain in Cork a few days earlier.[21]

THE BLACK AND TANS ARRIVE

The success of the IRA's campaign against the RIC can be measured by the fact that Winston Churchill, who was then the British Secretary of State for War, decided to reinforce the police in Ireland. Many British soldiers, demobilised after the end of the First World War and unable to find honest work, joined this reserve police force for the daily wage of ten shillings (a half of one pound). The main body of recruits came from London, Liverpool and Glasgow. Surprisingly some came from Ireland and were of the Catholic faith. Although the usual RIC training lasted for six months, the first recruits to this temporary force arrived in Dublin on 25 March 1920, after only a few weeks' training in Gormanston Camp, County Meath.

The first recruits to a reserve police force, which became known as the Black and Tans, arrived in Ireland on 25 March 1920, after only a few weeks' training.

As there was a shortage of police uniforms, the recruits were issued a mixture of clothing that included khaki and dark green, which quickly earned them the pejorative nickname 'Black and Tans'. Black and tan are the distinctive colours of the pack of Kerry beagles still used in the Scarteen Hunt in Limerick. Christopher O'Sullivan, a reporter with the *Limerick Echo* newspaper, wrote about one of the new recruits he had seen at Limerick Junction: 'He measured up to about 5 foot 6 and could scarcely weigh 10 stone. I would associate him with the Pallasgreen Scarteen Hunt [i.e. The Black and Tan Kerry beagles] to judge by the colour of his cap and trousers.'[22]

A group of Black and Tans in jovial form.

It is a myth that the Black and Tans were recruited from within the jail system in Britain. In fact, anyone with a police record was disbarred from joining. However, that did not disbar those who had been recruited from engaging in criminal activities such as looting, assaulting the public and murder. Many of the regular RIC men were uncomfortable with their new associates who shared barrack quarters with them. RIC Constable Eugene Bratton remembered the Black and Tans, 11,500 of whom served in Ireland, as 'a low-down lot of scoundrels'.[23]

It is often asked why the Tans were to swear the constable's oath for the RIC and not just act as a regular Army reserve (after all, eighty percent of them were ex-British Army). One reason is that police numbers were in decline. Between casualties, resignations resulting from intimidation, and low morale, RIC numbers needed to be increased. However, the main reason is that the British did not want the Army to fight the IRA directly as that would have legitimised the Irish cause; the British would have been officially on a war footing. The British Government preferred to state that the IRA was a criminal organisation and therefore should be tackled by the police. At a British Cabinet meeting on 30 April 1920, Lord French asked the Prime Minister if he would go so far as to declare war in Ireland. Lloyd George replied emphatically, 'You do not declare war against rebels.'[24]

INVESTIGATOR ALAN BELL

Michael Noyk was born in Lithuania but as an infant had immigrated to Ireland with his Jewish parents. He befriended Arthur Griffith sometime after finishing his studies at Trinity College, and following the Easter Rising became more involved with Sinn Féin. As a solicitor and legal advisor to Michael Collins, Noyk recalled later in life that 'the Dáil Loan was becoming more popular and making more strides' and that Dublin Castle desired to 'find out the source of that money'. To that end, in March 1920 the Castle employed a retired resident magistrate called Alan Bell who was known to be an effective operator despite his seventy years.[25] Bell's job was to track down accounts that held the Dáil Loan and, with that in mind, he summoned all of the bank managers in Dublin and held a private inquiry at the Police Courts on Inns Quay. Michael Noyk attempted to gain entry to the inquiry and reported back to Michael Collins that no one was allowed in.

It was clear to Collins that Bell needed to be stopped, but there was no way to identify him until the *Irish Independent* unwittingly published his photograph. The Squad received information from IRA Intelligence that Bell was living in Monkstown and commuted by tram daily. 'He used to get off the tram at Cook's, opposite Trinity College, where he would be met by two detectives who escorted him from there to the Castle.'[26] A decision was made to shoot Bell on his way into Dublin.

On the morning of 26 March 1920, Mick McDonnell, Jim Slattery and Vinny Byrne waited at the corner of Ailesbury Road in Ballsbridge for the tram. Also present were Liam Tobin and his fellow IRA Intelligence operatives, Joe Dolan, Joe Guilfoyle, Paddy Caldwell, and Owen Cullen. Tom Keogh came cycling at speed towards them and pointed out the tram on which Bell was travelling. The IRA men boarded the tram, and McDonnell and Tobin sat opposite Bell. Having asked him to confirm his name, they took him by the shoulders and brought him to the platform of the tram. Joe Guilfoyle pulled the trolley off the wipes and stopped the tram at the corner of Simmonscourt Road. Tobin and McDonnell then shot Bell, and the Squad and GHQ Intelligence members escaped towards Donnybrook.

A NEW CHIEF SECRETARY

Thomas Hamar Greenwood was born in Ontario, Canada, in 1870. At the age of twenty-five, he moved to England where he was called to the bar and elected an MP for the Liberal Party. He commanded a battalion for a short period during the First World War. As an avid supporter of Lloyd George, he was made Chief Secretary to Ireland on 12 April 1920, replacing Ian Stewart Macpherson, Lord Strathcarron. The Chief Secretary's role was essentially to implement the British Government's policies in Ireland. Sir Maurice Hankey, the Secretary to the British Cabinet, wrote in his diary in April that Greenwood 'talked the most awful tosh about shooting Sinn Féiners on sight, and without evidence, and frightfulness generally.'[27] Hamar Greenwood's arrival in Ireland coincided with the arrival of the Black and Tans and the worst year of violence during the War of Independence.

Greenwood presided over the Restoration of Order in Ireland Act, which became law on 9 August 1920. His desperate defence in the House of Commons of the violent reprisals carried out by British forces against civilians was farcical, and a phrase entered the vernacular: to 'tell a Hamar' meant to tell a lie. When asked about British policy in Ireland, Greenwood replied, 'there is no such thing as reprisals, but they have done a great deal of good.' The Squad planned to assassinate the Chief Secretary at a military sports meeting in Lansdowne Road. However, when the IRA men went to the meeting, there were armoured cars and machine guns in position. Realising that it would have been a death trap for them, they called off the shooting.[28]

MICHAEL COLLINS AND HIS MANY SAFE HOUSES

Throughout this time, Michael Collins continued to avoid arrest. There are many stories about his secret hiding places around Dublin. Tadhg Kennedy, who was Brigade Intelligence Officer for the First Kerry Brigade, remembered an occasion when he was meeting Collins in Dublin on Volunteer matters and he and Collins came close to being captured:

> I remember one day at 22, Mary Street, word came that the sector about Henry Street and Mary Street was completely surrounded by British forces and a house-to-house search was being carried out within the sector.

Mick Collins took me down to Henry Street and up the stairs in one of the houses. We went along a corridor till we reached what I took to be a bookcase. He touched a spring or something and opened up the bookcase and we went through into a darkened room, which I noticed had no windows. He closed the entrance and locked it firmly with a contraption of levers. He told me the escape room was constructed by Batt O'Connor, a Kerryman builder contractor settled in Dublin for some years previously. We heard the tramping of the British soldiers along the corridor and the sound of their rifles as they touched the floor.

We spent the whole night there and were not released until the following day. We slept on the floor, at least Mick did as I heard his heavy breathing. I know I didn't sleep much as I was feeling anything but happy.[29]

CHAPTER FIVE

Thrown Out in the Gutter

Cumann na mBan continued to be an integral part of the revolutionary movement, not only treating wounded IRA Volunteers but also carrying dispatches and arms at great personal risk. The establishment of 'Dáil' or republican courts and a special republican police force reinforced the position of Dáil Éireann as the legitimate government of Ireland. Although legal circles at the time were dominated by men, it is interesting to note that a number of women were appointed as judges and that the role of women was not restricted to 'supporting the men'. The republican police were at times the only force of law and order in parts of Ireland as many smaller RIC barracks had been evacuated because they were vulnerable to attack. In fact, in March 1920 the IRA celebrated Easter by burning around 300 evacuated police barracks and twenty-two income tax offices. Recruitment to the RIC was also proving a growing problem.

Throughout 1920, the Squad continued its campaign against the police, shooting Detective Dalton and Constable Kells in Dublin. The Limerick IRA attacked Ballylanders and Killmallock police barracks, and King's Inns was attacked in an audacious daylight raid by the Dublin IRA. The Cork IRA used a game of bowls as cover to ambush a patrol of British soldiers, and Captain Percival Lea-Wilson, who had abused the 1916 prisoners after the Easter Rising, was shot dead by the Squad in Gorey.

By the summer of 1920, the excesses of the British were proving too much for members of the RIC who mutinied in Listowel rather than obey orders to shoot as many people as possible; although not an ordinary police force in that its members were armed and in the frontline against the IRA, they were still Irishmen, and they objected to being asked to shoot their neighbours indiscriminately. Their mutiny was echoed four thousand miles away in India when the Connaught Rangers mutinied over the Black and Tan reprisals in Ireland. The IRA under Liam Lynch in Cork succeeded in capturing a brigadier-general of the British Army, who was treated with the utmost respect, in marked contrast to the fate that befell two IRA officers, arrested and brutally tortured by British soldiers in Bandon in July. As 1920 wore on, the hostilities escalated.

TREATMENT OF WOUNDED VOLUNTEERS

Cumann na mBan, the women volunteers of the Republican movement, undertook the care and treatment of IRA men who were wounded in action. Brighid O'Mullane, an active organiser and member of the Executive of GHQ, Cumann na mBan, recalled, 'Branches were always busy making field dressings and first-aid outfits. This was generally done in the girls' own homes.' O'Mullane also stated that women were often 'in the vicinity of an ambush, fully equipped with first-aid outfits to treat the wounded, if any, after the ambush. All this entailed a certain amount of danger for the girls', and sometimes 'they barely escaped with their lives from the scene of an ambush.'[1]

Early in 1920, Cumann na mBan set up a first-aid station in a house on South Frederick Street, which was the home of Gus Connolly of the Third Battalion Dublin IRA. Eileen Cooney was often on duty there. According to Annie O'Brien, 'On occasions after a street ambush wounded Volunteers were treated there, or girls on duty there were sent for to attend the wounded at other parts of the city.'[2] This station was one of a number in Dublin. Eilis Ní Riain recalled that her Branch of Cumann na mBan collected comforts for men on the run, organised safe houses and first-aid stations in Dublin city.[3] However, for serious cases the Mater Hospital, on the north side of the city, was usually used. The staff at the Mater were in sympathy with the Republican cause and endured many searches and much abuse by the British throughout the War.

REPUBLICAN COURTS AND REPUBLICAN POLICE

Arbitration courts or Sinn Féin courts, designed to undermine the established British judicial system, were authorised by Dáil Éireann in June 1919, but were not in operation until the following May. By then, Republicans were concerned that criminality was going unpunished, as the RIC was concentrating on fighting the IRA as opposed to fighting crime. Land agitation was on the rise, and cattle driving and removal of fences resulted in some Anglo-Irish landlords appealing to the Dáil for assistance. The Dáil courts, authorised by a new decree, replaced the arbitration courts on 29 June 1920; they were under the control of the Minister for Home Affairs, Austin Stack. The system entailed the use of parish, district, civil and supreme courts. No legal textbook published in Britain was allowed to be cited, and at parish level the judges were often IRA members or indeed local priests, in the hope that common sense would prevail. The courts were backed by a republican police force whose members wore no uniforms and were mostly unpaid. The Republican Police often enforced drinking regulations and crowd control.

Áine Ceannt, wife of Éamonn Ceannt who had been executed in 1916, was not only a member of the Executive of Sinn Féin, but also sat as a district justice in Dublin. Her colleague Áine Heron, who was a veteran of the Four Courts in 1916, was appointed as a justice in the

Pembroke and Rathmines district of Dublin, under the chairmanship of Erskine Childers; Childers was one of those responsible for landing arms in 1914 on board his yacht, the *Asgard*. Alice Cashel, another Cumann na mBan member, was a parish justice in Connemara. There were no jails as such, and sometimes sentences were served out in the wilds of a west of Ireland island. A letter from Lord Monteagle of Brandon in the *Freeman's Journal* of 5 July 1920 enthusiastically declared that the 'Sinn Féin courts are steadily extending their jurisdiction and dispensing justice even-handed between man and woman, Catholic and Protestant, farmer and shopkeeper, grazier and cattle driver, landlord and tenant.'[4]

The British in Dublin Castle were concerned that their courts were virtually defunct in many parts of Ireland. In more than one case, when British forces came across members of the Republican Police with prisoners, they released the prisoner, and in a number of cases shot the Republican policemen.[5] Increasingly, court sessions had to be held in secret locations. Circuit Judge Diarmuid Crowley, a member of the Irish Bar, who defied the RIC and sat openly in Ballina, County Mayo, was sentenced in a British-run court to two years with hard labour.[6]

DETECTIVE CONSTABLE LAURENCE DALTON AND CONSTABLE KELLS

The Squad received orders to shoot Detective Constable Laurence Dalton who was involved in political work. GHQ Intelligence provided evidence that the detective would be coming from Broadstone Station in Dublin on 20 April 1920. The IRA men waited in positions around the Black Church at St Mary's Place, off Dorset Street. When Dalton appeared, he had an escort with him. In the fusillade of fire, Dalton was killed outright. Squad member Vinny Byrne wondered later: 'How his escort escaped being plugged is a miracle. However, it was just as well, as he was not wanted.'[7]

Shortly prior to that, on 14 April, Constable Henry Kells had been shot dead. It is likely that Kells had recently been promoted to the rank of detective constable. Peadar Clancy, who was in Mountjoy Jail at the time, sent word that Henry Kells had been in the jail trying to identify who had shot Magistrate Bell (who had been investigating bank accounts). Clancy received a note from a friend telling him that 'he was going to Kells'; the note was signed 'MC'. (Kells is a town in County Meath, and MC was Michael Collins). On the morning of a one-day strike in support of hunger-strikers in Mountjoy Jail, the Squad went out specifically to look for Henry Kells. The men had information that Kells would be walking from his home at 7 Pleasants Street in the south of the city, as the trams were not running because of the strike. Paddy Daly recalled that Hugo MacNeill, the Director of Organisation and Training of Fianna Éireann, went with Joe Leonard to search for Kells. Daly recalled hearing shots and, moments later, seeing MacNeill and Leonard 'sauntering down as if nothing had happened'. MacNeill said to them, 'Kells is up there if you want him.' 'Where?' asked Daly. 'On the foot-path,' answered MacNeill.[8] Constable Henry Kells was found on Camden Street by a motorist who drove him to hospital; he was pronounced dead upon arrival.

ATTACKS ON BALLYLANDERS AND KILLMALLOCK BARRACKS IN LIMERICK

Tadhg Crowley, O/C Ballylanders Company, vividly recalled an attack on the local police barracks in his native village in East Limerick on 27 April 1920. Crowley reckoned that twenty-five men from his company and ten men from Galbally were involved, but in total 'about 60 or 70 people were in the village for the purpose of the attack'. In addition to this, large numbers of other IRA companies in the East Limerick Brigade were trenching roads and knocking trees to make it impossible for the enemy to approach. Crowley lived opposite the local RIC barracks and sent his mother off on a short holiday to Kilkee in County Clare.

His father was an old Fenian who had no objection to the IRA using his house to launch an assault on the police. Crowley recalled that his father 'told us that whatever we did we were not to forget to say our prayers'.[9] In charge of the attack and working under direct orders from Michael Collins was Tomás Malone (alias Seán Forde), from Tyrellspass in County Westmeath, a newly appointed organiser for the Dáil Loan, who had just been transferred to the area from IRA GHQ in Dublin.[10]

The IRA occupied Ballylanders village dispensary, broke out through the roof, and from there were able to drop heavy stones onto the roof of the police barracks next door. When they had made a hole of sufficient size, they dropped a bomb into the barracks, followed by petrol and torches. From the houses opposite, a fusillade of rifle fire was poured onto the barracks. The police returned fire and the battle raged for nearly half an hour before the five RIC men surrendered. Malone took the surrender and congratulated the RIC on the great fight that they had put up, but he also reminded them that the odds were against them. The IRA captured seven rifles, a good quantity of ammunition, and a number of Mills bombs (hand grenades) from the barracks.

On the strength of this success, the East Limerick Brigade decided to use the same tactics a month later in an attack on the police barracks in Kilmallock in south Limerick. The Kilmallock attack was one of the largest assaults carried out in Limerick, involving at least 200 Volunteers from five counties. The attack was planned by Brigadier Seán Wall, Tomás Malone, Ned Tobin, Mick Scanlon and Liam Scully. On 6 March 1867, Kilmallock Barracks had been attacked by a large force of Fenians and fifty-three years later, on 27 May 1920, another attack was undertaken by Irish Republicans. The usual preparations were made and all the outer-lying companies trenched and barricaded the roads for many miles around the centre of the attack. Tadhg Crowley remembered that his section took over the Provincial Bank, directly opposite the barracks on the main street. The bank manager, his wife and their family were in their beds, so the IRA explained to them that they would have to leave by the rear. After some time, the bank manager's wife came into the room the IRA men were occupying. Crowley thought she was worried about her jewellery and assured her that their belongings would not be interfered with. The woman replied, 'No, it's alright. I'm just looking for a stud for the boss's collar.'[11]

The Anglo-American Oil Company had a depot in Kilmallock and a cartload of petrol was procured from its premises and drawn up beside the barracks. A number of pint bottles were taken from O'Sullivan's Brewery and brought to Carroll's shop, adjacent to the barracks. Cornelius Kearney was given the task of filling the bottles with petrol and paraffin in the Carrolls' kitchen. He then handed the bottles to others on the stairway, where a relay of men extended up to the roof.[12] When the signal was given, at about half past eleven, all rifle fire was directed at the barracks from across the road at Clery's Hotel, Con Herlihy's shop and the Provincial Bank. Two powerful men, Ned Tobin and Michael Cleary, used a 28-pound weight, attached by ropes to their wrists, to smash the roof of the barracks.[13] Tadhg Crowley recalled:

> The fight went on for many hours. The barracks was blazing at one end after being broken by heavy weights and bombs, the pouring of petrol and the firing of petrol bottles from the roof which overhung the barracks ... Eventually the fight had proceeded so far that only one section of the barracks remained unburned, but still the police under Sergeant O'Sullivan ... held on. He doggedly continued firing although several of his men had been lost in the attack.[14]

Cornelius Kearney recollected:

> Paddy Hannigan called down from the roof for some water to drink, complaining that he was parched with the thirst. A container of water was promptly despatched up to him. At the same time, other containers,

filled with oil, were being passed along to him. On the way, the water became confused with the oil, and from the vessel, which was handed to Hannigan as water, he took a big gulp. He had drunk paraffin oil. The curses and abuse which he showered on us down below could be heard above all the din of the shooting and explosions, but, to make matters worse, he fixed the blame on me and threatened, amongst other things, to blow my brains out. However, he became so violently ill that, by the time he was brought down to the kitchen, he was in no mood to carry out his threat.[15]

Eventually the IRA decided to retire from the fight as it was six in the morning and there was a chance that the military might come to the aid of the RIC. Liam Scully, an IRA Volunteer from Ballylongford in County Kerry, went out firing into the street and was shot dead by the police. There were also two RIC men killed, Sergeant Thomas Kane and Constable Joseph Morton.

KING'S INNS RAID

Word had come to Brigadier Dick McKee and Vice-Brigadier Peadar Clancy that there were rifles, Lewis machine guns and ammunition stored in the King's Inns at the top of Henrietta Street in Dublin. The IRA Dublin Brigade decided to steal these weapons. A plan was devised to wait for a sunny day when the British soldiers tended to relax in the public park attached to the law school. Initially the date was set for 31 May, but it rained heavily that day. The following day, 1 June, was sunny, so at four o'clock in the afternoon, men from the Squad, GHQ Intelligence and the First Battalion Dublin Brigade were divided into four groups, all armed with revolvers. The first group surprised the British sentries, arrested them and headed for the guardroom where the weapons were stored. A second group disconnected the telephones and alarms. The third party protected the entrances and afforded cover for the raiding party, while the fourth group kept watch around Henrietta Street.[16]

The actual weapons were chained up, but George Fitzgerald of the First Battalion Dublin Brigade got the keys from one of the soldiers and unlocked the chains. Fitzgerald counted fourteen rifles, one Lewis gun and 'a fairly large quantity of ammunition which was in haversacks'.[17] Joe Dolan, GHQ Intelligence, reckoned the haul was twenty-five rifles, two Lewis guns and several thousand rounds of ammunition.[18] Seán Prendergast, First Battalion IRA Volunteer, saw the booty 'being brought out to the motor car — rifles, ammunition equipment and a machine gun'. He also remembered great joy and excitement, 'especially so when Kevin Barry, wearing a "tin hat" and carrying a machine gun, came out to the car — joking all the time.' Kevin Barry was executed five months later in Mountjoy Jail (see Chapter Eight). Prendergast was effusive in his praise for his Vice-Brigadier, Peadar Clancy, stating that 'his personality, his fine manly character and extraordinary methodical grip of military tactics, combined with a keen sense of placing men to the best advantage' all contributed to the success of the raid.

> [Clancy] always planned for success. More than that, he planned for the safety of his men. Every detail, however slight, was weighed, every possible contingency was considered, but always it was a fundamental law with him to register surprise, to strike at the right time and in the right place, and by utilising the minimum of men and material to apply guerrilla tactics to every form of military activity.

Prendergast had nothing but good to say of Brigadier Dick McKee either, who was a man 'of similar qualities, leadership and daring. He and Peadar were a complete pair militarily; each had the same military outlook, were guided by the same principles to fight whatever the cost, but never give in.'[19] The success of the King's Inns raid can be measured in the morale boost it gave to the Dublin IRA who captured much-needed munitions without suffering any loss themselves.

AMBUSH AT MILE BUSH

Michael Leahy, Commandant of the Fourth Battalion, Cork No. 1 Brigade IRA, recalled that 'there was no military party stationed in Midleton'.[20] There was, however, a strong RIC garrison in the town. A battalion of Cameron Highlanders arrived in Midleton on the morning of 5 June 1920, and took up quarters in a disused factory building on the Mill Road. Vice-Commandant of the Fourth Battalion Patrick Whelan remembered, '[the] Camerons lost no time in getting acquainted with their new surroundings, and that very evening, a cycle patrol of twelve, with an RIC man as a guide, left the town, on a routine journey through the district.'[21] Diarmuid Hurley, the local IRA O/C, assembled as many men of B Company as possible with a view to ambushing the cycle patrol and relieving the men of their rifles.

Joseph Aherne, a senior IRA officer, explained in his witness statement the background to the plan of attack:

> Bowl throwing is quite a popular game in Cork, which must not be confused with the English game. The contestants agree to throw the bowls over a certain distance along the road, which is usually two or three miles. The bowls are 28oz [0.79kg] metal spheres and the thrower taking the least number of throws is the winner. As the bowls are small, there is a danger of losing them in the long grass on the side of the road. Consequently, a number of men are sent out in front to watch them and to mark the road for the throwers. Hurley, who could always be relied on to think up a nice plan on the spur of the moment, thought that a bowling match would be a suitable method to employ to enable the Volunteers to get close enough to the cyclists. Hurley and Tadhg Manly were the contestants and the remainder spread out in front, ostensibly to mark the road and watch the bowls.[22]

At Mile Bush, the British patrol came upon the innocent-looking men playing bowls. Everybody carried on as if nothing was afoot and the patrol cycled unsuspectingly through the markers. When the head of the patrol reached the two throwers, Manly drew his gun and fired in the air, which was the signal to rush. The IRA men jumped on the cyclists who were unable to reach for their rifles in time. A few of the Camerons managed to escape over a small wall and a few seconds of firing ensued, until Hurley told the Lance Corporal to order his men to surrender. Another Highlander, who was behind the main group, did make an attempt to hold up the IRA, but a shot in his general direction dispatched him back to where he had come from. Twelve rifles and twelve hundred rounds of ammunition were captured, together with the bicycles. The soldiers, unharmed except for a few bruises, were allowed to return to their barracks.

Late that night, some of the soldiers began their terror campaign by occupying a position and pouring machine gunfire straight down the main street of Midleton. Two IRA Volunteers involved in the ambush were killed in Clonmult in February 1921 (see Chapter Ten). On 28 May 1921, O/C Diarmuid Hurley went to investigate reprisals carried out by the British in Carrigtwohill. He was alone and was surprised by the Black and Tans, who killed him.

A woman outside her ruined cottage in Meelin, County Cork, following a Black and Tan reprisal.

SHOOTING OF PERCIVAL LEA-WILSON

When the GPO and Four Courts garrisons surrendered in 1916, the Volunteers were held captive in the grounds of the Rotunda Hospital. A certain Captain Percival Lea-Wilson subjected the prisoners to a barrage of abuse and aimed his ire in particular at two signatories of the Proclamation, Thomas Clarke and Seán MacDiarmada. Frank Henderson, who had served under Clarke and MacDiarmada in the GPO, described Lea-Wilson's actions that night as 'savage'.[23] Liam Tobin, who was in the Four Courts in 1916 and witnessed Lea-Wilson abusing his comrades, 'registered a vow' to himself that he 'would deal with him at some time in the future.'[24]

After the First World War, Lea-Wilson left the British Army, rejoined the RIC and became District Inspector (DI) for Gorey. He appeared to be making life miserable for the local people including the IRA.[25] Michael Collins's Chief of Intelligence, Liam Tobin, and the Deputy Assistant Director of Intelligence, Frank Thornton, came down from Dublin on 12 June to shoot the DI. After three days in the company of three local IRA Volunteers they decided that the best time to shoot Lea-Wilson was in the morning, after he collected his mail and newspaper from the 9.35am Dublin train. The DI was always accompanied by a sergeant who usually walked only part of the way home with him. On 15 June 1920, under the pretence that local man Mick Sinnott's car had broken down, the two Intelligence men, together with Joe McMahon and Sean Whelan, waited for their quarry who 'opened his newspaper and was reading its headlines as he walked towards the place of execution'. The ambushers fired a number of times. According to Whelan, 'he must have been hit at least a dozen times, but just to make sure, we hit him again as he lay stretched full length on the footpath.' As they fled from the scene, Thornton started to sing a song written by Seán O'Casey, which mocked John Redmond, 'The Constitutional Movement Must Go On', and the rest of the men joined in the chorus.[26]

There is some debate as to why Lea-Wilson was assassinated. However, Thornton was definite that 'Wilson was shot because of the brutal treatment of IRA leaders during 1916 ... and finally because of his renewed activity in the Gorey district in 1920.'[27] Later on, Lea-Wilson's widow, Marie, received spiritual comfort from Fr Thomas Finlay, a Jesuit priest. As a token of gratitude, she gave the Jesuits a painting, which hung in their house in Leeson Street, Dublin, until the 1990s, when it was discovered to be a lost Caravaggio, *The Taking of Christ* (1602).[28]

LISTOWEL MUTINY

The RIC in Listowel received orders to vacate the Listowel RIC Barracks in favour of the British military. The rank and file decided not to co-operate. On 17 June, in defiance of Kerry RIC County Inspector Power O'Shea, fourteen police constables, under the leadership of Constable Jeremiah Mee, offered their resignations, which were refused. Two days later, Lieutenant Colonel Gerald Brice Smyth, Divisional Commissioner in charge of Military and Police for the province of Munster, arrived in Listowel. With him were General Henry Hugh Tudor, Inspector General of the RIC, and fifty members of the military and police who arrived in four Crossley tenders as a show of strength against the mutinous policemen. Lieutenant Colonel Smyth then addressed the RIC men in their barracks with a speech that Constable Jeremiah Mee recorded:

> Well, men, I have something of interest to tell you, something that I am sure you would not wish your wives to hear ... We must take the offensive and beat Sinn Féin at their own tactics. Martial Law, applying to all Ireland, is coming into operation shortly, and our scheme of amalgamation must be complete by 21 June ... If a police barracks is burned, or if the barracks already occupied is not suitable, then the best house in the locality is to be commandeered, the occupants thrown out in the gutter ... Police and Military will patrol the country roads at least five nights a week ... when civilians are seen approaching, shout 'hands up.'

Should the order not be immediately obeyed, shoot, and shoot with effect. If the persons approaching carry their hands in their pockets or are in any way suspicious looking, shoot them down. You may make mistakes occasionally and innocent persons may be shot, but this cannot be helped and you are bound to get the right persons sometimes. The more you shoot, the better I will like you, and I assure you that no policeman will get into trouble for shooting any man. In the past, policemen have got into trouble for giving evidence at coroners' inquests. As a matter of fact, inquests are to be made illegal so that in future no policeman will be asked to give evidence at inquests. Hunger strikers will be allowed to die in jail, the more the merrier ... A ship will be leaving an Irish port in the near future with lots of Sinn Féiners on board; I assure you, men, it will never land.[29]

Constable Mee took off his cap, badge and sword and shouted at Smyth that he was a murderer. Smyth ordered some RIC officers to arrest Mee, but he was rescued soon after by his comrades. Smyth and his party departed to address other RIC members in the area but at the RIC barracks in Tralee and in Killarney, they were met with shouts of support for the Listowel mutineers. Constable Mee sent a copy of Smyth's speech to Dublin to be published in newspapers. Despite an offer to increase RIC pay in Munster by fourteen shillings, after two weeks of mutiny five members of the RIC walked away from their jobs in Listowel.

On 10 July, Smyth's speech was published in the *Freeman's Journal*. Mee and some of the other ex-RIC men went to Dublin and met Michael Collins, Erskine Childers and Countess Markievicz. The Countess, as Minister for Labour, eventually asked Mee to run a new bureau for the purpose of finding jobs for ex-RIC men, which served to encourage more police to leave their positions.

Lieutenant Colonel Smyth had met Lloyd George two weeks before giving his speech; he was essentially explaining British Government policy to the RIC men in Listowel.

THE CONNAUGHT RANGERS

Coincidentally, thousands of miles from Listowel, a mutiny of members of the British Army began on 27 June 1920 in India. Joe Hawes recalled an informal meeting between a few men from C Company of the Connaught Rangers in the canteen of Jullundur Barracks. Hawes told his fellow soldiers some stories of British atrocities that were being carried out in Ireland. He explained to his comrades that 'we were doing in India what the British Forces were doing in Ireland'.[30] Initially five men agreed that, as a protest, they would no longer serve the British King. They were later joined by a large number of their comrades, and soon Jullundur Barracks was in the control of mutineers who elected a committee and drew up some rules to maintain order and discipline. Guards and sentry duties were maintained, but the only orders to be obeyed were those from the committee, who hoisted an Irish tricolour flag above the barracks.

Jullundur, now known as Jalandhar, is only fifty miles from Amritsar, which had been the scene of a bloody massacre when the British Army opened fire on unarmed peaceful protesters in April 1919. The official death toll of 379 'identifiable bodies' excluded hundreds of 'unidentifiable' victims. As a consequence, the local Indians were sympathetic to the mutineers, which caused great concern to the British authorities. Two mutineers went to Solon, 130 miles away, where the rest of the Connaught Rangers were stationed, to notify them of the mutiny. About forty soldiers in Solon raised a green flag over a hut, which they called Liberty Hall, and declared that their protest was peaceful. However, a rumour went around that the British Army was going to attack them so they marched towards the armoury during the night to raid it for weapons. They were halted by the officers and British soldiers on duty. One mutineer took a step forward and said, 'I'm James Joseph Daly of Tyrellspass, Mullingar, County Westmeath, Ireland and I demand ye to lay down your arms and surrender in the name of the Irish Republic.' Immediately the British officers and guards opened fire and two men, Peter Sears and

Patrick Smythe, were shot dead. The following day, Joseph Daly and his mutineer comrades were arrested and sent to Pune Jail.

In Jullundur, on 1 July, two battalions, a battery of artillery and a company of machine gunners surrounded the barracks. The British Army had arrived in a show of strength. The mutineers laid down their arms and 450 men were marched to a 'special camp' where they were allowed to continue their protest. The 'special camp' was nothing but a barbed-wire enclosed space about two hundred yards square. Machine-gun posts covered each side of the square. For the next week, the men suffered the extreme heat of the Indian summer. Every day a number of men were overcome by the heat and taken away to hospital. Eventually the majority of the mutineers simply gave up their protest and went to the guards to surrender. The last forty-eight of the Jullundur mutineers were taken by train to Dagshai Jail, where they were joined by forty of their comrades from Solon. The men were held in terrible conditions in Dagshai until late August when they were all tried by court martial. Fourteen men were sentenced to death but this sentence was later commuted to penal servitude for life for all but one of the men. Private James Joseph Daly, First Battalion of the Connaught Rangers, was executed on 2 November 1920. He was twenty-two.

The last of the Connaught mutineers were released in 1923, and some of them were given posts in the Free State National Army. In 1970, the remains of James Joseph Daly, Peter Sears and Patrick Smythe were reinterred in Ireland.

AN tÓGLACH APPEAL

In July 1920, as the war in Ireland continued, *An tÓglach,* the organ of the Irish Volunteers, issued an appeal for more members:

> Each individual Volunteer should endeavour to secure at least one recruit for the Republican Army ... There are many young men, sound Republicans, physically fit, who are not in the Volunteers but who should be.

In many cases they are not in because they were never asked and did not know how to get in touch ...Young men who, through apathy, timidity or from selfish motives remain outside the ranks should be shamed into 'doing their bit'. At a time when young men are facing prison and death, and many have shed their blood fighting for the Republic, the other young men who cheer their exploits but keep themselves safely out of the firing line should be made to feel themselves the selfish 'slackers' they are.[31]

CAPTURE OF BRIGADIER-GENERAL LUCAS

Hundreds of British soldiers were captured by the IRA throughout the War of Independence. They were usually released, except for Brigadier-General Cuthbert Henry Tindall Lucas of the Seventeenth Infantry Brigade, based at Fermoy Barracks. Liam Lynch was the O/C of Cork Number 2 Brigade IRA, and he and his Vice-Commandant, George Power, conspired to capture a high-ranking officer in retaliation for the arrest and imprisonment of Michael Fitzgerald, O/C of Fourth Battalion Cork Number 2 Brigade, who later died on hunger strike (See Chapter Eight). On 26 June 1920, Lynch, Power and two other officers from the Second Brigade, Seán Moylan (Newmarket Battalion) and Patrick Clancy (Kanturk Battalion), were driven by Volunteer Eoin Curtin to a spot five miles east of Fermoy where there was intelligence to suggest that some British officers were fishing on the banks of the River Blackwater. Lynch and his comrades first arrested Lucas's batman (personal servant) at a fishing hut, and then overpowered Lucas's two staff officers, Colonel Danford and Colonel Tyrrell, together with Brigadier-General Lucas himself. The IRA men had a car but they commandeered the British vehicle also, and drove the prisoners off, having given the batman a letter informing the British Army that the IRA had captured the officers as prisoners of war.

The British officers made a daring attempt to escape, causing one of the cars to crash. The driver, Eoin Curtin, was knocked unconscious, and the occupants were thrown from the car. Lynch was tackled by Lucas, and Danford attacked Clancy. Lynch managed to overpower his opponent and shot Danford in the face as he was strangling Clancy. Power and Moylan and the other prisoner returned to the scene. Colonel Tyrrell was left to tend to his wounded comrade, and when Curtin regained his senses he was sent to get a doctor for the wounded officer. Lynch, Power, Moylan and Clancy then drove off with their captive, Brigadier-General Lucas.[32]

Lucas was held for four weeks in total, during which time he was moved around between Cork, Limerick and Clare. He was treated with the greatest of respect by his IRA captors, who allowed him to play tennis, purchased his favourite type of tobacco and even brought him fishing on the River Shannon a number of times. When Mick Brennan was guarding him near Meelick in County Clare, he received a telegram for the prisoner:

General Lucas, c/o The Sinnfeiners, IRA, Cork. Born this morning a son. Both doing well.

Tomás Malone (alias Seán Forde) recalled that Lucas was gazing at the countryside one day when he admitted to Malone that if he were an Irishman, he would be in the IRA. Lucas even assured his captors that he would not tell where he had been lodged. After a month, the IRA let down their guard, perhaps even deliberately, and Lucas managed to escape on 30 July. Near Oola, he hailed a passing British Army vehicle, which was escorting a mail van. In a bizarre twist to the story, the IRA under Seán Treacy ambushed this small convoy and Lucas was wounded in the nose by a passing bullet; however, he lived to tell the tale. Despite the fact that the Seventeenth Infantry Brigade went on a rampage of destruction in Fermoy after their commander was captured, Lucas kept his word to the IRA and never divulged the details of his captors or where he had been held.

SHOOTING OF LIEUTENANT COLONEL GERALD BRICE SMYTH

Sean (Jack) Culhane, Intelligence Officer for Cork Number 1 Brigade, received a message from Ned Fitzgerald, a waiter in the Cork County Club, to the effect that Lieutenant Colonel Gerald Brice Smyth was staying there. Culhane met with a number of IRA Volunteers, including Daniel 'Sandow' Donovan, Daniel Healy, J.J. O'Connell, Cornelius O'Sullivan, Seán O'Donoghue, Leo Aherne, Martin Donovan and acting O/C 'Pa' Murray. A decision was made to attempt to exact revenge on Smyth for his Listowel speech. At ten o'clock on the night of 17 July 1920, Culhane met the waiter who confirmed that Smyth was seated in the bar. Culhane gave the signal to the others by removing his cap and running his hand through his hair. Culhane followed Fitzgerald 'as if at the point of a gun', and six armed men opened fire with revolvers. Daniel Healy recalled, 'Smyth tried to draw his revolver ... but without avail.'[33] Culhane, who also recalled their target making an effort to go for his gun, said that Smyth, somewhat disabled by an arm injury received during the war, 'must have died at once' in the barrage of gunfire.[34]

TOM HALES AND PATRICK HARTE

The Essex Regiment of the British Army captured Tom Hales O/C of the Third West Cork Brigade and Patrick Harte, the Brigade Quartermaster, at Hurley's farmhouse at Laragh, near Bandon in County Cork, on 27 July 1920. Incriminating documents having been found on them, the two men were beaten by the soldiers in a vicious assault and then taken to Bandon British Army Barracks. Hales recalled that when they arrived at the barracks, the British soldiers were howling for their blood. The men's hands were tied behind their backs and they were beaten again. The British soldiers then pretended to form up as if preparing for an execution. Captain James Kelly of the British Military Intelligence Department then stuck a British Union flag into the hand of Harte, who was very weak and could no longer see properly, and made him hold it up; a photograph was taken of the two men. Hales and Harte were then taken to a separate room where they were interrogated by Kelly and three lieutenants of the Hampshire (Hants) Regiment, Keogh, Green and Richardson.

The men's hands were tied behind their backs and they were whipped on their bare legs with canes. Harte was continually questioned about his brother Seán who was also in the IRA. The British officers used a set of pliers to pinch his fingernails, all the time bending and twisting his fingers. The torture continued for some time until, realising that Hales was not going to give any information, Lieutenant Keogh commenced to beat him vigorously, breaking four of his teeth. He continued to beat Hales on the ground until one of the officers told him to stop. Harte received the same treatment and never recovered from his ordeal.

The following day, both men were taken into a yard and told that they were to be shot. However, the British had a change of plan and sent them instead to the Military Hospital in Cork, where they shared a ward with a dozen wounded policemen who spent their day and night verbally abusing them. Hales believed that this had a very bad effect on Harte who suffered a complete mental breakdown. The IRA men were later tried and sentenced by court martial to two years hard labour in Pentonville Prison. Eventually the British took Harte's mental condition into account and he was incarcerated in Broadmoor Criminal Lunatic Asylum.[35]

CHAPTER SIX

A More Defiant Attitude

This chapter discusses the sectarian violence that erupted in Belfast after the funerals of Lieutenant Colonel Smyth and Inspector Swanzy who had been shot by the IRA. To some extent provoked by these and other IRA attacks, the mood of Ulster loyalists and Orangemen was whipped into a frenzy by the re-organisation of the Ulster Volunteers and the rhetoric of Sir Edward Carson. A protracted campaign of terrorism, which became known as the 'Belfast pogroms', continued for two years and resulted in 470 people being killed, the majority of them Catholics.

If the Black and Tans were ruthless, they were surpassed in their violence by the Auxiliaries, former British Army officers under the command of Frank Percy Crozier, who arrived in August 1920 to act as an aggressive gendarmerie against the IRA. Reprisals continued into the autumn. Following the IRA shooting of a policeman, 150 drunken members of the Black and Tans sacked and destroyed the town of Balbriggan in Dublin. In County Clare, the IRA ambushed the police at Rineen, and the reprisals carried out by the British saw four towns suffer a night of burnings and killings. Meanwhile, communications between IRA GHQ and the country were maintained by Cumann na mBan who ran an effective postal service throughout Ireland.

BELFAST 'POGROMS'

In 1688, Prince William of Orange, together with his wife Mary II, acceded to the Crowns of England and Scotland, deposing the Catholic King James II, who was Mary's father. Thus began the Williamite–Jacobite War, which culminated in a famous battle across the River Boyne near Drogheda, in County Louth. Protestant King William III or 'Dutch Billy' won a famous victory over James on 1 July 1690. The Pope at the time, Alexander VIII, supported the Protestant king and had *Te Deum* hymns of thanksgiving sung in the Vatican when he heard that William had been successful. James, on the other hand, was unpopular even with the Irish Catholics who called him 'Séamus a' Caca', which translates as 'James the Shit'. While it was not a sectarian battle, it became a sectarian victory. The Loyal Orange Institution, or Orange Order, founded in 1795 to maintain the Protestant Ascendancy, traditionally celebrates the battle on 12 July, the discrepancy in dates resulting from the later adoption of the Gregorian calendar in 1752.

While Orange parades in Belfast on 'The Twelfth' had at times passed peacefully, in 1920 tensions were high. The IRA had acted more in a defensive capacity in Belfast, knowing that even the smallest action on its part brought massive retaliation against Catholic communities. Unemployment was high and there were many former soldiers of the British Army who were idle. Moreover, many Loyalists were incandescent with rage at actions of the IRA.

A popular Loyalist leader, Edward Carson, one of the founders of the Ulster Volunteer Force (UVF), gave a dangerous speech in Belfast on 12 July 1920, in which he said, 'We in Ulster will tolerate no Sinn Féin.' He further stirred the emotions of the Orange crowd with a clear threat to the nationalists, saying, 'we will take the matter into our own hands.' A week later, on 19 July, Derry was the scene of terrible riots against Catholics. The following day, in Banbridge, County Down, the funeral of Lieutenant Colonel Gerald Brice Smyth caused more violence.

As we saw in Chapter Five, Smyth had been shot by the IRA in Cork for his infamous Listowel speech. After his funeral, Catholic homes and businesses in Banbridge were attacked and burned.

On 21 July, Protestant shipyard workers gathered at Workman and Clark's at lunchtime for a meeting organised by the Belfast Protestant Association. Following rousing speeches, Protestant workers formed a mob and turned on their 'Sinn Féin' co-workers. The Inspector-General of the RIC reported that the Catholic workers were hunted, severely beaten and thrown in the water. Men had their clothes torn to see if they were wearing rosary beads.[1] Burning hot rivets, nuts and bolts, or 'Belfast confetti', rained down on workers, simply because of their religion. Any Protestant workers, some of whom were socialists, who tried to defend the Catholics were immediately branded as 'Rotten Prods' and beaten

Members of the IRA Northern Division pose for a photograph.

and expelled from the shipyards. Three days of sectarian rioting ensued. Over 7,000 workers were expelled from the shipyards, most of whom would never return to work there. For the next two years, a spark was all it took to reignite what came to be known as the 'Belfast pogroms' — sectarian murders and violence against a sector of society because of their religious affiliations. In the two-year period 1920–22, 470 people were killed, nearly 60 percent of whom were Catholic, although Catholics made up only 25 percent of Belfast's population.

THE AUXILIARY DIVISION OF THE ROYAL IRISH CONSTABULARY

As discussed in Chapter Five, Winston Churchill, Secretary of State for War, had been responsible for the arrival in Ireland of the Black and Tans. He also suggested that a 'special emergency gendarmerie' was required to help police Ireland. General Nevil Macready, as Commander-in-Chief of the British Army in Ireland, rejected the idea, but Lieutenant General Tudor, the 'Police Advisor' in Dublin Castle, liked it. Known as the Auxiliary Division of the Royal Irish Constabulary (ADRIC) this new force consisted of former British Army officers. The 'temporary cadets' or 'Auxies', who wore distinctive glengarry hats, were to act as aggressive counter-insurgents and bring the fight to the IRA.

Although their initial training period seems minimal at six weeks, it was soon reduced to six days. Over the course of the war, 2,100 Auxiliaries signed up for duty but their total strength by the time of the Truce was about 1,500. Under the command of Brigadier General Frank Percy Crozier, they were divided into nineteen companies, named after letters of the alphabet and scattered around Ireland. They were very well armed and carried machine guns, Lee-Enfield rifles and revolvers, which they wore low slung around their waists in the fashion of North American cowboys. Their wage of £1 per day was twice as much as the Tans earned and nearly three times as much as an RIC constable. Nonetheless, they

Members of the Auxiliary Division of the RIC at Beggars Bush Barracks. Under the command of Brigadier General Frank Percy Crozier, the Auxies were well armed and well paid.

seemed to enjoy a policy of not paying for anything while they were in Ireland, with countless reports of the Auxiliaries spending days drinking in hotels and simply refusing to pay for their drink.

The Black and Tans were often blamed for the excesses carried out by British forces in Ireland, such as Bloody Sunday at Croke Park in November 1920 or indeed the Burning of Cork the following month. In reality, it was often the Auxiliaries at the forefront of reprisals, followed by a mixture of Black and Tans and RIC. There was a tendency to lump them all together, under a sort of catchall term, 'The Tans'.

POLICE COMMANDER H.H. TUDOR

Sir Henry Hugh Tudor was a lieutenant general who had commanded the artillery of the Ninth Scottish Division and planned the first large-scale tank battle in the First World War. Small of stature but plucky, Tudor was known for being on the front line of battles. He cared little for authority but was a personal friend of Winston Churchill's. On 15 May 1920, Tudor was made 'Police Advisor' in Ireland. When the RIC Inspector General, Thomas James Smith, retired in November 1920, Tudor essentially took over his position.

Tudor was unsure of his position as 'advisor', and his inexperience of policing gained him few friends. He attempted to control the Dublin Metropolitan Police, the Royal Irish Constabulary, the Black and Tans and Dublin Castle's intelligence network, which was a heavy burden. Ultimately, his inability to control the reprisals and murders carried out by his forces earned him the opprobrium of the press and the people of Ireland.

AUXILIARY COMMANDER FRANK PERCY CROZIER

Frank Crozier spent most of his childhood at the homes of relations in Ireland. At the age of nineteen, he fought with the British Army in the Second Boer War and later served in Nigeria. Having emigrated to

Canada in 1909, he returned a few years later to campaign against Home Rule and he became a commander in the Ulster Volunteers, the unionist army founded in 1912. When war broke out in Europe, he fought with the Thirty-Sixth Ulster Division and was later promoted to Brigadier-General. On 3 August 1920, he assumed command of the Auxiliary Division of the Royal Irish Constabulary.

SHOOTING OF DISTRICT INSPECTOR OSWALD ROSS SWANZY

At the beginning of August, instructions were given to the IRA for the execution of District Inspector Oswald Ross Swanzy who had been indicted by a jury for the murder of Lord Mayor Tomás MacCurtain earlier in the year. Swanzy had been moved from Cork to Lisburn for his own security. 'Lisburn is a small market town with a predominantly Protestant population ... At this time a state of tension prevailed, Catholics had been beaten and others threatened and information was therefore difficult to obtain about the police movements.'[2] Roger McCorley O/C First Brigade, Third Northern Division, recalled that he and his Belfast comrades, Thomas Fox and Seán Leonard, were joined by Sean Culhane and Dick Murphy from Cork in a mission to ambush Swanzy after he had attended church on Sunday, 22 August. Whilst Leonard kept the getaway car (his own taxi) running, the other four armed IRA men waited outside the chapel.

When Swanzy was spotted, the first shot was fired, as agreed, by Sean Culhane using Tomás MacCurtain's revolver, which had been brought up from Cork.[3] As the IRA delivered a further volley of shots, a large crowd of angry church-goers began to pursue the gunmen. McCorley halted and fired into the mob. He was then 'attacked by an ex-British Officer called Woods who seemed to have plenty of courage'. Woods assailed McCorley with a blackthorn stick but 'by a fluke' McCorley 'shot the stick out of his hand'. Luck continued on the side of the IRA when the police gave chase in a car and one of its wheels came off. However, Seán Leonard's luck was short lived. He had devised a cover story to say that the IRA had hijacked his taxi but the police became suspicious and Leonard was eventually sentenced to be hanged for the shooting of the District Inspector. His defending barrister Tim Healy took the matter up with Lord French and the sentence was commuted to twelve years.

For the small Catholic and nationalist community in Lisburn, the shooting of Oswald Ross Swanzy meant that 'the pogrom was pursued with increased activity, practically every business and house of a Catholic in Lisburn being burned to the ground....'[4] Belfast, meanwhile, was the scene of ten days of rioting, which resulted in the deaths of over thirty people. Dáil Éireann reacted by voting for a boycott of Belfast firms, in order to exert financial pressure on businesses to force them to seek a halt to the violence.

CUMANN NA mBAN

Of the 276 women who were active in the 1916 Rising, the majority were members of Cumann na mBan, which was founded in 1914. Their activities during the conflict from 1919 to 1921 were numerous and included first-aid duties, provision of safe houses, communications, fund-raising, propaganda, storing arms, spying and administrative duties. They were women of immense courage. dignity and strength of character. Brighid O'Mullane was responsible for setting up 'a secret line of com-munications between Dublin Headquarters and each District Council by which despatches were carried.' She explained how it worked:

> For example, information from Athlone would be conveyed by a Cumann na mBan cycle despatch carrier to the nearest Cumann na mBan Company Captain on the route, who, in turn, would pass it on similarly to the Adjutant of Mullingar District Council. The latter would then take over control of the messages and ensure their safe and secret

despatch to Dublin. In this way, most important intelligence work for the IRA was done by Cumann na mBan. The Cumann na mBan had various ways of collecting information; some of the girls, being employed in local post offices, were able to tap wires from police barracks.

Cumann na mBan 'also stored arms and ammunition in safe dumps, and kept the rifles and revolvers cleaned and oiled. If required by the IRA, they were utilised to transport arms to and from the dump before and after engagements….'[5] Historian Pádraig Óg Ó Ruairc notes that 'Women undertook dangerous work transporting arms and explosives during the War of Independence but the only occasion that women were permitted by their male comrades to play a direct role in attacking the enemy appears to have happened during the IRA attack on Kilmallock RIC Barracks….'[6] (see Chapter Five.)

THIRD TIPPERARY BRIGADE

On 12 September 1920, a meeting of the Third Tipperary Brigade was in session at a farm belonging to the Meagher family of Blackcastle. This brigade council was attended by three officers from each battalion, and the entire brigade staff was also present. They gathered in a 'haggard' normally used to store crops. Two senior IRA officers who were on their way to the IRA meeting, Edmond McGrath, Commandant of the Sixth Battalion, Third Tipperary Brigade, and his Battalion Adjutant, William Casey, ran into a patrol of Lancers from Cahir British Army Barracks. McGrath pretended to have a punctured tyre on his bicycle, which allowed him time to size up the situation. They cycled through the by-roads to get to Blackcastle where they reported what they had seen to the Third Tipperary Vice-Brigadier, Seán Treacy, who assured them that there were plenty of armed guards protecting the meeting.

Just as Treacy said that, there was a commotion, as scores of British Lancers came galloping towards them. Tom Meagher immediately slammed a large gate, which forced the Lancers to dismount from their horses.

Seán Treacy ordered the IRA officers to collect up all the IRA books and documents. IRA officers Jack O'Meara, Con Moloney, Arty Barlow, Tadhg Dwyer and Jerome Davin grabbed what they could and then dashed in various directions.[7] Moloney unleashed a volley of shots in the direction of the British. Treacy quickly loaded his Parabellum (Luger pistol) and he also opened fire on the British. Jack O'Keefe recalled in his witness statement that this action of Seán Treacy's enabled most of those present at the meeting to get away.[8]

The IRA men retreated as best as they could across the fields. Treacy stopped running every now and then and fired his pistol until the British ceased their pursuit. Three important men from the Third Tipperary Brigade of the IRA were captured in the event which became known in Republican lore as 'The Blackcastle Races': Edmond McGrath, Commandant of the Sixth Battalion, Séamus O'Neill who commanded the Second Battalion and Jack O'Keefe who was Adjutant of the Eighth Battalion.[9] All three were sentenced by court martial to two years' hard labour in English prisons.

THE SACK OF BALBRIGGAN

Balbriggan, a small town with a population of 2,200, situated twenty miles to the north of Dublin, witnessed a night of terror on 20 September 1920. Head Constable Peter Burke was celebrating his promotion to District Inspector with his brother Sergeant Michael Burke. The brothers, who were from County Kerry, had taken a taxi from Dublin, which they left outside while they went drinking in Mrs Smyth's public house. There were several Black and Tans in the pub, and when the taxi driver went in to ask for his fare, he was abused by the police. Michael Rock, the local Commandant of the IRA, got word that the Tans and the Burkes were abusing the cabman and 'terrorising everybody in the public house, and making the men go down on their knees and sing God Save The King!'[10] Michael Rock, William Corcoran and John Gaynor armed themselves, entered the pub and ordered the drunken Tans to clear out. Instead of doing so, the Tans made a rush at the IRA men, and Rock was left with no option but to fire.[11] Peter Burke was killed and Michael Burke was severely injured.

At least a hundred and fifty Tans who were quartered at Gorman-ston military barracks, three miles away, arrived that evening seeking revenge. Looting and burning ensued and terrified residents ran from their beds in fear of their lives. The *Drogheda Independent* recorded that 'Clonard Street suffered most extensively and here some 20 houses of all type were set alight.'[12] Twenty other houses and pubs and a hosiery factory, Deeds, Templers & Co., that employed a couple of hundred people were also destroyed by the rampaging Tans. Sinn Féin activists James Lawless, a hairdresser, and John Gibbons, a dairy farmer,

Destruction in the small town of Balbriggan, County Dublin, following a night of terror as members of the Black and Tans sought revenge for the deaths of two RIC men.

were dragged from their beds and brought to the barracks. They were severely beaten and eventually brought out and shot on Quay Street. The *Drogheda Independent* reported: 'As they lay on the ground, their bodies were stabbed again and again, even after the last breath of life had gone.'[13] From 11.45pm to 5am, the Black and Tans terrified the town of Balbriggan. They then went to nearby Skerries, where they murdered another two men. Their reprisal policy and the destruction and violence they inflicted was recorded by the media and brought wide-scale condemnation.

RINEEN AMBUSH

The Mid-Clare IRA had intelligence that a police tender travelled between Ennistymon and Miltown Malbay, County Clare, every Wednesday morning. An ambush site at Rineen, two miles from Miltown Malbay, where there was a curve in the road, was selected. Of the eight companies in the Fourth Battalion, each was to supply seven men for the ambush planned for 22 September 1920. The IRA parties arrived before daybreak, and the plan of attack was explained by Battalion O/C Ignatius O'Neill who, with the assistance of John Joe Neilan, O/C, Ennistymon Company, allocated positions to the men. It was the intention to attack the tender on its way to Miltown Malbay. However, a wrong signal had been transmitted, and the phrase 'Ford lorry travelling' was interpreted as 'four lorries travelling'.[14] As the positions the IRA occupied were not suitable for an attack on a convoy, Ignatius O'Neill called off the attack. However, the IRA waited patiently to ambush the tender on the return journey.

The ambush a few hours later lasted less than a minute. In a barrage of fire, six RIC men were killed, including a member of the Black and Tans. When the firing was over, the IRA men quickly captured 'six Lee Enfield rifles, six .45 revolvers, a couple of thousand rounds of .303 ammunition and some Mills bombs'.[15]

They also set the police lorry on fire. However, after a short time, they were surprised by ten British Army lorries, out searching for Captain Lendrum, a resident magistrate who had been killed by the West Clare IRA earlier that day near Doonbeg. They had obviously heard the firing and seen the smoke from the burning Crossley tender. The British placed a machine gun in position at the top of Dromin Hill and poured a steady stream of fire at the IRA. A small number of IRA Volunteers returned fire, and they managed to hold off the British for long enough to give their comrades time to retreat, suffering only two wounded.

Patrick Kerin, O/C Glendine Company, Fourth Battalion, Mid-Clare Brigade IRA, recalled the British reprisals: 'After the Rineen Ambush, the British forces in the area of Miltown Malbay and Ennistymon ran amok. They burned and looted several houses in these towns and in the village of Lahinch, and also murdered a number of innocent persons, some of whom were only on a holiday in the locality.'[16] The Town Hall of Ennistymon was set on fire. Tom Connole, the local secretary of the Irish Transport and General Workers' Union, was dragged from his house with his wife and two young children. He was tied up and murdered on the street by the Tans, who then set his house on fire and threw his corpse into the flames.

Having looted Flanagan's shop for alcoholic spirits, the RIC and Tans began to order people out of their houses, which they then set on fire. They captured and shot dead a fifteen-year-old boy, P.J. Linnane and also murdered a farmer called Joseph Sammon who was in Ennistymon on his holidays. Patrick Lehane, who had been one of the IRA ambushers earlier in the day, was burned alive when the RIC again turned their attention to Flanagan's shop and set it on fire. Lehane had been hiding in the attic of the shop.[17] A *Cork Examiner* reporter wrote that Miltown Malbay was 'completely wrecked' and that several houses had been burned to the ground. His report stated that Lahinch, Ennistymon and Liscannor 'were also wrecked' and that rifle fire went on from 11pm until 4.30am. Residents ran from the towns to seek refuge in the countryside. According to the *Cork Examiner*, the estimated damage in financial terms was £40,000.[18]

The night of terror in Miltown Malbay, Lahinch, Ennistymon and Liscannor strengthened the resolve of the IRA and the people of Clare who refused to be cowed by the British. Musing on the event, Anthony Malone, one of the IRA ambushers, said that there were two direct results: 'The enemy became more hostile and active, but he used large convoys when travelling. The people became very much embittered against him and adopted a more defiant attitude towards the Military and the Black and Tans.'[19] The *Irish Independent* reported that the Bishop of Galway 'deplored the fatal outbreak at Rineen as both unwise beyond measure and a grave breach of the law of God, except, of course, if it occurred in lawful self defence'. He also, it was reported, 'deplored and condemned the destruction of lives and property of innocent people perpetrated in reprisal by British forces, all the more because of its seeming toleration and encouragement by those who, as professing to govern, are bound beyond all else to protect life and property'.[20]

CHAPTER SEVEN

Trench Coat, Bandolier and Leggings

By September 1920, republican courts or Sinn Féin courts were effectively replacing the British judicial system in most of Ireland. The British were losing control of the country to the Republicans. Moreover, the war in Ireland had dragged on for over a year and a half, and newspapers in Britain were questioning the brutality of the British forces in Ireland; English horror at what was happening in Ireland would ultimately be a factor in bringing the war to an end, as public pressure was increasingly brought to bear on the situation.

Newspapers in Ireland also carried daily reports of the killings, ambushes and burnings carried out by the IRA and the British. A typical front page of any newspaper from the time makes hard reading but illustrates the extent of the war and how it affected daily life. The IRA began to form 'flying columns', small groups of mobile Volunteers who would live away from home and spend their time in the field, staging regular ambushes on British patrols. The IRA, under Liam Lynch, temporarily captured a British Army barracks in Mallow, and the town was attacked and burned the following night in a reprisal by the British. Two of the IRA Volunteers who had fired the first shots of the war, Dan Breen and Seán Treacy, had a miraculous escape after their safe house in Dublin was raided by the British, but Breen was badly wounded in the encounter. Treacy was shot dead two days later outside the Republican Outfitters on Talbot Street. As reports of hostilities continued, the Republicans were winning the propaganda war decisively.

TYPICAL WAR REPORTS FOR ONE DAY

The front page of *The Liberator* newspaper, published in Tralee, County Kerry, on 30 September 1920, gives a flavour of the intensity of the war at the time. Ardrahan village in County Galway was attacked by the Black and Tans in a reprisal for an ambush on the RIC. Shots were fired in Dingle, County Kerry, during the night. A civil guard made up of civilians was formed in Trim, County Meath. Seven RIC men were ambushed by masked men in Waterville, County Kerry, and a policeman was shot in the face. Two policemen were shot dead by the IRA in Templemore, County Tipperary. An RIC man, Sergeant Dee, who had been shot five times in the chest in Drimoleague, County Cork, was still alive but in a critical condition in hospital. The condition of eleven IRA hunger strikers in Cork Gaol was reported as being very grave.

Nor were those the only incidents reported in that edition of the newspaper. A British Army officer had been wounded in an ambush in Dundrum, near Limerick Junction. Five men had been arrested in Galway by the RIC, and charged with being members of the Republican Police. Persons unknown had set fire to Dingle railway station in County Kerry. A jury had returned a verdict of murder against a British Army officer and sergeant (who did not attend an inquest) for the shooting of seventy-year-old James Connolly at Unshinagh, Kinlough in County Leitrim. A raid had been carried out in the Wicklow Hotel, Dublin, by the British Army and men in plain clothes who were 'searching for a man'. The report noted that one of the men in plain clothes was masked. 'Armed men' had attacked Arva Barracks, Cavan, where the RIC surrendered and the building was burned to the ground. (Those 'armed men' were the Longford IRA under

Seán MacEoin, the 'Blacksmith of Ballinalee'). The newspaper goes on to report on the sacking of Mallow town in County Cork by the British Army, where the Cleeves Condensed Milk Factory (whose owners were Unionists) was amongst the destroyed business premises; the total damage in Mallow was estimated at £100,000.

On a lighter note, the paper reported on how some ordinary people in Ireland were reacting to the war. A public meeting in Clonmel, County Tipperary, had been held, at which it was unanimously decided to arrange for the taking of a total abstinence pledge in the town until such time as Ireland was free of British rule.

IRA FLYING COLUMNS

Organisation Memo No. 1 (1920) was issued by Óglaigh na hÉireann (Irish Volunteers or IRA) GHQ on 4 October 1920. It concerned the formation of flying columns:

> At the present time a large number of our men and officers are on the run in different parts of the country. The most effective way of utilis-ing these officers and men would seem to be by organising them as a Flying Column. In this way ... they would become available as standing troops of a well-trained and thoroughly reliable stamp, and their action could be far more systematic and effective. Permanent troops of this kind would afford an exceedingly valuable auxiliary arm to the remainder of the Republican Army, which is in great measure only a part-time service militia. These Flying Columns would consist of only first-rate troops as the work required of them would be very exacting.[1]

However, it should be noted that flying columns were already in opera-tion in June 1920, several months before the GHQ issued these orders. The historian Thomas Toomey notes that the 'founding of the first flying column, and the whole concept of flying columns, is generally accepted as having originated in east Limerick.'[2]

Members of the West Mayo IRA Flying Column.

A typical IRA flying column would use bicycles, which were relatively cheap, light enough to carry over fields, and most importantly a very popular mode of transport; there was nothing suspicious about a few men cycling together. Vast distances could be covered by a flying column, which ideally consisted of twenty-six combatants. The duties of flying columns would comprise two distinct types of action, auxiliary and independent. For auxiliary action the Brigade commandants would assign the flying column as an invaluable extra force for a local attack in his area. Independent action would comprise attacks on hostile patrols and raids on postal deliveries and enemy stores. Commanders of flying columns had wide discretion but were to keep in contact with local O/Cs to avoid interference with each other. Except 'by definite arrangement with the Brigade Commandant of a neighbouring Area, which offered an opportunity for action', flying columns were to remain in their own Brigade area.

The West Connemara Brigade IRA Flying Column wearing the uniform of trench coats, bandoliers and leggings.

Dan Breen recalled that a member of a flying column could always be recognised

> … not only by the rifle and revolver which he usually carried, and the
> trench coat, bandolier and leggings which were part of his regular outfit,
> but also by the razor and toothbrush which he carried after the manner
> of a fountain pen, standing up in his breast pocket. Discipline in this
> matter was very strict, cleanliness was considered essential. A column man
> with a dirty or unshaven face was unheard of.[3]

CAPTURE OF MALLOW BARRACKS

On 22 November 1919, the original Cork Brigade was divided into three Brigades. Mallow became the Fourth Battalion attached to the Second Brigade IRA. On 28 September 1920, Liam Lynch, Commandant of Cork Number 2 Brigade, led the only capture of a British Army Barracks during the War of Independence. Two IRA men, Richard Willis and Jack Bolster, were working as civilian contractors in Mallow Barracks, and they took note of the movements of the Seventeenth Lancers, a British mounted regiment. The Lancers used to exercise their horses every morning on the outskirts of Mallow; when they were doing so, there were only fifteen men left in the barracks. On the morning of 28 September, Lynch's men went into action. One of his staff officers, Owen Harold, had been billeted for some time in a house facing the barracks, where he watched the movement of the troops.[4] Lynch posted a sniping party in Mallow Town Hall in order to get a line of sight on O'Brien Street where the local RIC barracks was. If the police were tempted to go to the aid of the military, they were to be fired upon.

Willis and Bolster were inside the army barracks with Paddy McCarthy, who was posing as the foreman of the job but who was actually an IRA quartermaster. All three were armed with revolvers. Another staff officer of Lynch's Brigade, Ernie O'Malley, approached the door of Mallow Barracks under the pretence of delivering a letter. As the sentry opened the door, O'Malley and a couple of others pushed the door in and overpowered the soldier. Lynch and the rest of the IRA piled into the barracks. A British sergeant by the name of Gibbs ran to the guardroom but was mortally wounded. Meanwhile, the three 'workers', Willis, Bolster and McCarthy, ran into the guardroom and arrested the soldiers.

When the British had been rounded up and locked in the stables, the IRA set the guardroom on fire using petrol and hay. The raid enabled them to commandeer a large haul of equipment: twenty-seven rifles, two Hotchkiss light machine-guns, a revolver, a large quantity of ammunition and a number of Verey light pistols (flare guns).[5]

SACKING OF MALLOW

The capture of Mallow Barracks by the IRA was a blow to the British morale and they took their anger out on the civilians of the town. The night following the raid was one of terror in Mallow. British Army

British Army armoured car blocked by a tree felled by the IRA.

detachments from Buttevant and Fermoy indulged in an orgy of drinking, looting and burning.[6] Drunken British soldiers rampaged through Mallow, throwing petrol bombs into the homes and businesses of the town. The Town Hall was destroyed and the local creamery, Cleeves, where several hundred people were employed, was burned to the ground. The ashes were still smouldering in other towns that had been looted in the previous days and weeks: Balbriggan, County Dublin (20 September), Miltown Malbay, Lahinch, Liscannor and Ennistymon in County Clare (22 September), and Trim, County Meath (27 September). *The Liberator* carried a report on the 'Terrible wreckage in Mallow' inflicted by the British Army. In fairness to the RIC, the newspaper reported that the police had provided refuge in their barracks for civilians, and noted: 'an extraordinary feature of the attempts to save burning houses after the wreckers had departed was the active participation with the townspeople of the local police, including the Black and Tan section.'[7]

Two days after the burning of Mallow, several houses and two creameries in Tubbercurry, County Sligo, were burned by the Black

British Army officers inspect damage to a bridge on the Ballinspittle road in County Cork, following an IRA attack. Local labourers can be seen carrying out repairs.

and Tans in revenge for an IRA ambush which had seen the death of an RIC district inspector, James Brady. It was clear that reprisals against civilians were part of British policy in Ireland.

THE CAFÉ CAIRO

The Café Cairo on 59 Grafton Street was often used for meetings by Dublin Castle spies and informants. There are many references in modern Irish history books to the 'Cairo Gang', and indeed there are some images referenced as being the 'Cairo Gang'. However, the term was rarely used by the IRA or the British during the war. The exception is Dan Breen who made reference to it in his recollections, *My Fight for Irish Freedom,* published in 1924: 'Major Smyth had been on service in Egypt. He applied for intelligence work in Ireland, was accepted, and brought over eleven picked men with him to avenge the death of his brother. They became known as the Cairo Gang.'[8]

George Osbert Stirling Smyth, decorated by the British and the French for gallantry during the war, was the brother of Lieutenant

Colonel Gerald Brice Smyth who had been shot in Cork on 17 July 1920 (see Chapter Five). George Smyth, a serving British Army Brigade Major in Egypt, was determined to avenge his brother's death, and arrived in Ireland in August 1920, but there is no evidence to suggest that he brought men with him from Egypt. There is no mention of a 'Cairo Gang' in the Bureau of Military History witness statements or in pension records. It seems more likely that the term 'Cairo Gang' used by Dan Breen derived from the café as opposed to the capital of Egypt.

Another place the British secret service agents, British Army intelligence officers and Auxiliary intelligence officers frequented was Kidd's Back (or Kidd's Buffet), which could be accessed from Nassau Street or from Grafton Street, via Adam Court. IRA Assistant Director of Intelligence Tom Cullen, and Frank Thornton, Deputy Assistant Director of Intelligence, together with their comrade Frank Saurin, an IRA intelligence officer, regularly ate and drank in Kidd's Back. David Nelligan introduced the three IRA intelligence men to all the British spies in Kidd's, referring to them as his touts and giving them false names. As discussed in Chapter Three, Nelligan worked in Dublin Castle but was actually an IRA operative. Discussions in Kidd's Back were all about Michael Collins and the Dublin IRA, and the British often dropped the names of touts that they were using, which was very useful information for the IRA to have.

Frank Thornton recalled in his witness statement a particular day in Kidd's when one of the British turned to him, Tom Cullen and Frank Saurin and said in an exasperated tone, 'Surely you fellows know these men — Liam Tobin, Tom Cullen and Frank Thornton — these are Collins's three officers and if you can get these fellows we would locate Collins himself.' Thornton realised then while the British may have known the names of the IRA GHQ Intelligence, they quite clearly did not know what they looked like.

'FERNSIDE' ESCAPE

Dan Breen and Seán Treacy often stayed with the Fleming family who lived above their grocery shop at 140 Drumcondra Road, 'which was a noted place for all men on the run'.[9] However, word came that Fleming's was under constant watch, and that no one was to stay there for a while. Instead, the duo spent the night of 11 October with the family of Professor John Carolan, at 'Fernside', 37 Upper Drumcondra Road. Treacy and Breen let themselves in a little after the eleven o'clock curfew and quietly made their way to a bedroom at the top of the house, where they attempted to sleep.

At two in the morning, the glass in the front door was smashed and a raiding party led by George Osbert Stirling Smyth (brother of Gerald Brice Smyth) came rushing into the house. Smyth grabbed Professor Carolan on the landing and demanded to know who was in the house. The British fired a couple of shots into the room where Treacy and Breen were frantically trying to dress and make a plan for escape. The IRA men fired back through the door to hold the raiders off. Seeing that there were British outside in the rear too, Breen came out onto the landing firing wildly down the stairs at point blank range. He recalled, 'One bullet grazed my forehead, another passed through the fleshy portion of my thigh, two hit me in the calves of my legs and one lodged in my right lung. But I still kept my stand and fired at the raiders until the gun was empty.'[10] Two of the attackers were mortally wounded, Smyth and Captain A.P. White of the Surrey Yeomanry. Treacy and Breen made their escape through the bedroom window, crashing down on the conservatory roof. Both men lost each other in the rush to escape.

Treacy made his way to the home of Phil Ryan in Finglas, where his wounds were tended to. Ryan sent a messenger to Fleming's to see if they could get word of Breen about whom Treacy was very concerned, fearing that he might even be dead. However, Fleming's was under assault by the remainder of the raiding party still alive after the shooting at 'Fernside'.

In their anger, the British trashed the Fleming home and shop, demanding to know where Breen and Treacy were. James Fleming defied the British who tried to plant a gun on him and he was arrested along with his brother, Michael. Kitty Fleming remembered that one of the British officers appeared to be distraught, saying that he had 'lost five of our best men'. The raiders ransacked the shop and eventually left with their prisoners. Word came to Fleming's that Professor Carolan was mortally wounded and wanted the Fleming sisters, Dot and Kitty, to come and see him in hospital. Carolan told them that the British had made him stand against a wall in the bedroom where he had sheltered Breen and Treacy, and had shot him in the neck. The Professor also made this statement to Joseph Penrose who was on the staff of the *Freeman's Journal*.[11]

Meanwhile, Dan Breen, suffering some serious blood loss, ended up wading through the Tolka river in a delirious state until he came to the back of a row of houses on Botanic Avenue. Fred Holmes and his wife Kathleen took sympathy on Breen and gave him shelter. Kathleen even took a message to IRA Brigadier Dick McKee, via Phil Shanahan's public house, and McKee arranged for Breen to be collected by car. Plans were made for Breen to be looked after at the Mater Hospital. However, the hospital was being raided by the British Army, so instead Breen was driven to a shed down a lane on Mountjoy Square. Joseph Lawless, the driver of the car, recalled the scene in the dark shed: 'Dan in his delirium was all the time grieving over the loss of his best friend and gallant comrade Seán Treacy, and by this time further administrations of brandy were having little or no effect in keeping him quiet.'[12] But Mick McDonnell of the Squad soon brought Treacy to see Breen. Lawless remembered that reunion between Treacy and Breen as an 'emotional climax'. Breen later lamented: 'Little did I think on that evening that never again on this earth would I set eyes on my faithful friend, one who was dearer to me than a brother.'[13]

SEÁN TREACY SHOT

On the evening of 12 October, Dan Breen was secretly brought to the Mater Hospital, where he was hidden by the staff who were also caring for Professor Carolan. Breen later said of Carolan that he was 'generous, noble and patriotic' and regretted that 'he met such a sad death' a few days later. Meanwhile, the British were still scouring Dublin for him and Treacy. They knew that at least one of them was injured, so on 14 October they carried out a series of raids on the Mater Hospital, Beaumont Convalescent Home, Jervis Street Hospital and even the Clarence Hotel. Armoured cars patrolled the streets around the Mater, and a strong force of British military, Tans and Auxiliaries searched the hospital for three hours. Michael Collins and the Squad made hurried preparations to rescue Breen if the British should find him. Dick McKee and Peadar Clancy were using Clancy's drapery shop, The Republican Outfitters at 94 Talbot Street, as a point of contact to send and receive messages. The Brigadier and Vice-Brigadier had been 'active at the Mater Hospital and in Talbot Street organising and directing the mobilisation of all the available Dublin men.'[14]

Seán Treacy, meanwhile, was rushing around the city, unconcerned for his own safety and all the time thinking about his wounded comrade, Dan Breen. Treacy collected a new coat and bike from Jim Kirwan's pub on Parnell Street, courtesy of Denis Patrick Walsh. Walsh urged him to 'lie low' as the British had spies all around the streets looking out for him. Jim Kirwan, who had established his public house in March 1920, employed only IRA staff. The premises was used as an arms dump and Michael Collins held regular meetings of the GHQ of the IRA there. Kirwan also warned Treacy that the British were scouring the streets for him. Just as Treacy was leaving Kirwan's, two lorry loads of British soldiers came slowly moving past the pub. Treacy drew his Parabellum, ready for a fight, but the British were raiding a house further down the road. Kirwan remembered Treacy saying, 'They have been after me all day.' Treacy then headed for a meeting with Dick McKee in the Republican Outfitters.

Seán Brunswick had been running messages between the Mater and Talbot Street all day. He noticed that the shop was under observation and reported to Peadar Clancy that a British intelligence officer called Francis Christian and other suspicious-looking individuals were loitering in the area. Brunswick recalled the men he had seen in the Republican Outfitters: George and Jack Plunkett, both veterans of the Rising, whose brother Joseph had been executed in 1916; Leo Henderson who had also fought in the GPO in the Rising; Joe Vize who was O/C IRA Scotland and was responsible for the importation of arms from Britain; and Brigadier Dick McKee and Vice-Brigadier Peadar Clancy.

Sometime after four o'clock, an armoured car and two lorries carrying British soldiers, Auxiliaries and plain clothes British intelligence men came sweeping at speed into Talbot Street from Sackville Street. Dick McKee, Leo Henderson and Joe Vize were chatting in the doorway of the Republican Outfitters. McKee said, 'They are coming — Get Out!' Seán Treacy was further from the door than the others. By the time he got outside, the British were at the shop. Treacy ran to grab a bicycle but took one that was too large for him and he stumbled as he tried to mount it. Francis Christian jumped from one of the trucks and grappled with Treacy who fired his pistol into the stomach of his attacker; Christian collapsed. Treacy fired at two more of the British, one of whom, Gilbert Albert Price, wrestled with him. The military in the lorries and the armoured vehicle unleashed a fusillade of gunfire at the struggling group, without much regard for their own men. Seán Treacy was shot in the head and died instantly, as did Price. After a few minutes, when the firing had ceased, Seán Brunswick cleverly pretended to be a medical student and attended to Treacy. He quickly retrieved ammunition, dispatches and a field message book from the dead man's pockets.[15]

CHAPTER EIGHT

They Who Can Suffer Most

The Lord Mayor of Cork, Terence MacSwiney, died in Brixton, London, after seventy-four days on hunger strike, bringing worldwide outrage and condemnation of the British, and international attention to the Irish cause. This increased attention also reflected the work of the Dáil's department of publicity and propaganda, producer of the *Irish Bulletin,* which was sent weekly to hundreds of international papers (see Chapter Three). Two other men, Michael Fitzgerald and Joseph Murphy, also died on hunger strike around the same time, further bolstering public support for the IRA and Sinn Féin.

MacSwiney's death set the stage for what was to become the worst month in the entire War of Independence. In early November 1920, the town of Tralee was besieged by the Black and Tans and Auxiliaries who terrorised the civilian population for ten days, again bringing condemnation from afar. When Kevin Barry was hanged in Mountjoy Jail, he was the first person to be executed by the British since the Easter Rising. His case aroused deep emotion in Ireland and abroad. Michael Collins ordered the Squad and the Dublin IRA to shoot a number of British agents in Dublin. In reaction to this, the Black and Tans, Auxiliaries and British Army attacked Croke Park football stadium, killing fourteen people on what became known as Bloody Sunday. The Auxiliaries also captured Brigadier Dick McKee and Vice-Brigadier Peadar Clancy of the Dublin IRA and murdered them in Dublin Castle. When Arthur Griffith and Eoin MacNeill, considered moderates within Sinn Féin, were arrested and held in Mountjoy Jail later that month, it was seen as a sign of the desperation of Dublin Castle and the British forces in Ireland who were frustrated by their inability even to come close to arresting Michael Collins. At the end of the month, in one of the most infamous incidents in the west of Ireland, two brothers, Patrick and Harry Loughnane, were tortured, mutilated and murdered by the Auxiliaries.

HUNGER STRIKES

Hunger strikes proved to be a potent propaganda weapon for the IRA. However, they were not an official policy, and were not directed by IRA GHQ; Cathal Brugha was against them and no official order was ever given to prisoners to commence fasting. Instead, each hunger striker made an individual decision to strike. While in London's Wormwood Scrubs prison, Edmond McGrath, who had been arrested after the Blackcastle Races (see Chapter Six), received word from Michael Collins that he could not order a hunger strike but that it would be a damn good thing if it came off. McGrath and about seventy Irish republicans went on hunger strike and also smashed up their cells. After about twenty days, most prisoners were taken to hospitals in London and, having received treatment, were released.

TERENCE MACSWINEY

Following the murder of Tomás MacCurtain on 20 March 1920 (See Chapter Four), Terence MacSwiney had replaced him as Lord Mayor of Cork. MacSwiney, an accountant, playwright and author of pamphlets on Irish history, had been active with the Irish Volunteers since their foundation; he was Commandant of Cork Number 1 Brigade when he was arrested on 12 August 1920. Charged with possessing an

The funeral of Lord Mayor of Cork Terence MacSwiney, who died in Brixton Prison following a hunger strike.

incriminating document, he received a two-year prison sentence. Sixty Republicans in Cork Gaol had commenced a hunger strike the day before MacSwiney's arrest, to protest their internment. Eleven more, including MacSwiney, joined them. MacSwiney continued his fast even when he was transferred to London's Brixton Prison, where he died on 25 October 1920 at the age of forty-one.

As an elected member of Dáil Éireann and Lord Mayor of a major city, MacSwiney knew that his struggle would gain worldwide attention. In his acceptance speech as Lord Mayor on 30 March, he famously said, 'This contest of ours is not on our side a rivalry of vengeance but one of endurance — it is not they who can inflict most but they who can suffer most will conquer....'[1] His death after seventy-four days of suffering caused a wave of revulsion; it also brought condemnation from political and religious leaders from other nations. Thousands lined the streets as his body was brought to St George's Cathedral, Southwark, for requiem mass attended by Catholic hierarchy including Archbishop Mannix of Melbourne. Three hundred British police and a force of Auxiliaries sent over from Dublin intercepted his funeral at Holyhead. They roughed up the chief mourners and sent the coffin to Cork by steamer, fearful of the animosity and antagonism that would follow if the body travelled through Dublin.[2] McSwiney's body lay in state in Cork City Hall where thousands came to pay their respects. On 31 October, he was buried beside his comrade, Tomás MacCurtain, in St Finnbarr's Cemetery.

MICHAEL FITZGERALD AND JOE MURPHY

Terence MacSwiney was not alone in the sacrifice he made for his cause. Two of his comrades, Michael Fitzgerald and Joe Murphy, also died on hunger strike. Fitzgerald was O/C Fourth Battalion Cork Number 2 Brigade and died a week before MacSwiney, on 17 October 1920. On Easter Sunday, 1919, Fitzgerald had led the capture of Araglin RIC Barracks, which was stripped of arms and ammunition. He was also part of the group of IRA men under Liam Lynch who had captured weapons from the military on their way to the Wesleyan Church in Fermoy, resulting in the death of a British soldier (see Chapter Three). Held on remand, Michael Fitzgerald believed that the only way to fight for his release was to go on a hunger strike. He lasted for sixty-seven agonising days before his death.[3]

Twenty-four-year-old Joe Murphy, a Volunteer with C Company, Second Battalion, Cork Number 1 Brigade, died on 25 October, a few hours after Terence MacSwiney. When Murphy's home was raided, the British found a dud bomb used for throwing practice. He lasted a staggering seventy-nine days on hunger strike, and his comrades managed a volley of shots over his grave in defiance of the British. Frank Hynes, IRA Captain of Cork Number 1 Brigade, recalled:

After this incident every young man in the area joined our Company. When Terence MacSwiney … was brought home to be buried in Cork, I had 169 men on parade at the funeral. There was no limit to the number at the funeral. They lifted the ban for the occasion. The Volunteers were used to line the route on each side of the two miles to the cemetery.[4]

Four men died on hunger strike between 1917 and 1920. Throughout the twentieth century, twenty-two Irish republicans died on hunger strike.

SIEGE OF TRALEE

From Sunday, 31 October to Wednesday, 10 November 1920, 'Tralee was in a state of siege; armed military went through the town firing volleys as they sped by, public and private buildings were razed to the ground, civilians were shot dead on the streets.'[5] Two Black and Tans had been captured by the IRA in the town and were later shot and secretly buried.[6] The police, Black and Tans and Auxiliaries went on a shooting rampage. To add fuel to their anger, the IRA had killed RIC men in Ballyduff and Killorglin, and wounded police in Abbeydorney, Causeway and Dingle. The British set fire to a number of key buildings in Tralee, including the old County Hall. Other buildings and houses were looted and ransacked.

On Monday, 1 November, a holy day of obligation, mass-goers were harassed, beaten and shot. John Conway, a father of six children, was shot dead on Upper Rock Street. The British posted notices around Tralee:

Take notice of the warning that unless the two Tralee policemen in Sinn Féin custody are returned before 10 a.m. on the second instant, reprisals of a nature not yet heard of in Ireland will take place in Tralee and surroundings.

On Tuesday, the violence against civilians continued. Former British soldier Tommy Wall was beaten by the British and told to run, whereupon he was shot in the stomach, dying the following day. The Black and Tans and Auxiliaries maintained an embargo on trading, so all shops were closed and the people of Tralee began to suffer from the lack of food.

By Saturday, the situation remained the same, with the Tans still rampaging through the streets, engaged in a drunken orgy of violence and retribution. In Ardfert, a young man named Maguire was taken by the Tans and murdered; his body was found in Causeway. Just north of Tralee, in Kilflynn, a farm labourer called Archer was shot dead as he worked in a field.[7] The *New York Times* reported on the terror being inflicted on the people of Tralee, and when the siege was finally lifted on 10 November, the world could see that the Black and Tans, Auxiliaries and RIC were out of control. That evening, a young IRA Volunteer, Frank Hoffman, was found by the Tans, placed standing against a fence, then bayoneted and shot dead, the last murder in the Siege of Tralee.[8]

KEVIN BARRY HANGED

On 1 November 1920, the day after Terence MacSwiney was buried, eighteen-year-old Kevin Barry was hanged in Mountjoy Jail, Dublin. Barry, who had been an active Volunteer for a couple of years, had been involved in a number of raids, including that at King's Inns on 1 June 1920 after which twenty-five British were released by the IRA under Peadar Clancy (see Chapter Five). A medical student at University College Dublin, Kevin Barry was due to sit an examination at 2pm on 20 September 1920. However, he was also scheduled to take part in an ambush that morning.

On 20 September, a British Army truck was due to collect bread from Monk's Bakery on Church Street, and H Company of the First Battalion Dublin Brigade IRA was lying in wait for the truck, intending to capture the soldiers' weapons. The ambush resulted in a shoot-out. Barry's .38 Parabellum jammed and he ran for cover under the British Army lorry. Three privates died: Harold Washington was killed in the ambush; Marshall Whitehead and Thomas Humphries succumbed to their wounds later. Barry was captured by the British and brought to the North Dublin Union where, although he was horrifically abused and tortured, he refused to divulge the names of his comrades. Under the orders of Dick McKee, his Brigadier, a signed affidavit concerning his torture was smuggled out of Mountjoy Jail by his sister: 'When I lay on the floor, one of the sergeants knelt on my back, the other two placed one foot each on my back and left shoulder, and the man who knelt on me twisted my right arm, holding it by the wrist with one hand, while he held my hair with the other to pull back my head. The arm was twisted from the elbow joint.'[9]

Under the Restoration of Order in Ireland Act, Barry was sentenced to be hanged. No revolutionary had been executed in Ireland since the Easter Rising of 1916. With characteristic insensitivity towards a pre-dominantly Catholic nation who loved its martyrs, the British set the date for Barry's execution: 1 November, All Saints Day.

Michael Collins, who was beside himself with anger and worry over Barry, formulated a daring idea to liberate him two days before his execution. Barry's sisters were to have been 'on the inside' but the unexpected arrival of a visiting priest, a friend of Barry's, who was brought to see him first, ruined the timing of the attack which centred around the changing of the guards.[10] The rescue plan was reluctantly called off by Captain Charlie Byrne.

GHQ and Barry's comrades decided on another desperate plan the following day, which involved using a mine to blow a hole in the wall of Mountjoy Prison and rushing the armed British guards. The men ready to die rescuing young Barry included IRA Volunteers of the calibre of Collins himself and three members of the Squad, Tom Ennis, Charlie Byrne and Tom Keogh, as well as Barry's close friend in H Company, Frank Flood, who would face a similar fate in Mountjoy Jail less than five months later (see Chapter Ten). All were willing to do anything to save Barry. IRA Chief of Staff Dick Mulcahy, Brigadier Dick McKee,

Vice-Brigadier Peadar Clancy and Seán Russell, who was Director of Munitions, were also ready to go through with the rescue. Others who had volunteered for the operation included veterans of the Rising like Paddy McGrath (executed in Mountjoy Jail on 6 September 1940) and Joseph Plunkett's brothers, George and Jack, and many others including Barry's H Company. Gathered in premises adjoining the jail, the IRA men realised that whoever was first through the hole was bound to be shot, and every one of these men was prepared to sacrifice himself in this way. Dick McKee, as O/C of the operation, chose that role for himself.

Unfortunately a constant stream of people was gathering in the vicinity of the jail to pray for Barry, and despite whispered words to send them away, the crowds grew. The attempt to free Barry was called off because too many innocent people might have died. The IRA rescue party was devastated by this failure. Lieutenant Seán O'Neill of H Company wrote later: 'Every man there cried like a child. The same scene took place in all the positions which were taken up by our men, and I believe it was pitiful to see such strong and gallant men … break down and cry like children when they found the attempt at rescue was off. Kevin Barry had to die for Ireland. It was God's will.'[11]

THE BLACKSMITH OF BALLINALEE

Meanwhile, in Longford on Halloween night, RIC District Inspector Philip Kelleher, a war hero, was shot by the IRA in Kiernan's Hotel in Granard. According to Seán Sexton, 'Kelleher had been bragging that he had complete information about the IRA and was biding his time to make a clean sweep of the lot.'[12] The following day, 1 November 1920, Constable Peter Cooney, who was in plain clothes and had been spying in Ballinalee, was shot in Granard.[13] Everyone expected that the Black and Tans would burn Granard and Ballinalee in reprisal. An attempt was made to set fire to a premises in Granard, and the IRA fired at the RIC and Tans and sent them back to their barracks. Word came that Ballinalee would be attacked so local blacksmith and O/C Longford IRA Seán MacEoin prepared to defend his town. The night of 2 November was a very wet and dark one, and the British were expected to come from the Longford side. The plan was to allow them into the village, and then to hem them in and attack them.

At about two in the morning, no fewer than eleven truckloads of Tans arrived. When they stopped and alighted, MacEoin, in the pitch dark, shouted, 'Surrender to the IRA', even though there were just five IRA men.[14] When the Tans refused, the IRA lobbed a couple of Mills Bombs in their general direction, and a two-hour gun battle at close quarters ensued. The Tans had a Maxim machine gun and a Lewis gun, and the IRA had about 100 rounds of ammunition each. Seán Sexton understood why none of the other IRA outposts came to their assistance: they could not tell friend from foe; 'I would like to emphasise that the darkness was intense during the fight. It was raining very hard and visibility was only about ten yards or so.'[15]

Just as MacEoin and his few men were down to their last rounds, the Tans finally withdrew, and Ballinalee was left in the hands of the IRA for nearly a week. This was the first and only time during the War of Independence that a town was successfully held and defended by the IRA. Seán MacEoin, known as 'the Blacksmith of Ballinalee', said that his men also found a great supply of items left behind by the Tans: 'About the area in which the lorries had been drawn up were pools of blood, and strewn all over it were items of military equipment, revolvers and thousands of rounds of .303 ammunition.'[16]

Ballinalee may have been protected by the IRA, but in Granard practically every house in the town was robbed and looted. Many houses were also burned, most likely by the same Black and Tans who had been ambushed by the IRA under Seán MacEoin.

THE 'B SPECIALS'

James Craig was a leading member of the Orange Order and also a member of the British Cabinet as Parliamentary and Financial Secretary to the Admiralty. He suggested to Lloyd George that a special police force would provide some assistance in the northern region of Ireland and that this would relieve the pressure on the RIC men who were stretched in the fight against the IRA. The Prime Minister agreed and, on 1 November 1920, the Ulster Special Constabulary was formed. The Specials were to operate in six counties in the northern area of Ireland comprising Armagh, Antrim, Down, Fermanagh, Tyrone and Derry. The force was made up, almost entirely, of Protestant men, many of whom were members of the Ulster Volunteer Force. Members of the Catholic nationalist population were not encouraged to join, either by the British Government or, indeed, the IRA.

In all, some thirty-two thousand men joined the Ulster Special Constabulary (USC). About five thousand of those were in the A Specials and acted as full-time paid members, serving alongside the RIC in their local areas. Nineteen thousand were members of the notorious B Specials and were part-time members who served under their own command structure. The rest of the men, called C Specials, were older individuals who undertook lighter duties. The Specials were involved in many reprisals against nationalists and, in many ways, behaved in the same unruly manner as the Black and Tans and the Auxiliaries, terrorising the Catholic minority of the Six Counties, not only between 1920 and 1922, but throughout the period up to 1970.

In Belfast, on 23 March 1922, two A Specials were shot dead by the IRA. The following day, Friday, 24 March, suspected members of the USC burst into the McMahon home on Kinnaird Road in Belfast. Owen McMahon was a successful businessman, owner of the Capston Bar and a director of Glentoran Football Club. He was considered quiet and apolitical but he was a Catholic and that was all the Specials needed.

They herded Owen McMahon, his six sons and a friend and employee, Edward McKinney, into one room, separating them from the women of the house. The Specials opened fire on the men and boys for a full five minutes. Edward McKinney, the barman, was killed. Owen McMahon and his sons Frank (24), Patrick (22) and Gerard (15) were also killed. Bernard McMahon (26) died of his wounds later. The youngest son, twelve-year-old Michael, was shielded behind some furniture and feigned death. The murders caused revulsion, even in the House of Commons, but no police were ever charged.

A few days later, after the shooting of an RIC man, George Turner, on the Old Lodge Road, ten RIC men went on the rampage in nationalist areas. On Stanhope Street, they broke into a house and shot Joseph McRory in his kitchen. Bernard McKenna, a father of seven children, was shot in his bed at his home on Park Street. On Arnon Street, the murder gang smashed its way into the home of William Spallen who had just buried his wife, a victim of the conflict. The policemen shot the seventy-year-old man in front of his grandson who saw them take £20 intended to pay for William's wife's funeral. The police then used a sledgehammer to break into the house next door where they bludgeoned Joseph Walsh to death in front of his children. A six-month-old baby, Robert, was also killed in the attack. That evening, the gang shot John Mallon, a sixty-year-old Catholic, on Skegoneill Avenue.

The chief suspect, according to an IRA report, was District Inspector John William Nixon from Brown Street Barracks, who 'made the lives of the people unbearable by permitting the men in the Barracks to snipe at the residents on their way to mass or to work.'[17] Nixon was rewarded by the British Crown with an MBE (Member of the Order of the British Empire) for 'services rendered'. In 1924, DI Nixon was dismissed from the police after he gave a political speech at his Orange Hall, contravening police regulations.

BRITISH SPIES SHOT IN DUBLIN

As Dublin was flooded with British intelligence officers, IRA GHQ decided to eliminate as many as possible in one swoop. These spies or agents, who mostly wore civilian attire and mingled with Dubliners, had carried out a number of killings. Often erroneously referred to as the 'Cairo Gang' (see Chapter Seven), these men were out to get Collins who was left with little choice — kill or be killed. Piaras Béaslaí recalled that a list of names and addresses of British agents was carefully compiled in which only those whose guilt was certain were included.[18] Michael Collins used men from the Squad and handpicked individuals from the four Dublin Battalions to carry out this meticulously planned operation.

On 21 November 1920, the Sunday morning silence was shattered by the sound of the guns of the IRA. Most of the shooting was carried out in the well-to-do Georgian southside areas of the city. Lieutenant Henry Angliss, alias McMahon, suspected of killing a Limerick Sinn Féin councillor, was killed at 22 Lower Mount Street by Tom Keogh. A passing lorry of Auxiliaries surrounded the house, and Frank Teeling was wounded and captured. Two Auxiliaries, Frank Garniss and Cecil Morris, were shot dead as they were running to Beggars Bush Barracks for reinforcements.[19] However, word got to the barracks anyway, where General Crozier was inspecting the Auxiliaries, and Crozier himself was one of the first on the scene.[20]

On Lower Baggot Street, two spies were killed. At number 92, Bill Stapleton and Joe Leonard shot Captain William Frederick Newberry. At number 119, Captain Geoffrey Thomas Baggallay was killed. The media reported that 'Captain' John Fitzgerald was shot at 28 Earlsfort Terrace. The man was, in fact, RIC Sergeant John J. Fitzgerald who was recovering from an assassination attempt by the IRA in County Clare.

Lieutenant Donald Lewis MacLean and Thomas Smith, the owner of the house, were killed at 117 Morehampton Road, and Lieutenant Peter Ames and Captain George Bennett were shot dead at 38 Upper

Mount Street. Six spies were shot at 28 and 29 Upper Pembroke Road. Three survived but Captain Leonard Price and Major C.M.C. Dowling died; Lieutenant Colonel Hugh Montgomery died a few weeks later from his wounds. The only operation carried out on the northside of Dublin was at the Gresham Hotel where Captain Patrick MacCormack and Leonard Wilde were shot dead. The three Cooney sisters, Annie, Lily and Eileen of Cumann na mBan, waited at University Church on St Stephen's Green to take charge of a number of revolvers used in the attack.[21]

Altogether fourteen men were killed and one died later.[22] Most of the killings were carried out at nine o'clock, when the men were lounging in bed, which would tend to engender sympathy. However, Michael Collins wrote later: 'By their destruction the very air is made sweeter … For myself, my conscience is clear. There is no crime in detecting and destroying in wartime the spy and the informer. They have destroyed without trial. I have paid them back in their own coin.'[23]

BLOODY SUNDAY AT CROKE PARK

Perhaps the worst reprisals of the war were carried out that afternoon when a combined force of Black and Tans, Auxiliaries, RIC and British Army entered Croke Park during a football match between Tipperary and Dublin. There were some links between local GAA clubs around Ireland and the Volunteer movement; however, this was no excuse for the murderous rampage in which the Crown forces engaged. Officially, the British Army, under Lieutenant Colonel Robert Bray, were to be used as 'crowd control' during a planned search (of an entire stadium of football supporters) by the RIC, Tans and Auxies. It was more obviously going to be a reprisal for the shooting of British spies that morning. A military aeroplane flew over Croke Park and fired a flare, presumably a signal for the British forces. The Army was first to arrive, followed soon by the police. Major Edward Lawrence Mills, in charge of the Auxiliaries, and Major George Vernon Dudley, in charge of the Black and Tans, arrived in their trucks.

As the trucks screeched to a halt, people outside the ground scattered. The Auxiliaries and Black and Tans dashed into the ground, firing immediately. Croke Park was the scene of a bloody massacre, with indiscriminate shooting at men women and children, GAA supporters and players alike. Fourteen people lost their lives.

Twenty-six-year-old Jane Boyle, who worked in a butcher's shop, was the only woman to die. A laundry worker from Arbour Hill, forty-four-year-old James Burke, was also killed. Michael Feery, a former Royal Marine who was about forty, struggled down the road from Croke Park, but succumbed to his mortal wounds. Twenty-four-year-old Michael Hogan, who was playing for Tipperary that day, was shot dead, and as Thomas Ryan, a gas company labourer, said an Act of Contrition into Hogan's ear, he too was murdered. Jeremiah O'Leary, who was only ten years of age, was shot in the head and killed. John William Scott, only four years older than him, was killed too. James Mathews, a labourer by trade, aged forty-eight, was also shot in cold blood, as was another builder's labourer, fifty-seven-year-old Patrick O'Dowd. Another victim was Joseph Traynor, who was in his twenty-first year.

Not surprisingly, the crowds rushed for the exits, but only to be met by machine-gunfire from outside, which caused those at the front to turn and try to get back into the ground. James Teehan, who was twenty-six, was crushed so badly that he died. William Robinson, only eleven, died two days later, on 23 November, from wounds he received in Croke Park, as did thirty-year-old Daniel Carroll, manager of a pub. Thomas Hogan, no relation to Michael Hogan, was a mechanic from Bruree in Limerick and an IRA Volunteer. He died five days after Bloody Sunday from wounds he had received in Croke Park.

MEDIA REACTION

The *Weekly Irish Times* reported 'Bloody Sunday' in detail the following Saturday. Interestingly, the *Times* used the word 'murdered' to describe the manner of death of the fourteen spies but the word 'killed' to describe that of the thirteen civilians. The *Times* printed the 'Official Report', which emanated from Basil Clark, the head of propaganda at Dublin Castle. In the report, Clark claimed that the British had been fired upon by pickets who were guarding the approach to Croke Park, and that the people inside the ground were killed in the crossfire. In the same paper, 'statements by onlookers' told a different story:

> According to what can be gathered from inquiries, the match had been in progress for about fifteen minutes when a force of armed men arrived in lorries and armoured cars … armed men in uniform arrived simulta-neously at the four corners of the field. Almost immediately afterwards there was firing … armoured cars and military lorries moving about … shots were fired from machine guns in armoured cars and from rifles car-ried by the occupants of the lorries.[24]

According to an *Evening Herald report:*

> Some minutes before the fire was opened at Croke Park an aeroplane twice circled the playing pitch at fairly low altitude. At the sound of the rifle fire a great mass of people swept on to the playing pitch like an ava-lanche … Women and children were trampled on … The exits from the grounds were choked, and the men and women fainted in their efforts to get away. The cries of the weak and the shrieks of the female folk struck terror into the hearts of the people.[25]

CLANCY, MCKEE AND CLUNE MURDERED IN DUBLIN CASTLE

On the eve of Bloody Sunday, Collins, Dick McKee and Peadar Clancy were in Vaughan's Hotel, finalising plans for the execution of the British spies. Vaughan's Hotel at 29 and 30 Parnell Square was 'Joint No. 1' and was regularly used by Michael Collins and the Dublin Brigade.[26] Not long after Collins, McKee and Clancy left, the hotel was raided, and a young Gaelic

League scholar visiting from Clare, Conor Clune, was arrested by the Auxiliaries. Later that night, the British scored a coup and arrested Brigadier McKee and Vice-Brigadier Clancy; all three were brought to a room at the Detective Branch offices in Exchange Court, adjoining Dublin Castle. The following day, the three men were beaten and murdered by the Auxiliaries as a reprisal for the assassinations carried out by the IRA that morning.

Michael Lynch, O/C of the Fingal Brigade of the IRA, recalled:

> I saw Dick McKee's body afterwards, and it was almost unrecognisable. He had evidently been tortured before being shot. Peadar [Clancy] had a clean bullet wound in the temple and apparently was put out of pain at once. News leaked out that, after the shooting in Mount Street, the auxiliaries, infuriated at the loss of so many of their special agents, endeavoured to force information out of Dick and Peadar. They must have beaten Dick almost to pulp. When they threatened him with death, according to reports, Dick's last words were, 'Go on, and do your worst!'[27]

HOUSE OF COMMONS REACTION

On 22 November, the House of Commons was treated to lurid descriptions of the killings by the IRA on Bloody Sunday. Irish Secretary of State Hamar Greenwood read through the list of the dead, pausing slowly for effect and whipping the House into a frenzy, with the use of phrases such as 'possibly a hammer was used as well as shots to finish off this gallant officer'. After much discussion and calls for further powers to be extended to the military and police, Joe Devlin, Irish Party MP for the Falls Road area of Belfast, rose to ask Lloyd George and Greenwood why there had been no mention of the killings in Croke Park. There were shouts of 'sit down' from hundreds of MPs, and Greenwood whispered something to his fellow MP, Major John Molson, who lunged at Devlin, grabbing him by the neck and pulling him over the bench, egged on by shouts of 'kill him, kill him' from MPs.[28] The official report stated: 'Grave disorder having arisen, Mr. Speaker suspended the Sitting under Standing Order No. 21.'[29]

ARTHUR GRIFFITH AND EOIN MACNEILL ARRESTED

Arthur Griffith was Acting President of the Irish Republic while Éamon de Valera was in the US. Often regarded as a moderate, Griffith was, however, seen by the British as being supportive of the IRA's campaign. He was mentioned in the British House of Commons by Irish national-ist MP T.P. O'Connor on 20 October 1920: 'I do not think the Chief Secretary believes that Mr. Arthur Griffith has anything whatever to do with or approves of this campaign of murder.' Hamar Greenwood was quick to reply: 'He never condemns it.'[30] There may have been no direct link but Griffith was arrested a month later, on 25 November 1920, and imprisoned in Mountjoy Jail until the following July.

Another moderate, Eoin MacNeill TD (who had countermanded the order to muster on Easter Sunday, 1916) was also arrested in November and, like Griffith, was held in Mountjoy until the following summer. MacNeill was the former Minister for Finance (succeeded by Michael Collins) and at the time of his arrest he was Minister for Industries. His only connection with the IRA was that three of his sons were active members in County Clare during the war.

According to Patrick Moylett, who was IRB President for a couple of months in late 1920, British Prime Minister Lloyd George and some members of the British Cabinet were annoyed by the arrest. Moylett was already in secret discussions with C.J. Phillips who was H.A.L. Fischer's secretary.[31] Fischer was Chairman of the Cabinet Committee of Ire-land. In essence, a line of communication had been opened up between Dublin and London, albeit with no direct contact yet.

INTERNMENT CAMPS

Lord French, in a discussion on the situation in Ireland, suggested to the British Cabinet on 30 April 1920 that it 'would be more effective to put the struggle on a war basis, as had been done in the Boer War when the rebels were seized and put into concentration camps'.[32] Horrific as that idea was, the British did, however, run a number of internment camps in Ireland during the War of Independence; these included Ballykinlar (in County Down), Rath Camp (the Curragh, County Kildare), Gormanston (County Kildare) and Spike Island (County Cork). Ballykinlar, a disused British Army barracks, was the largest of the internment camps set up in the immediate aftermath of Bloody Sunday in November 1920. Two large sections of the barracks, with nearly forty wooden huts in each, were ring-fenced with barbed wire. Two thousand IRA internees were held in groups of twenty-five in each hut for a little over a year. The camp conditions were as brutal as might be expected, and some prisoners did not make it out of the camp alive. On 17 January 1921, an IRA internee, Joseph Tormley, was shot dead by a British sentry without warning. The bullet passed through him and into the neck of his comrade, Patrick Sloan, who also died. Tadhg Barry, Secretary of the Cork Branch of the Irish Transport and General Workers' Union (ITGWU), was shot dead on 15 November 1921 for the crime of standing too close to the barbed-wire fence.[33]

Patrick Colgan, a veteran of the Easter Rising, was the first O/C of the IRA prisoners, and he organised the Ballykinlar internees along the lines of any prisoner-of-war camp. Educational classes were held in Irish, music lessons were given by the prisoners, and there was even an amateur dramatics group which put on a number of plays. The IRA men produced their own newspapers, *Ná Bac Leis* (Don't bother with that) and *The Barbed Wire*. Although the British tried to break the spirit of the internees, the prisoners managed to establish a community within the camp. The internees came from a cross-section of Irish society, with boot-makers, tailors, carpenters, barbers, and many other skilled men all contributing to make the poor conditions bearable. As money was not allowed, the prisoners devised a clever monetary system with coins made of printed cardboard. The Society of Friends (Quakers) supplied a large number of books, which built up into an impressive camp library run by Denis McCullough.

It was Tadhg Barry of the ITGWU who organised the May Day celebrations in Ballykinlar. Barry had to agree with the British that no red flags would be flown; however, Alec Bradley from County Monaghan was carried around on a door with a red flag on a makeshift pole, followed by a procession of prisoners, as Bradley played 'The Red Flag' on his melodeon.[34]

Escape committees were formed and a large tunnel had been constructed before it was discovered by the British. Colgan and Maurice Donegan managed to escape dressed in British Army uniforms procured from a sympathetic guard. The duo hired a car in the village of Dundrum and made it to Drogheda before they were arrested by the British at a checkpoint.[35]

In July 1921, no fewer than fourteen elected members of Dáil Éireann were in Ballykinlar. Most of the 3,600 internees in the camps around Ireland were released a few days after the Treaty was signed in December 1921. In Ballykinlar, the three special trains that brought the prisoners home were attacked by armed Loyalist mobs.

MURDERS IN GALWAY

Hidden amongst the horror stories emanating from Dublin, the *Evening Herald* of Monday, 22 November reported the random shooting of a young boy, Thomas Lyons, by Black and Tans or Auxiliaries on a passing lorry.[36] The *Evening Herald* also reported on the discovery of the dead body of Fr Griffen, a priest who had been abducted by the British on 14 November. Fr Griffen's body, with a gunshot wound to the head, was found in a bog four miles from Galway. That night, near to where his body was found, 'a mysterious party of cyclists' destroyed seven cottages in nearby Barna, no doubt as a warning from the Auxiliaries to locals, in case anyone might have witnessed the dumping of Fr Griffen's body.

During the War of Independence, hardly a day went by without reports in the newspapers of random shootings, many of which received only a few cursory lines on the inside pages of the nationals. One of the most infamous incidents in the west of Ireland occurred when Patrick and Harry Loughnane were arrested by the Auxiliaries on 27 November 1920. The brothers were IRA Volunteers and had taken part in an ambush at Castledaly, County Galway, which had resulted in the death of an RIC man. Partick and Harry's mutilated corpses were found, three days after their arrest, in a pool of water at Umbriste, near Ardrahan. Their hands were missing fingers, their arms and legs were broken, they had been set alight, and hand grenades had been exploded in their mouths.[37] Photographs taken by locals of

Mourners with the charred remains of brothers Harry and Patrick Loughnane who were abducted, tortured and killed by Auxiliaries in Galway in November 1920.

the Loughnanes in their coffins are amongst the most gruesome of all the images from the war. Local priest Father Nagle received a letter saying that the brothers had 'escaped from custody the night they were arrested' by the Auxiliaries.

CHAPTER NINE

Kill Or Be Killed

The heavy-handed tactics of the British merely succeeded in eliciting more support both for Sinn Féin and for the IRA. The harsh reprisals carried out by the Black and Tans and Auxiliaries increased the determination of those fighting them. Having heard someone describe the Auxiliaries as 'invincible', Tom Barry and the Third West Cork Flying Column planned an ambush in Kilmichael, which not only inflicted devastating losses on the British, but also proved that the Auxiliaries could be defeated. Nonetheless, Fermoy, perhaps inevitably, suffered a night of reprisals following the ambush, including the murder of innocent civilians.

The British government had sought to suppress organisations it declared to be illegal by imprisoning men and women convicted, or even suspected, of political 'crimes'. However, although hundreds of arrests were made, there were always other men and women ready to step into the gap. In a further effort to turn the people against the IRA, and in direct response to the Kilmichael ambush, Lord French, the Viceroy, declared Munster to be under martial law. General Macready announced that anyone aiding or abetting the IRA would face the penalty of death. Coinciding with these measures, the reprisals of the Auxiliaries, Black and Tans and British Army reached a crescendo with the destruction of Cork in an orgy of violence and murder. In the House of Commons, Sir Hamar Greenwood, the Chief Secretary, blamed the IRA for the burning of the city.

Lloyd George's legislative response to the crisis was the Government of Ireland Act, which replaced the Home Rule legislation, suspended because of the war in Europe. The Government of Ireland Act provided for two Home Rule parliaments, one in Dublin and one in Belfast, thus splitting Ireland along the six-county border. Although the Act retained provision for the unification of Ireland if the two parliaments agreed, it fell far short of Sinn Féin's demands.

De Valera, fresh from his lengthy sojourn in the United States where he had raised millions of dollars in aid, arrived back in time for Christmas; the timing of his arrival was probably partly in response to Griffith's arrest the previous month, but he was undoubtedly also influenced by the length and harshness of the war. Even as the year drew to a close, the conflict continued. In Dublin, in December, selected IRA men were formed into an Active Service Unit to ambush British patrols. And the year ended on a brutal note in Clare and also in Limerick where a dance in aid of the IRA was raided by the Black and Tans, British Army and RIC who engaged in violent attacks against those in attendance.

TOM BARRY AND THE KILMICHAEL AMBUSH

The first, and most successful attack carried out by the IRA against the Auxiliaries took place on 28 November 1920, near Kilmichael, County Cork, under the direction of Tom Barry. Barry was Commandant of the Third West Cork Flying Column, having risen speedily through the ranks of the IRA despite the fact that he was a former British soldier who had fought in Mesopotamia (Iraq) during the First World War. 'Of all the ruthless forces that occupied Ireland through the centuries, those Auxiliaries were surely the worst,' Barry wrote, referring to the hundred and fifty who had commandeered Macroom Castle as their barracks since August 1920. He stated that the Auxiliaries were openly established as a terrorist body and were habitual looters, describing their technique:

> Fast lorries of them would come roaring into a village … firing shots
> and ordering all the inhabitants out of doors. No exceptions were
> allowed. Men and women, old and young, the sick and the decrepit were
> lined up against the walls with their hands up, questioned and searched.
> No raid was ever carried out by these ex-officers without their beating
> up with the butt ends of their revolvers, at least a half-dozen people …
> For hours they would hold the little community prisoners, and on more
> than one occasion, in different villages, they stripped all the men naked
> … and beat them mercilessly with belts and rifles.

Barry considered it strange that the IRA had not engaged the Auxiliaries properly since their arrival in August, allowing them to 'bluster through the country for four or five months killing, beating, terrorising, and burning factories and homes'. He resolved to challenge them, spurred on by the stories he heard from locals who described the Auxiliaries as 'invincible' and 'super-fighters'.[1]

Thirty-six Volunteers were assembled for the flying column and undertook special training for a week before the Kilmichael attack. Barry himself rode out by horse to establish the best place from which to ambush the enemy; however, he needed to figure out how to slow the Auxiliaries down on the road to give the IRA an opportunity to engage them. Paddy O'Brien had a very fine IRA officer's tunic and Barry decided that if he borrowed it and stood out on the road, the Auxiliaries would be bound to stop and investigate. It was an audacious and risky plan.

Having marched for five hours in terrible rain, the column reached the ambush position on 28 November at 8.15am. Barry explained to his men that the position they occupied offered no line of retreat:

> [The] fight could only end in the smashing of the Auxiliaries or the
> destruction of the Flying Column. There was no plan for a retirement until
> the Column marched away victoriously. This would be a fight to the end,
> and would be vital not only for West Cork, but for the whole nation …

> The Auxiliaries were killers without mercy. If they won, no prisoners would
> be brought back to Macroom. The alternative now was kill or be killed …[2]

The column was split into three main sections and, despite the lack of cover, the men managed to stay hidden in their soaked clothing for the next eight hours. A scout signalled the approach of the British just around five o'clock. As the first Crossley tender turned the bend, it slowed down when the driver spotted Barry standing in the middle of the road. An IRA Mills bomb was hurled into the driver's cabin. As it exploded, a barrage of fire was unleashed on the Auxiliaries. Close-quarter fighting ensued, the Auxiliaries with their hand guns and the IRA using rifle butts and bayonets.

The nine Auxiliaries in the first lorry were wiped out and Barry and his men went to assist the other IRA sections, whose men were engaging the second lorry. Some of the Auxiliaries shouted, 'We surrender', and two IRA Volunteers stood up only to be shot by the British, who recommenced firing. Incensed by the false surrender, Barry gave the order to commence rapid fire and not to stop until he commanded it. The Auxiliaries were sandwiched between the IRA sections and some of them called out 'surrender' again. However, Barry ordered his men to continue firing until eventually two lorry loads of British lay silent on the road.

The driver of the second Crossley tender, Cecil Guthrie, escaped. Guthrie had murdered an innocent civilian, Jim Lehane, in Ballyvourney less than a month earlier and had openly boasted that he 'got the bastard'.[3] Guthrie was captured by the First Cork Brigade IRA later that night and executed. Only one Auxiliary survived, Lieutenant H.F. Forde, who was found the following day and brought to hospital; he was later awarded £10,000 compensation.

Of the IRA men, Michael McCarthy and Jim Sullivan were dead and sixteen-year-old Pat Deasy lay dying from his wounds, which would prove fatal later that night. The men of the IRA column were quick to collect eighteen rifles, thirty revolvers, 1,800 rounds of ammunition and a haul of Mills bombs. They then set the two trucks on fire.

Barry, somewhat used to the horrors of war from his time in Mesopotamia, realised that his men were in danger of shock from the battle. He ordered them to march up and down the road, halting them, marching them and drilling them until a sense of normality and discipline returned. The Flying Colum then marched through the rain for eleven miles and camped in an unoccupied cottage at Grannure. The men had been without a decent meal for thirty-six hours, had marched twenty-six miles, and were soaked through from the rain, but they had shown the people of Ireland that the Auxiliaries were not invincible.

The *Cork Weekly Examiner* reported on the funeral of the Auxiliaries as the cortège passed through Cork, for the coffins to be brought to England by sea. All businesses were ordered to close for three hours as sixteen coffins 'shrouded in Union Jacks' passed by. The eight Crossley cars, with two coffins on each, were observed in silence by an unusually large number of people on the streets. 'At more than one point a youth or two had not had his head gear removed as the first coffins passed. A member of the guard of honour gave the order "remove your hat" which was immediately complied with.'[4]

REPRISALS FOR KILMICHAEL

Not surprisingly, the British were incensed by the successful ambush of two lorry loads of Auxiliaries. For days after, the area was awash with British forces who, in keeping with official policy, carried out reprisal attacks on the local people and their properties. The only farmhouse near the ambush site was burned to the ground. On 1 December, the Auxiliaries issued an order from Macroom Castle that all male inhabitants of Macroom were liable to be shot for having their hands in their pockets.

That same night, a party of Auxiliaries created havoc in Fermoy. They murdered the proprietor of the Blackwater Hotel, Nicholas de Sales Prendergast, a former captain in the British Army, who had fought in the First World War. Four Auxiliaries beat him up in the bar of the Royal

Hotel and then dumped his body in the Blackwater river. When his wife called at a number of hotels seeking her husband, she was callously told by the drunken British to 'try the Blackwater'.[5] The following night, the Auxies, who were drunk again, dragged a shop owner, Mr Dooley, from his premises and threw him into the river as they had done with Prendergast. Dooley, however, managed to swim to safety despite the Auxiliaries shooting at him in the river. The Auxiliaries then went to his shop and set it on fire alongside two other premises.[6]

MARTIAL LAW IN MUNSTER

With the approval of the British Cabinet and on the order of Lord French, the Lord Lieutenant, martial law was declared on 10 December 1920 for certain counties in Munster, namely Cork, Tipperary, Kerry and Limerick. French's proclamation, issued from Dublin Castle, specifically mentioned Kilmichael and contained some false accusations against the IRA intended to gain the sympathy of the populace. It falsely referenced 'attacks on His Majesty's forces, culminating in the ambush and massacre and mutilation with axes, of sixteen cadets of the Auxiliary Division, all of whom had served in the late war, by a large body of men who were wearing trench helmets and were disguised in the uniform of British soldiers', and went on to appeal to 'all loyal and well-affected subjects of the Crown to aid in upholding and maintaining the peace of this Realm and the supremacy and authority of the Crown, and to obey and conform to all orders and regulations of the military authority, issued by virtue of this proclamation.'[7]

On the strength of this, General Macready, Commander-in-Chief of the British Forces, issued an order on 12 December that all arms and ammunition must be surrendered by 27 December. Those who were found in possession of such items would be 'liable on conviction of a military court to face DEATH' (Macready's capitals). Any person guilty of aiding and abetting the IRA would also face the penalty of death.

Macready announced that the 'Forces of the Crown in Ireland are hereby declared to be on Active Service'.[8]

THE BURNING OF CORK

The Burning of Cork by the Auxiliaries on the night of 11 December 1920 may have been in reprisal for Kilmichael but it was very much prompted by an IRA ambush of the British at Dillon's Cross that evening. A particularly vicious group of Auxiliaries, K Company, had been making life miserable for the people of Cork. They had engaged in beatings, robberies, floggings and looting of public houses. The IRA understood that Captain James Kelly, the intelligence officer for the British in Cork, was due on patrol with the Auxiliaries.[9] At 8pm, six IRA Volunteers under Seán O'Donoghue ambushed the Auxies' Crossley tender as it left Victoria Barracks in the north district of the city. One Auxiliary, Spencer Chapman, was killed and a dozen were wounded. The Auxies and British soldiers were incensed and went on a rampage of violence first in the Dillon's Cross area and then in the city centre.

Florence O'Donoghue, an intelligence officer for the IRA, wrote later about what happened:

Auxiliaries, Black and Tans, soldiers — some were half drunk, many were shouting and jeering, all were wild, furious, savage, exultant in the urge to destruction. A tram car going up Summerhill, full of passengers and on its last journey for the night, was set upon by Auxiliaries and Black and Tans; the passengers were dragged or pushed out upon the road, searched, threatened, abused, beaten with rifle butts and fired upon. A priest who was a passenger in the tram was singled out for special attention. He was put up against a wall, his overcoat, jacket and vest and collar were torn off; he was knocked sprawling upon the ground and told to say 'To hell with the Pope.' He refused and was told he would be shot. Another group intervened; he was kicked again and told to run ... he was fired at [while attempting to run].

O'Donoghue described how '... hordes of armed men now issued forth, lorries laden with petrol tins swept through the empty streets and over the river bridges into the main thoroughfares. From the city police barracks other groups emerged, and soon the central streets of the city were overrun by swarming masses of violent men intent upon loot and destruction.'[10]

Hamar Greenwood, the Chief Secretary of Ireland, first said that it was the IRA who had burned Cork, and then decided to blame the people of Cork themselves. However, witnesses recalled that the group who had set fire to Grant's department store marched up to the building in military formation under the command of Auxiliary officers. The British who had set fire to Cash's did so under sharp military commands. Before long, though, all discipline relaxed and an uncontrolled orgy of burning and looting began. One after another, all the principal businesses on Patrick Street were set on fire. At the Munster Arcade, where a number of people resided, shots were fired through the doors, the windows were smashed and bombs were thrown into the buildings.

The fire brigade did its best to cope with a situation far beyond the capabilities of its resources. The firemen tried to confine the fires at some points, but their efforts were hampered by the British who slashed their hoses with bayonets and even shot at the firemen themselves. One wounded fireman was taken away by ambulance, which in turn was fired upon.

Cork City Hall was attacked and the Auxiliaries and Tans placed explosives and petrol cans throughout the building, ensuring its total destruction. They then turned their attention to the Carnegie Library next door, where thousands of books were burned. Some firemen managed to get a hose onto the library but they were hampered by a group of RIC men who kept turning the hydrant off. Two IRA Volunteers, Con and Jeremiah Delaney of Dublin Hill, were taken out of their beds at two in the morning and shot dead by a party of military men with English accents.

Locals gather on the burnt-out streets of Cork following a night of violence and destruction by the Auxiliaries and Black and Tans.

W. D. HOGAN,
6, HENRY ST.,
DUBLIN.

The financial cost of the reprisals was estimated at three million pounds, similar to the cost of the destruction of Dublin during the 1916 Rising. A few hundred houses were destroyed and forty major business premises were wrecked. Later, the British military's investigation into the burning of Cork, the 'Strickland Report', laid the blame on the Auxiliaries, but the British Government refused to publish the findings.

The British media, with few exceptions, were happy to collude with the government story that fires had spread from Patrick Street to City Hall, although this would have meant that the fires had skipped five hundred yards of buildings and crossed the River Lee. A fake map, repositioning City Hall beside Patrick Street, was even published in the newspapers in Britain. Without doubt, the culprits were members of K Company, who were removed from the city to Dunmanway. As a mark of disrespect to the people of the city they had set on fire, they wore a piece of burnt cork on their glengarry bonnets.

MURDER AT DUNMANWAY

On 15 December 1920, Patrick Brady, a resident magistrate from Skibbereen, was driving his car to Bandon Barracks, where he had official business, when he suffered engine trouble near Dunmanway, County Cork. The local parish priest, Rev. Canon Thomas Magner, who was out walking, stopped to chat, and then a young farmer and member of Cork No. 3 Brigade of the Volunteers, Timothy Crowley, came along to help.[11]

Two Crossley tenders carrying K Company Auxies were making their way to Cork for the funeral of Spencer Chapman who had been killed at the Dillon's Cross ambush. As they passed the three men, Auxiliary Section Leader Vernon Hart stopped the lorry, disembarked, approached Timothy Crowley and shot him in the head. He then turned to the priest, made him kneel down and murdered him. Brady, the RM, survived only by running for his life. Hart, a close friend of Chapman's, was subsequently tried in a military court and was declared guilty but insane.

VIOLENCE IN COUNTY CLARE

On 6 December, Five Crossley tenders of Black and Tans raided the village of Craggaknock, near Kilkee in County Clare. Information provided by a spy led them to believe that William Shanahan, an IRA officer, was attending a Republican court as a member of the Republican police. IRA scouts managed to warn Shanahan and he escaped moments before the Tans burst into the court. Enraged that they had failed to capture Shanahan, the Tans opened fire on the civilians and killed one man, Thomas Curtin. Twelve days later, they captured Shanahan and another IRA Volunteer, Michael MacNamara, in Doonbeg. The two men were held in the RIC Barracks in Kilrush, where they were subjected to five days of torture and interrogation. Three days before Christmas, the two men were driven towards Ennis in a Crossley tender. The Tans took Michael McNamara off the lorry at Darragh and told him he was free to go, but they shot him dead. They then bayoneted his corpse, tied it to the back of the tender and dragged it to Ennis. The other prisoner, William Shanahan, was brought to Ennis Jail where his brutal treatment continued. On a trip to the latrine, he was shot in the head at point blank range by Sergeant David Finlay.[12]

FORMATION OF THE DUBLIN ACTIVE SERVICE UNIT OF THE IRA

In December 1920, IRA GHQ decided to form an Active Service Unit made up of selected Volunteers from the four battalions of the Dublin Brigade. Members of the ASU were to be paid £4 per week and would be full-time. The ASU did not replace the Squad, which would continue to assassinate targets. Instead, it was designed to carry out ambushes. Typically the ASU members would wait on the streets in civilian attire and, as soon as the Auxiliaries or Black and Tans drove by in their trucks, the ASU would attack them with hand grenades followed by a rapid small-arms fire. About fifty IRA Volunteers, divided into four sections, made up the ASU, which was under the command of Paddy Flanagan. In the first ASU attack, two sections ambushed two Crossley tenders carrying Auxiliaries on Bachelors Walk in January 1921.

VIOLENCE AT IRA DANCE

The violent year 1920 ended with an attack by the RIC on a dance near Bruff, County Limerick. The unoccupied stately home of the Viscounts O'Grady at Caherguillamore was chosen for a dance on St Stephen's Day. The purpose of the dance was to raise money for the Third East Limerick Battalion of the IRA, and the venue was not generally known until the 240 carefully selected guests were brought there by a guide. However, the local RIC, British Army and Black and Tans had managed to hear about the dance and, despite the secrecy of the plans, were informed of the venue. They surrounded the large house in huge numbers. Volunteers Harry Wade and Daniel Sheehan, acting as sentries, were shot and died the following day, while John Quinlan, another sentry, was shot dead. The British poured volleys of shots through the windows, and glass and bullets rained down on the young dancers.

The British then burst into the building, firing wildly in all directions. Éamon Moloney, an IRA Volunteer, shot one of the Tans, Alfred Hogsden from London, but Moloney was then shot dead himself. Volunteer Martin Conway, who was 'on the run', tried to escape but was shot on the road by the Black and Tans. There were some reports that he crawled, badly wounded, for miles but was found by the Tans and their bloodhounds and was then shot dead.

In the house, following the death of their comrade Hogsden, the Black and Tans went wild, engaging in violent retribution against the unarmed people at the dance. All the men were forced, one at a time, to run a gauntlet through RIC and Tans who severely beat them with rifle butts, whips and broken banisters and spindles. Each man was interrogated and beaten viciously. Their ordeal lasted for the entire night.

All the women were held upstairs by drunken Tans, with the sound of their friends' cries echoing through the house. Over the next couple of weeks, sixty men who had attended the dance were sentenced to between three and six months' imprisonment. A further fifty-nine men were sentenced to jail in England for five years.[13] The action of the RIC and Black and Tans was an acute blow to the East Limerick Battalion who lost so many Volunteers in one night. An IRA Volunteer later recalled that the 'IRA swore vengeance, and in a short time a three-to-one toll of the Tans was exacted at Dromkeen'[14] (see Dromkeen Ambush, Chapter Ten).

GOVERNMENT OF IRELAND ACT, 1920

With the European war over, the suspended Home Rule legislation was due to be enacted. However, much had changed since 1914. The Easter Rising of 1916 had contributed greatly to the meteoric rise of Sinn Féin. The Irish Parliamentary Party was defunct and the IRA was waging a guerrilla campaign against the British Empire. The Government of Ireland Act, 1920, replaced the Home Rule Act. It was introduced to the House of Commons on 25 February and was designed to appease the minority Unionist population in Ireland who opposed the notion of a Dublin Parliament. The Act provided for two parliaments, one in Dublin and one in Belfast, which essentially split the country.

Northern Ireland, a hitherto non-existent geographic region, would include the six counties of Armagh, Antrim, Derry, Down, Fermanagh and Tyrone, the new entity being based entirely on a Unionist majority. Thus Unionists would still be part of the United Kingdom, and Britain would retain its economic interests in Ulster linen and, even more importantly, the Belfast ship-building industry. The Act included an oath of allegiance to the British Crown; if a majority of the parliamentary representatives failed to swear it, direct rule would be imposed.

The Act was not designed to appease Irish nationalists. The arch Conservative F.E. Smith, or Lord Birkenhead, served on Ulster Unionist MP Walter Long's committee which formulated the new policy for Ireland. Lord Birkenhead remarked that he was absolutely satisfied that the 'Sinn Feiners' would refuse it. British Prime Minister Lloyd George initially wanted 'Northern Ireland' to include all nine counties of Ulster but he bowed to Craig's wishes for a six-county Protestant-dominated state. On the positive side, the Act provided for a Council of Ireland, which would include representatives from both parliaments to discuss matters pertaining to the whole island. However, the Unionists chose to ignore the Council. The Government of Ireland Act, ensuring the partition of Ireland, became law on 23 December 1920. Elections for the two houses of Parliament, North and South, were due to be held in May 1921 (see Chapter Eleven).

RETURN OF ÉAMON DE VALERA

Meanwhile, Éamon de Valera's nineteen months of travelling and lecturing, raising awareness and money in the United States, had come to an end. He secretly left the US on the *Celtic* and, despite British parties searching for him, he evaded arrest and was in Ireland for Christmas Day.[15] De Valera had raised over a million pounds in the US, some of which went to fund the fledgling underground Irish State. Lloyd George, who rejected the idea of negotiating with Michael Collins for fear that this would recognise the legitimacy of the IRA, might be more inclined to treat with de Valera. In Lloyd George's mind, de Valera was an acceptable face of Sinn Féin and was more of a politician than the 'gunman' Collins.

CHAPTER TEN

The Demesne Walls Were Tumbling

At the end of 1920, a tentative peace initiative had begun, involving Archbishop Patrick Clune as an intermediary (see Chapter Eleven). However, Prime Minister Lloyd George was heading a coalition government and coming under both military and Conservative pressure to destroy the IRA. His precondition that IRA arms should be surrendered before talks began was rejected outright. Following military advice, in January 1921, four more counties of Ireland were subjected to martial law, and the first executions were carried out under the orders of special military tribunals. In Dublin, the Igoe Gang carried out extensive searches of the city in pursuit of IRA suspects, some of whom they imprisoned and others of whom they shot. The IRA fought back. However, the Dripsey Ambush in Cork was a disaster for the IRA when information on their plans was passed to the British Army, resulting in the capture of a number of IRA Volunteers and the shooting of the informants by the IRA.

The distribution of land in Ireland was very uneven with large farms and estates owned by a small number of landlords, who extracted rents from their tenants, which enabled them to maintain 'big houses', many of which dotted the landscape, fuelling resentment and providing an obvious target for the IRA. A policy of burning the 'big houses' of the landed gentry was pursed by the IRA in order to exact revenge for the British policy of burning houses as reprisals. Hundreds of them were burnt down during the War of Independence and the subsequent civil war. The pursuance of this policy, especially in Cork, is discussed in this chapter, together with the specific case of Maria Lindsay, executed for informing.

The war raged on, with ambushes by flying columns increasing in number. While arrests and imprisonments also continued, so too did efforts to assist prisoners, as for example when three IRA men escaped from Kilmainham Gaol in Dublin with the help of a couple of sympathetic guards from the Welsh Regiment of the British Army. The IRA suffered a setback when Volunteers unintentionally killed a number of civilians in an attack on a train at Upton, which did little for public support. However, the actions of the Black and Tans and Auxiliaries continued to offset such setbacks, arousing public horror and outrage. In February 1921, General Crozier, the Commander of the Auxiliaries, resigned his position over atrocities being committed by the men under his command.

However, the worst of the conflict was by no means over. On 20 February, a dozen IRA Volunteers were killed when they were surrounded at Clonmult, near Midleton in County Cork, in one of their deadliest encounters with the British. At the end of that month, IRA men went on a mission in Cork city to shoot as many British soldiers as they could, in revenge for the executions being carried out under the military tribunals. The following month, in an attack that had echoes of the shooting of Tomás MacCurtain, another Sinn Féin mayor, George Clancy of Limerick, was murdered by the Auxiliaries in his own home. Violence against women was also commonplace during the War of Independence, as will be discussed in more detail below.

MARTIAL LAW EXTENDED AND BRITISH MILITARY TRIBUNALS ESTABLISHED

On 5 January 1921, martial law was extended to Clare and Waterford, thus ensuring that the whole of Munster was under British Army rule. The two Leinster counties of Kilkenny and Wexford were also included. Internment had already been introduced all over Ireland after Bloody Sunday, meaning that anyone could be held without trial. The way was also paved for the arrest of anyone who was a member or even a supporter of Sinn Féin. Now, in areas under martial law, special military tribunals had the power to execute IRA suspects. Fourteen men were to die by firing squad in Cork and Limerick over the next six months. The first of these was Cornelius Murphy, on 1 February 1921, in Cork Detention Barracks. Murphy had been arrested for carrying a loaded revolver.

Less than a month later, six more IRA Volunteers were executed in the same manner in the same place, Cork Detention Barracks. Seán Allen, arrested for carrying a weapon, was shot by firing squad on 28 February 1921. He was executed with five others who had been captured during the Dripsey Ambush (see below): Thomas O'Brien, Daniel O'Callaghan, John Lyons, Timothy McCarthy and Patrick Mahoney. Four more IRA men were shot by firing squad on 28 April 1921, namely Maurice Moore and Patrick O'Sullivan who had both been captured at Clonmult (see below) and Patrick Ronayne and Thomas Mulcahy who had been captured at the Mourne Abbey Ambush (see below).

Patrick Casey was captured during an ambush at Knockanevin near Kildorrery on 1 May 1921 and was executed in Cork Detention Barracks the following day. Daniel O'Brien was captured on 11 May, when the British Army surrounded a house in Aughrim, County Cork. Five days later, on 16 May, he was shot by firing squad in Cork Detention Barracks. O'Brien had been a participant in the Kilmallock Ambush in April 1920 (see Chapter Five).

The only man executed in Limerick was IRA Captain Thomas Keane. He was with his comrade Henry Clancy when they were both captured by the Black and Tans at Ballysimon on 1 May. Clancy tried to make a run when the Tans were distracted but they shot him dead at close quarters. Thomas Keane, Captain of C Company, Second Battalion of the Mid-Limerick Brigade of the IRA, was executed by firing squad in the New Barracks, Limerick, on 4 June 1921.

IGOE GANG

Charles Dalton of IRA GHQ Intelligence recalled: 'Towards the end of 1920 a young Irish Volunteer officer by the name of Howlett, who had

arrived at Broadstone railway station from the West, was waylaid and shot dead by men dressed in civilian clothes.'[1] In the IRA's investigation into the matter, it was discovered that Howlett had been shot by a man called Eugene Igoe and a number of RIC men from the country. They came to be known as the Igoe Gang, although officially called the Identification Branch of the Combined Intelligence Service, and under the command of the Dublin Castle

Eugene Igoe of the Identification Branch of the Combined Intelligence Service at Dublin Castle.

head of intelligence, Colonel Ormonde Winter. Máire Gleeson ran a small shop and tearooms, the West End Café, which was adjacent to the main entrance of the Phoenix Park. A member of Cumann na mBan, Máire reported that several plainclothes policemen who were living in the police depot in the Phoenix Park often ate at her restaurant. Although a plan to attack the Igoe Gang there was considered, their movements were too erratic and it was decided that Parkgate Street was not the best place to stage an ambush.

Patrick Moylett, who succeeded Harry Boland as President of the IRB when the latter went to the US, had known Igoe as a boy. He came from Attymas, about three miles outside Ballina, County Mayo. Moylett also knew him later in Galway where Igoe was stationed in the RIC. Moylett recalled an occasion when, on O'Connell Bridge in Dublin, he had bumped into Igoe and his girlfriend, Miss Elwood, who worked in a shop in Galway. When Michael Collins heard of this meeting later that day, he was astonished that Igoe had been walking the streets without his gang and told Moylett that he was lucky that Igoe had not shot him. Collins reckoned that 'Igoe felt miserable any day he did not shoot a man.'[2]

By January 1921, Collins, as Director of Intelligence, had transferred a Volunteer by the name of Thomas Newell (also known as Sweeney Newell) to Dublin, as he also knew Igoe personally.[3] Charles Dalton recalled that Newell ran into 4 Crow Street and said that he had seen Igoe and his gang heading up Grafton Street. Newell, who had reason to recall the date, remembered that it was 9.30am on 7 January 1921. Instructions were sent to the Squad HQ in Upper Abbey Street to assemble at St Stephen's Green in the hopes of ambushing the Igoe Gang. However, as Dalton and Newell were making their way towards Stephen's Green, they were captured by Igoe's men and questioned on Dame Street. Vinny Byrne and other members of the Squad spotted them but did nothing. Bill Stapleton remembered, 'On looking to the left we saw Charlie Dalton and Sweeney Newell standing, smoking, against the wall of an insurance building and chatting to one or two others.'[4] The Squad mistook the Igoe gang for friends of the two IRA men.

During the interrogation, Newell realised that he had been recognised and said, 'I know you, Igoe, and you know me.' At this point, Dalton was released as the gang believed his story that he was a solicitor's clerk. Newell was marched at gunpoint all the way up to the Four Courts area, constantly being questioned about his activities. He recalled that when they reached Greek Street, Igoe told him to run. Newell refused, knowing they would shoot him. Igoe gave him 'a hell of a punch', which sent him several yards into Greek Street where the gang unleashed a volley of shots at him. A police van arrived and brought the wounded Volunteer around the corner to the Bridewell police station, where they knocked several of his teeth out with the butt of a revolver.

Newell was eventually brought to hospital where he underwent eleven operations.[5] Bill Stapleton mulled over the lost opportunity to get Igoe: 'I am sorry to say that this was the nearest we ever got to the Murder Gang and I think, if we have any disappointments, I consider this to all of us would be one of the major ones.'[6] Charlie Dalton considered Igoe's group very capable: 'Igoe's party were effective in their duties and picked up a number of Volunteers, many of whom, fortunately, were imprisoned. This party became one of the most difficult and dangerous forces opposed to the IRA in Dublin.'[7]

SETBACK FOR THE IRA

Frank Flood, the IRA Lieutenant with the No.1 Section of the Dublin Active Service Unit (ASU), planned to attack a couple of RIC lorries at the Royal Canal Bridge in Drumcondra, on 21 January 1921. Having waited for an hour, at 9.30am, Flood and the ASU section moved a few hundred yards north only for an RIC truck to appear. Taking up new positions opposite St Patrick's College and Richmond

Road and Drumcondra Road, they waited for a second lorry. Flood noticed a DMP sergeant on patrol but thought that the policeman was oblivious to them. At 11am, the ASU section again decided to retire but then spotted an RIC lorry. The IRA men threw their grenades and opened fire. Suddenly a British Army armoured car and a Crossley tender of Auxiliaries from I Company came on the scene from the North Dublin Union, having been alerted by the patrolling DMP sergeant, who had, in fact, seen the IRA men and suspected that they were up to something. The first armoured car and tender were joined by two tenders of K Company Auxiliares and another armoured car from Dublin Castle.

Flood and the ASU attempted to disperse as they were hopelessly outnumbered by the British. Mick Magee, who had fought in the Four Courts in 1916, was mortally wounded by the British machine gunfire and he died the following day. After a chase, Frank Flood, Thomas Bryan, Patrick Doyle and Bernard Ryan were captured; they were subsequently hanged in Mountjoy Jail. Dermot O'Sullivan was also captured but his death sentence was reprieved as he was only seventeen years of age.

DRIPSEY AMBUSH

The Sixth Battalion of the First Cork Brigade suffered a heavy defeat in an ambush at Dripsey on 28 January 1921. A flying column from the seven companies of the Battalion had been formed in late 1920 and there were about sixty IRA Volunteers involved in it. They planned to attack a British convoy of seven Crossley tenders, which travelled the road every morning between Macroom and Cork. In preparation for the ambush, it was decided to give the flying column an intensive course of training, which lasted two weeks. The O/C, Jackie O'Leary, and his second in command, Frank Busteed, trained their comrades in '(i) Use of ground and cover, (ii) occupation of and withdrawal from a position,

(iii) security measures, including scouting and field signalling, and (iv) Fire Control', while the men were permanently billeted in the nearby parish of Donoughmore.[8] On the morning of the ambush, the men of the flying column waited in their positions for the British. Trees had been sawn through and held fast by ropes, which were to be dropped once the enemy was in position, thus trapping the trucks. The River Lee, impassable at the point of the attack, ran parallel to the road, thus providing the perfect trap. Snipers and signallers waited for the arrival of the Crossley tenders.

However, the British Army had been warned of the planned attack; seventy-year-old Maria Lindsay of Leemount House and her chauffeur James Clark had informed on the IRA that morning. Seventy men from the Manchester Regiment of the British Army, accompanied by two armoured cars, descended on Dripsey. The IRA spotted the British a little too late as they were almost wholly surrounded, except for a narrow laneway. Under intense fire from the front and rear, most of the IRA men battled their way to relative safety. 'Ultimately, after all night fighting, the Column reached safety ... where a check was made of men and material. There was sadness in our camp as many of our comrades were wounded and many more in enemy hands.'[9] Five of those men who were captured were sentenced by courts martial to be executed.

On 20 February, Maria Lindsay and James Clark were taken prisoner by Jackie O'Leary and the local IRA. They were held for a few days in Goulane, Donoughmore and later moved to the Rylane district.[10] The IRA sent an ultimatum to the Commander of the British Army in Cork, Edward Peter Strickland, warning him that if the IRA prisoners were executed, the same fate would befall Lindsay and Clark.[11] Strickland consulted with Nevil Macready, the Commander of the British Army in Ireland. Macready told him not to treat with the IRA. In his memoirs, he explained his rationale: 'I could not listen to such a proposal, which would have resulted in the kidnapping of loyal or influential persons every time a death sentence was passed on a rebel.'[12]

Seán Allen and the five men captured at Dripsey — Thomas O'Brien, Daniel O'Callaghan, John Lyons, Timothy McCarthy and Patrick Mahoney — were executed in Cork on 28 February 1921. That day, the IRA in Cork exacted revenge on the British by shooting six British soldiers in Cork city (see below). A couple of weeks later, the IRA executed Maria Lindsay and James Clark as spies. Michael O'Donoghue of the Second Battalion Cork IRA wrote in his witness statement that 'stark military necessity obsessed the British Army of occupation, while desperate instincts of self-preservation and stark ruthless resistance motivated the merciless retaliation of the Irish Republican Army.'[13]

BURNING OF THE 'BIG HOUSES'

Maria Lindsay's large mansion was set alight by the IRA in revenge for the fact that she had told the British about the Dripsey ambush. She was a loyalist, loyal to the British Empire and to Ireland's place in the United Kingdom. She was also a member of the Church of Ireland and her chauffeur, James Clark, was a Presbyterian. They were shot as spies and not as Protestants, their religion being irrelevant.

The burning of Lindsay's house was part of IRA tactics. Between January 1920 and the Truce in July 1921, nearly eighty Big Houses were set alight and destroyed. These houses represented Anglo-Irish landlordism and those who lived on large estates in comfort and wealth were viewed as a manifestation of imperialism and personified as 'The English'. The Big Houses were often generous hosts to the local British Army and, in the case of Maria Lindsay's home, could be trusted by the forces who were fighting an enemy that tended to be drawn from the small farming classes or, in Dublin, the workers.

The Cork IRA pursued with a particular vigour this policy of destroying the large houses on estates. Indeed, nearly a third of all the mansions destroyed during the war were in Cork. Edward Horgan described an attack on Dunsland, the palatial Glanmire residence of

The remains of the Pike mansion in Cork, destroyed by the IRA. Between January 1920 and the Truce in July 1921, nearly eighty 'big houses' were set alight and destroyed.

Joseph Pike, chairman of the City of Cork Steamship Company and a leading member of the Irish Unionist Alliance in Cork: 'This was a well-known rendezvous for British officers, the Pikes being strong loyalists.'[14] About thirty Volunteers carrying tins of petrol 'ordered all the occupants (about twenty) out of the building at the point of a revolver, and set fire to the place, completely destroying it.'

Meanwhile, the British were actively engaged in burning the homes of IRA suspects. Besides their wanton destruction of Cork city in November 1920 (see Chapter Nine), Tom Barry, O/C Third West Cork Flying Column, recalled that 'the destruction of Republican homesteads was an important plank of British terrorist policy, aimed to intimidate the Irish people into their old submissions. Farmhouses, labourers' cottages and shops went up in flames as the British fire gangs passed, leaving desolation and misery in their wake.' Barry recounted how the IRA in Cork sent a note to the British Commander informing him that for every Republican home destroyed, the homes of two British loyalists would be destroyed. As a consequence of that, the 'British Loyalists were paying dearly, the demesne walls were tumbling and the British Ascendancy was being destroyed.'[15]

Tom Ryan, a member of Number 2 Flying Squad of the Third Tipperary Brigade, remembered the British burning a few houses following an IRA ambush. Ryan and his comrades decided to burn a local Big House that belonged to a landlord named Perry. Ryan recalls that Perry was in his pyjamas when they called to his house but was somewhat relieved that the IRA had 'merely come to burn down the house, at which he smiled all over and requested us to give him permission to take a glass of spirits … When he drank his whiskey, he told us that he had a very valuable library of books and requested permission to save these from the flames … and about ten men were detailed to remove the books from the house, following which straw was spread around the rooms and other men came to sprinkle this with petrol.'[16] In Limerick, Dan Doody remembered four houses belonging to 'prominent supporters' of the IRA being burned by the British after an ambush in May 1921. The IRA 'carried out a counter reprisal in the same month, burning Springfield Castle, belonging to Lord Muskerry'.[17]

DROMKEEN AMBUSH

On the first Thursday of every month, two lorry loads of Black and Tans and RIC men left Pallas Barracks in Limerick for Fedamore, with money to pay the police. The Mid-Limerick and East Limerick flying columns decided to ambush the police at Dromkeen on 3 February 1921. Richard O'Connell recalled ushering civilians into local houses to keep them out of harm's way.[18] There were about six IRA Volunteers in a farmhouse at a bend in the road beside a graveyard where a number of the East Limerick Brigade were in position. The lorries would have to come down a hill for about three hundred yards where the road then split into two. Both of these roads were blocked off by the IRA.

When the ambush began, the first lorry careered into a wall, and the driver and the local District Inspector, Thomas Sanson, were thrown clear and ran for their lives. Seán Meade said Sanson 'buried himself in a heap of horse manure, heaped in a field. In the excitement he was not noticed and escaped.'[19] The police in the first lorry were mostly killed by a grenade that the IRA flung into it. The second Crossley tender was attacked midway up the hill. 'After it had been fired on for a time, the occupants seemed to have all been killed, except one RIC man who got out and lay by the front wheel ... and he was blazing away ... Johnny Vaughan got down on one knee and got him.'[20] However, Maurice Meade, a member of Roger Casement's Irish Brigade and a former British soldier, says in his witness statement: 'It was I actually who took this fellow out from under the lorry and shot him on the road.'[21]

When all the firing was done, the IRA walked amongst the wreckage, and 'two tans, who had been shamming death, started to get up and run.' They were quickly captured and court martialled on the spot. According to O'Connell, Maurice Meade was appointed to carry out the executions: 'Maurice put one Tan behind the other and shot the two of them with one bullet, because, he said, there was no use wasting ammunition on them.' However, Maurice Meade himself told a different, more plausible, story:

Donncadh O'Hannigan called me and said, 'Here, Maurice, will you shoot one of them?' I agreed to do so. He gave Stapleton the job of executing the other. I took my man down the road and shot him. Then I went down to see how Stapleton was getting on, and found that he disliked the job and did not want to do it, so I took this fellow over and executed him also. The reason for shooting these Tans after they had surrendered was that O'Hannigan had an order from GHQ in Dublin that we were to shoot all Tans and Peelers who fell into our hands.[22]

Eleven policemen and Tans were killed in the ambush at Dromkeen. When reinforcements of the Tans arrived from Pallas Barracks, they burned eleven houses in the district.

THE DRUMCONDRA MURDERS

James Murphy and Patrick Kennedy, two men with no connection to the IRA, were apprehended on Talbot Street, Dublin, on 9 February 1921, after an evening at a cinema. They were arrested by F Company of the Auxiliaries and taken to Dublin Castle. Hours later, Murphy and Kennedy were found by the Dublin Metropolitan Police in Clonturk Park, Drumcondra. Metal buckets had been placed on their heads and they had been shot at close range and left for dead on the street. James Murphy, however, was still alive and managed to say before he died that Captain W.L. King of F Company had taken them from Dublin Castle and told them that they 'were going for a drive'. King, alongside two of his fellow Auxiliaries, Herbert Hinchcliffe and Frederick Welsh, were charged with what the newspapers called 'the Drumcondra murders'.

The court martial of the accused Auxiliaries was held in City Hall on 12 to 14 April. Witnesses in Dublin Castle had seen the accused mistreating the murdered men and also reported seeing King, Hinchcliffe and Welsh get into a car with Murphy and Kennedy. The Auxiliaries had been heard to say that they were 'going out to shoot'. The *Irish Independent* reported that 'peculiar statements' had been made by a number of Auxiliaries at the court martial, who swore that the accused had been in the Castle at the time of the murders. The court martial ruled that Murphy's evidence was inadmissible and, despite the evidence pointing to their guilt, all three men were acquitted.

ESCAPE FROM KILMAINHAM GAOL

Kilmainham Gaol (jail) is very significant in Republican lore as Robert Emmet spent his last night there before his execution. As discussed in Chapter One, Emmet was the leader of a very small uprising on 23 July 1803, and he was captured in August and sentenced in September to be hanged and beheaded. This punishment was carried out on 20 September 1803 outside St Catherine's Church on Thomas Street in Dublin after he had been taken from Kilmainham Gaol. Fourteen men were executed in the stone-breakers' yard in the jail after the Easter Rising in 1916, further adding to the status of Kilmainham as a shrine to Irish revolutionaries.

One of the most audacious escapes carried out by the IRA during the war was from Kilmainham Gaol in February 1921. Simon Donnelly, Vice-Commandant of the Third Battalion, Dublin Brigade related how he was captured on 10 February by the British, and brought initially to Dublin Castle where he was questioned by the notorious Captain 'Hoppy' Hardy who was infamous as a bully and for his brutal methods of attempting to force information from prisoners. Donnelly was then taken to Kilmainham Gaol, suspected of involvement in the shooting of British spies on Bloody Sunday. There he met with Ernie O'Malley, Commandant General of the Second Southern Division of the IRA. Donnelly described O'Malley, who was using the alias Bernard Stewart, as 'one of the bravest and most resourceful soldiers who had fought for Irish Independence'.[23] Frank Teeling, who had been wounded and captured on Bloody Sunday and was due to be executed, was also being held in the jail. Other IRA prisoners housed in Kilmainham at the time were Frank Flood, Thomas Bryan, Patrick Doyle and Bernard Ryan from the Drumcondra Ambush (see above), and Thomas Whelan and Paddy Moran who were also held on a charge of murder. It was imperative that Frank Teeling should escape, and so a plan was devised.

Prisoners Thomas Whelan and Paddy Moran pose with their prison guards. Both men were executed in March 1921.

Thanks to two sympathetic Welsh soldiers, communications were established with the IRA on the outside, and Oscar Traynor, O/C of the Dublin Brigade, coordinated a plan of escape. A bolt-cutters, procured by Volunteer Mick Smith, with the handles cut off and detachable tubular steel handles fashioned in their place, was smuggled in and given to the prisoners by one of the Welsh soldiers. This was to be used to break open the padlock on the outer gate of the prison. The British tended not to lock the cells, knowing that the gates to the prison were always locked. Perhaps to save time, or just out of laziness, the warders tended to push home the bolts on the cell doors and leave the padlocks open. Donnelly realised that a prisoner could slip his hand out through the peephole and ease back the bolt from its socket. In addition, a 'Plan B' was formulated; this involved a rope and a rope ladder, which could be thrown over the wall from the outside of the prison. The night of 13 February was chosen and, rather than risk a mass breakout, the numbers were kept low to increase the chance of escape for Frank Teeling, Ernie O'Malley and Simon Donnelly.

Members of F Company of the Fourth Battalion were waiting in the vicinity when the three prisoners made their way to the side gate in the jail where they needed to break open a padlock. However, the makeshift handles on the bolt-cutters had been wrongly fitted and did not give enough leverage to cut through the lock. Whispering quickly to their comrades, they decided to try the rope-ladder plan. The rope attached to the ladder was thrown over the high wall but it sank into a groove in the masonry at the top of the wall and, when they pulled hard on it, the rope broke away. The three men returned, dispirited, to their cells.

The following day, one of the sympathetic Welsh soldiers went to Oscar Traynor to explain what had gone wrong, and Traynor again demonstrated the method for fitting the handles to the bolt-cutters. That evening at 6.30pm, to show his loyalty to the prisoners, the Welshman himself cut the lock for the escapees. Their problem now was that the bolt was heavily rusted. Using butter rations that they had saved, they greased up the bolt and, after much pressure, managed to loosen it quietly. The three prisoners escaped and the soldier slipped back into the jail.

Perhaps the saddest aspect of this escape is that Oscar Traynor wanted the escape to include Paddy Moran, O/C of D Company, Second Battalion. Donnelly did try to encourage Moran to join them in the escape but Moran had lots of alibis and was convinced that he would get a fair hearing at his court martial. It was not to be and Paddy Moran was executed in Mountjoy Jail on 14 March 1921, a month after the Kilmainham Gaol escape (see below).

General Macready was livid when he heard about the escape. In a letter to Sir John Anderson, the joint Under-Secretary at Dublin Castle, he wrote:

> We have had a real disaster. The man Teeling and two other unimportant men escaped last night from Kilmainham Prison and got clean away. It is about the worst blow I have had for a very long time, and I am naturally furious ... it is perfectly obvious that the escape could not have been made without the collusion of the men of the Welsh Regiment who were on duty there. I will certainly take the most drastic action against those responsible.[24]

And what of the British soldiers who helped the IRA? Patrick Kennedy remembered them as Paddy Holland and another by the name of Storkman. Kennedy recalled in his witness statement that he had introduced them to Oscar Traynor in Kirwan's pub. Kennedy wrote that one of the soldiers deserted the British Army and the other was sentenced to eight years in prison but was released in 1923 and received a gratuity from the Irish Free State of a few hundred pounds.[25]

MOURNE ABBEY AMBUSH

Tuesday, 15 February 1921 was a bad day for the Second Cork Brigade. An ambush was arranged in the Mourne Abbey district to attack a British convoy which was expected 'to be escorting General Cummings, O/C Buttevant Military Post, to a conference of the officers commanding the British Forces in the Southern Command'.[26] John O'Sullivan recalled that instructions were issued by the Battalion O/C, Tadhg Byrne, to mobilise at Jordan's Bridge on the main Cork–Mallow road at 5am. Selected men from the Burnfort and Analeentha companies received similar instructions.[27] 'The Volunteers from the Burnfort Company under Tadg Looney were in position at the eastern side of the road on a high projection of rock more or less directly over the position selected to hold up the convoy,' recalled Jeremiah Daly, Vice O/C Mallow Battalion, Second Cork Brigade IRA.[28] Daly remembered hearing shots some time after 11am and, when he looked in the direction of the shooting, seeing about forty or fifty soldiers walking in extended order across the fields at the rear of the party from Burnfort Company at what was known as Leary's Rock.

The Burnfort IRA men were almost completely surrounded in a short space of time. They endeavoured to withdraw in the direction of their home districts but met with considerable opposition. It was only their intimate knowledge of the area that saved them from complete annihilation. Three Volunteers from the Burnfort Company were killed:

Patrick Dorgan, Patrick Flynn and Edward Creedon. Michael Looney was mortally wounded and died later.[29] Eight prisoners were arrested by the British and two of them were executed in Cork Detention Barracks: twenty-four-year-old Patrick Ronayne and Thomas Mulcahy who was eighteen.

UPTON TRAIN AMBUSH

Whilst the IRA enjoyed the support of the majority of the people of Ireland in their fight for freedom, sometimes ambushes resulted in heavy civilian casualties, which affected their popularity. One such occasion was the Upton Train Ambush in Cork, which also took place on 15 February 1921. A company of IRA Volunteers, consisting of ten local men armed with rifles and hand-guns, planned to ambush a train carrying British soldiers between Cork and Bandon. Two scouts with bicycles were stationed at Kinsale Junction to report the number of military on the train to the men at Upton.[30] The train was due in Upton at 9.30am so ten minutes beforehand some of the ambushers waited in the station whilst a few others waited in a goods store and behind a low wall beside the railway line.

In the event, the scouts on the bicycles at Kinsale Junction failed to make Upton before the train. Instead of the small party of military in the central carriage, there were fifty British soldiers scattered throughout the train. Amongst these were a large number of civilians. As soon as the train stopped at Upton station, the IRA opened fire. The British military were quick to respond and, very soon, two Volunteers, Seán Phelan and Batt Falvey, had been killed. Three others received terrible wounds; they were Pat O'Sullivan, John Hartnett and Dan O'Mahoney. The Brigade O/C, Charlie Hurley, received a very serious wound to the face when he was firing on the train from an overhead bridge. Tom Kelleher opened rapid fire on the British soldiers who were advancing in all directions, but after ten minutes of shooting, the IRA retreated from what was a hopeless engagement.

Sadly, six civilians, including two railway workers, lost their lives in the shooting. Two more died later from their wounds. IRA Volunteer Dan O'Mahoney died a few years later as a result of his wounds. Pat O'Sullivan was eventually brought to Cork Hospital with a bad wound in the stomach. Diarmuid O'Leary recalled in his witness statement that he was in hospital with O'Sullivan. According to O'Leary, 'One night, following an ambush in Cork city, in which some soldiers were killed, a few military came into the room and proceeded to beat this man unmercifully with the butts of their revolvers. He died from the effects of the beating.'[31]

Patrick Coakley, an IRA captain turned informer, was 'arrested' at the scene by the British. He then gave the British information on the location of the Third Cork Brigade HQ that led to the capture and death of Charlie Hurley and the Battle of Crossbarry (see Chapter Eleven). It is possible that Coakley had also given the British advance warning of the planned ambush at Upton.

RESIGNATION OF GENERAL CROZIER

General Frank Percy Crozier, Commander of the Auxiliaries, was becoming increasingly despondent about the discipline of his force. Seamus Finn, Adjutant of the Meath Brigade IRA, wrote that a garrison of Auxiliaries and Tans posted in Trim 'gave real hell to the townsfolk'.[32] The Auxiliaries of N Company looted Chandler's public house in Trim on 9 February 1921. They beat up Bob Chandler and kicked him down the stairs. The bottles of spirits they didn't drink they smashed. They ill-treated Chandler's elderly invalid mother, stole many valuables, made a bonfire of clothing and furniture, and set the pub on fire. In an attempt to instil some much-needed discipline, Crozier dismissed eighteen Auxiliaries from N Company. However, Hugh Henry Tudor, as Commander of the RIC, reinstated them. On 19 February 1921, Crozier resigned as Commander of the Auxiliaries. He maintained that the Auxiliaries he had dismissed had threatened that they would make revelations about all the assassinations that had taken place under the aegis of the English regime, and especially about those of Kennedy and Murphy (the Drumcondra murders). Crozier reckoned that the British Government was 'obliged to reinstate these Auxiliaries', leaving him with no choice but to resign.[33]

CLONMULT

The Active Service Unit or flying column of the Fourth Battalion of the First Cork Brigade, under the orders of Commandant Diarmuid Hurley, took possession of a disused farmhouse overlooking the village of Clonmult, seven miles northeast of Midleton, County Cork. The house had a thatched roof, and a large cowshed was attached to the building at one end; the other end adjoined a small grove of twenty trees. About twenty IRA Volunteers drawn from various companies in East Cork were taking part in intensive training as an active service unit.[34] Hurley and a couple of his officers were away scoping out the potential for an assault on the British and he left Captain Jack O'Connell in charge of the men, with instructions to break camp on Sunday, 20 February. At 4.15pm that day, Michael Desmond and John Joe Joyce were filling water bottles for their comrades when they realised that British soldiers were surrounding their encampment. They shot their way back towards their comrades and warned them, but the wounds they received in the attempt proved fatal.

After about an hour of intense fighting, the acting O/C, Jack O'Connell, decided to lead a small charge out of the building at the British, in the hope that someone might break through the lines and get help. The five IRA men in the charge were met by a hail of gunfire, and Michael Hallahan, Richard Hegarty and James Aherne were killed in the attempt. Diarmuid O'Leary recalled how he 'got out into the haggard, but, seeing the other boys fall, decided there was no hope of escape and dashed back into the house amidst a hail of bullets'.[35] Jack O'Connell did manage to break through the British cordon and made contact with some local Volunteers.

Members of the East Cork Flying Column, many of whom were killed in Clonmult on 20 February 1921. Left to Right: Michael Desmond (killed in action at Clonmult), Pat Higgins (shot after surrender at Clonmult, survived but was sentenced to death but reprieved because of the Truce), James Glavin (killed after surrender at Clonmult), Donal Dennehy (killed after surrender at Clonmult), Joseph Aherne (Vice-Commandant), Richard Hegarty (killed in action at Clonmult), Joe Morrissey (killed after surrender at Clonmult), Michael Hallahan (killed in action at Clonmult), Maurice Moore (captured at Clonmult and executed on 28 April 1921) and Paddy White.

The British called on the trapped Volunteers to surrender but were greeted with a chorus of 'The Soldier's Song', and the battle raged on. After an hour, instead of the hoped-for IRA reinforcements, a company of Black and Tans arrived to reinforce the British Army. The roof of the cottage was set on fire, and 'Through the doors and windows British lead poured in a relentless stream'.[36] An attempt was made to break through the gable but Volunteers James Glavin and Diarmuid 'Sonny' O'Leary were wounded and fell back into the cottage, O'Leary becoming unconscious. There was nothing to do but surrender.

Pat Higgins, Liam Aherne, Jeremiah Aherne, David Desmond (brother to Michael), Christopher O'Sullivan, Donal Dennehy, James Glavin and Joe Morrissey came out. Pat Higgins recounted the horror:

> We were lined up alongside an outhouse with our hands up. The Tans came along and shot every man … A Tan put his revolver to my mouth and fired. I felt as if I was falling through a bottomless pit. Then I thought I heard a voice saying, 'This fellow is not dead, we will finish him off.' Only for the military officer coming along, I, too, would be gone.[37]

The other seven men were dead, murdered at point-blank range by the Tans. Two more IRA men, Patrick O'Sullivan and Maurice Moore, who were carrying their wounded comrade, Diarmuid O'Leary, came out just as a British Army officer ordered the Tans to stop shooting. The North East Cork IRA column did eventually arrive but it was too late and all they found was the cottage on fire.[38]

Clonmult ranks as one of the deadliest attacks on the IRA. Five IRA Volunteers were killed in the battle. After surrendering, seven others were murdered. Two more, Patrick O'Sullivan and Maurice Moore, were executed by firing squad in Cork on 28 April.

SIX BRITISH SOLDIERS SHOT IN CORK CITY

Michael O'Donoghue recollected a mobilisation order received by the members of A Company, ASU, on 28 February 1921. By 6.30pm all had reported at College Tower, University College Cork, and were issued with small firearms and ammunition from an IRA dump. Their instructions were clear and simple: to shoot on sight every British soldier and policeman in uniform on the streets of Cork city. A Company was not alone as all the Cork city companies of the Brigade were given the same orders. Their mission was to 'exact bloody revenge for the execution by firing squad of the six republican prisoners that same morning'.[39] A Company ASU was to operate around Patrick Street and the adjoining streets between South Mall and Coal Quay, a particularly dangerous section as there were a number of police barracks in the area. O'Donoghue remembered that '[an] air of grim foreboding seemed to overhang the whole place. No policeman in uniform was anywhere to be seen in the whole section.' Seven o'clock was zero hour and, at that exact time, shooting seemed to 'break out all over'. Three British soldiers came running towards the A Company IRA. Two were shot immediately and the third, in a blind panic, ran for his life into a shop where he was followed by O'Donoghue who remembered the soldier huddled 'crying in a corner against the counter' just before he shot him dead.[40] In total, six British soldiers were killed that evening in revenge for the six IRA men who had been executed that morning.

VIOLENCE AGAINST WOMEN

Violence, physical and sexual, against women is a terror device used by men especially during times of conflict when they know that they are unlikely to suffer recriminations for their actions. It was commonplace during the war in Ireland. Often, women were subjected to having their hair roughly shorn by British forces. The IRA also employed this as a punishment for women who were seen to have fraternised with the enemy. Although physical violence was discussed, rape and sexual assaults were rarely reported. There are many reasons for this; victim blaming and Catholic guilt complexes might be part of it. However, there was also the fact that any woman who reported sexual assault was liable to be targeted by the perpetrators of the crime. George Berkeley from the Peace With Ireland Council recalled in his diary in 1921 that he 'received a letter from Mrs. Corbally describing a case of rape in Ireland. A woman was raped and when she made a complaint [to the authorities] her house was burnt as a reprisal.'[41]

In Limerick, James Maloney remembered that 'IRA men's sisters and other girls had to go on-the-run fearing rape.'[42] Seamus Fitzgerald, a TD in the First Dáil, was asked to collate atrocities carried out in Cork and also recalled two cases of sexual assault — one the rape of a pregnant woman in Blackpool 'and in the same locality a middle-aged woman successfully resisted a similar attempt.'[43] In December 1920, Kate Maher was violently raped and murdered by British soldiers in Dundrum, County Tipperary. It is clear that, besides murder and intimidation, British forces also subjected the women of Ireland to sexual assaults during the war but we will probably never know the full extent of this barbarity.

MAYOR OF LIMERICK KILLED

George Clancy was a Gaelic League enthusiast who, while a student at the Catholic University in St Stephen's Green, included among his friends James Joyce, Francis Sheehy-Skeffington and Tom Kettle. With Arthur Griffith he joined the Celtic Literary Society. Having joined the Irish Volunteers in 1913, Clancy was arrested after the 1916 Rising and imprisoned in Cork, but after a hunger strike was released before he came to trial. He and his wife Máire organised for the Dáil Loan in the Limerick area.

In the municipal elections of 1920, Clancy was offered the mayoralty but declined as he felt he was inexperienced; Michael O'Callaghan was made Mayor of Limerick city instead. Both men were Sinn Féin councillors and worked closely together. O'Callaghan's life was threatened after the murder of Tomás MacCurtain, the Lord Mayor of Cork (see Chapter Four), and Clancy ensured that armed guards were placed at the Mayor's house. However, when curfew was imposed on Limerick by the military authorities, any person found out of doors after 10pm was liable to arrest and, if in possession of weapons, liable to be shot. In January 1921, Clancy replaced O'Callaghan as Mayor of Limerick. The Clancy home had been raided innumerable times by the Auxiliaries and the RIC. Now that he was the Mayor, the raids became more frequent and threatening in manner.

On 6 March 1921, Máire Clancy buried her father; in the early hours of the following morning, three tall men wearing motor goggles, with their caps drawn down over their faces, barged into the home. Máire and George had opened the door and the men demanded that Clancy come outside. He refused and one of the Auxiliaries shouted at him, 'Then take this' and fired three shots at Limerick's Mayor.[44] Máire tried to come between the gunman and her husband but to no avail. She remembered hearing seven shots in all. Máire was wounded and George died in her arms some time later.

George Clancy was one of three people murdered that night in their homes in Limerick. His comrade Michael O'Callaghan, the previous Mayor, was shot by the same men. Joseph O'Donoghue, a city clerk, was also killed that night. George Clancy was immortalised in James Joyce's A *Portrait of the Artist as a Young Man* as the character Michael Davin, a friend of the protagonist Stephen Dedalus.

AN tÓGLACH, MARCH 1921

The organ of the Volunteers, *An tÓglach*, remained defiant in March 1921:

It is now generally realised and even admitted by the enemy that his new campaign of intensified terrorism, massacres and burnings and drastic military measures has proved a hopeless failure. The high hopes treasured by the champions of savagery have not been realised. Their confident predictions of an early breakup of the Irish Republican Army, of a disintegration of Republicanism, of a rapid breaking of the spirit of the people of Ireland, have not been fulfilled ... Today the Irish people's spirit remains unbroken, their loyalty to the Republic undiminished, today the Army of the Irish Republic is stronger, better armed, more efficient and more active than ever before.[45]

BRITISH EXECUTIONS OF IRA

Besides the executions in areas under martial law, nine IRA men were also hanged, like their comrade Kevin Barry, in Mountjoy Jail, Dublin. On 14 March 1921, six Volunteers were hanged. Twenty-two-year-old Thomas Whelan from Galway was accused of the Bloody Sunday shooting of Captain G.T. Baggallay, an army prosecutor who had been a member of the military courts that sentenced Volunteers to death. Paddy Moran, a greengrocer's assistant who had fought in Jacob's in 1916 under Thomas MacDonagh, was charged with the shooting on Bloody Sunday of Lieutenant Peter Ames, an American working as a British military intelligence officer. Both men protested their innocence but were found guilty.

Four of the Volunteers were charged in connection with the ambush in Drumcondra, Dublin on 21 January 1921 (see Chapter Ten). They were: Frank Flood, Lieutenant in the ASU and a UCD student and great friend of Kevin Barry's; Patrick Doyle, ASU (whose brother was killed in the attack on the Custom House in May 1921); twenty-year-old Bernard Ryan, ASU; and Thomas Bryan, a former hunger striker and ASU Volunteer. Thomas Traynor was captured during an IRA ambush of Auxiliaries on Great Brunswick Street. A father of ten children, he was tortured and beaten by the Igoe Gang and hanged in Mountjoy Jail on 25 April 1921. Traynor had fought in 1916 in Boland's Mills, under Éamon de Valera.

Edmond Foley was tried twice, as was Patrick Maher, for the shooting of the RIC men during the Knocklong rescue. Their third trial was by court martial and they were hanged on 7 June 1921 in Mountjoy Jail.[46] The ten IRA men hanged in Mountjoy Jail were given state funerals on 4 October 2001, and nine of them were reinterred in Glasnevin Cemetery. Patrick Maher was reinterred in a family plot in Ballylanders, County Limerick.

THE MAYO IRA

Support for the Volunteers in County Mayo was strong and the county had its fair share of killings and reprisals. In July 1920, the Mayo Brigade of the Irish Volunteers had been reorganised into four brigades: North, South, East and West. Commandants Tom Maguire (South Mayo), Tom Ruane (North Mayo), Seán Corcoran (East Mayo) and Tom Derrig (West Mayo) were chosen by GHQ to command them. Commandant Michael Kilroy was later selected to replace Tom Derrig after his capture by the British.

By the spring of 1921, the Mayo brigades were equipped and seeking action with the RIC and British troops. The first successful ambush was carried out on a Border Regiment lorry travelling from Ballinrobe to Castlebar at Kilfaul, near Partry, by Commandant Tom Maguire's South Mayo Brigade. The British policy of bloody reprisal became clear in the aftermath when farmer Thomas Horan was shot in the head and mortally wounded by Black and Tans as they searched his home in Shrah.

On 29 March, a Black and Tan called William Stephens was mortally wounded by the IRA in Ballyhaunis. Two days later, masked men dragged an IRA Volunteer, Michael Coen, from his home at Lecarrow near Ballyhaunis. He was severely beaten and stabbed to death by bayonets.

TOURMAKEADY AMBUSH

In May 1921, Tom Maguire, O/C South Mayo Flying Column, took over Tourmakeady village in preparation for an ambush on an RIC patrol. Maguire's men were mostly armed with shotguns. They did, however, kill two Black and Tans, Constables Hubert Oakes and Christopher O'Regan, and they mortally wounded RIC Sergeant John Regan. Another IRA section opened fire on a Crossley tender and killed Constable William Power. The RIC managed to make it to Hewitt's Hotel and the IRA retreated towards the Partry Mountains. The police alerted the RIC in Ballinrobe and called for reinforcements.[47]

Two lorries containing British soldiers arrived at Tourmakeady and another couple of trucks made their way to the northern end of the Partry Mountains. Further British reinforcements were called for from Castlebar and from the RIC Barracks at Westport. The British Army was advancing on the flying column and Lieutenant Ibberson, a cross-country runner, took off his officer's tunic and ran at speed towards the retreating IRA. He managed to shoot and wound Tom Maguire and killed IRA Section Commander Michael O'Brien. The IRA returned fire on Ibberson. Although wounded seven times, he remained standing but retreated, covered in blood. Meanwhile, two IRA men from the ambush, Patrick King and Philip Hallinan, were captured by the British. They were severely beaten on the spot and in Ballinrobe RIC Barracks, and many homes in the area were burned out.

When darkness fell, the IRA managed to escape, and the British spent the following days searching for the elusive South Mayo Flying Column.

CHAPTER ELEVEN

Broke in All Directions

By 1921, the flying columns had become the backbone of the IRA campaign, with ambushes on barracks and convoys serving not alone to strike at the British but also to seize their much-coveted arms. Tom Barry of the Third West Cork Flying Column was one of the most successful of all the flying column leaders. It was he who was in command when, as outlined below, the British very nearly captured his entire flying column of over one hundred IRA Volunteers at Crossbarry on 19 March. Instead, despite their superior firepower, the British ultimately lost their opportunity to achieve a major triumph against the IRA flying columns. Arms were always an issue for the IRA, who relied heavily on attacks on barracks to seize much-needed weaponry. The Thompson submachine gun (tommy-gun), the development of which was funded by the IRA, could have changed the course of the war if the shipment ordered had arrived in time; such an effective weapon would have bolstered the IRA and destroyed the morale of the British forces in Ireland.

Elections were held in Ireland on 2 May 1921. These elections were supposed to be for seats in the British-mandated houses of commons in Belfast and Dublin, as established by the Government of Ireland Act (see Chapter Nine). However, Sinn Féin, rather than boycott them, treated the elections as being for seats in the illegal Dáil Éireann; the results, as outlined below, were unsurprising. Later that same month, the Dublin Brigade of the IRA set fire to one of the economic symbols of British rule in Ireland, the Custom House, where hundreds of thousands of taxation records were stored. There was a fierce fight between the IRA and the British, and many IRA men were taken prisoner, leaving numbers depleted. Both sides were now being pushed towards negotiation. Lloyd George, having concluded that, for various reasons discussed in this chapter, the British military campaign could not continue, decided to drop his precondition of arms surrender before any negotiation could take place. This made it possible for peace talks to begin and, on 11 July 1921, the British offered a truce, the details of which are discussed below. Even in the last hours before the truce, the bitter hostilities continued. Margaret Keogh, a member of Cumann na mBan, was fatally wounded in a raid on her house by the British. Meanwhile, four British soldiers were apprehended and killed by the IRA.

BATTLE AT CROSSBARRY

In the run up to St Patrick's Day, Tom Barry, Commandant of the Third West Cork Flying Column, Liam Deasy (Brigade Adjutant), and Tadhg O'Sullivan (Brigade Quarter Master) asked the piper Florence Begley (Assistant Brigade Adjutant) to join their flying column and help celebrate the national feast day in style by ambushing some lorries to the accompaniment of his uilleann pipes (Irish bagpipes pumped with the elbow).[1] However, the planned ambush at Shippool, Innishannon, on 17 March 1921 did not come to fruition as the British were informed of the plans and returned to their barracks at Kinsale. The IRA flying column marched north towards its Ballymurphy HQ.

The British Army in Cork, under Lieutenant General Strickland, had captured an IRA company captain, Patrick Coakley, during the Upton Ambush (see Chapter Ten). Coakley divulged the whereabouts of the Third Cork Brigade HQ.

After a day of resting, the IRA flying column arrived in Ballyhandle, beside Crossbarry, County Cork, at 1.30am on 19 March, and retired to billets, which were basically beds provided by people in the local area. After about half an hour, the alarm was raised. British lorries were reported to be slowly approaching their position from various directions. An area of about four miles in circumference was taken in by the British troops, whose plan was to arrest every man and boy they came across in all the houses in the district, moving slowly but thoroughly.

The IRA officers decided to wait in ambush for the British at Crossbarry, eight miles from Bandon and twelve miles from Cork. The column was divided into sections of fourteen men. Seán Hales, John Lordan, Mick Crowley, Denis Lordan, Tom Kelleher, Peter Kearney and Christy O'Connell were each in command of a section. The residents of the area were sent to safety while barricades were built, mines laid down and positions allocated to each section. Soon the lorries were spotted on the Bandon–Crossbarry road but the British were also coming from other directions. No fewer than twenty-four lorries of military left Bandon, six hundred military came from Cork and Ballincollig, and three hundred from Kinsale.[2]

The IRA flying column lay in position from about 4.30am and at about eight o'clock a long line of British lorries drove slowly towards their positions. Michael O'Driscoll recalled in his witness statement: 'When the first lorry was opposite our position … soldiers started to get out of the lorries. We got orders to open fire and we gave it to them at point blank.'[3] Florence Begley proceeded to play the uilleann pipes and continued to do so whilst the firing lasted. O'Driscoll recalled that the pipes had a great effect on the IRA and he felt that they could have tackled the whole British Army. The superior firepower of the British did not come into play, though, as the IRA men were very fortunate that a bullet penetrated the drum of an enemy machine gun, which was in a position on a lorry, thereby jamming it. Edward White, a civilian prisoner in one of the lorries, managed to escape during the battle and carried the machine gun away. When the firing ceased, the IRA went onto the road to collect arms and set fire to the British vehicles.

The second wave of attack came from two hundred British on the left flanks of the IRA, but they were tackled by the section under the command of Denis Lordan. Peter Kearney's section was moved up to reinforce this position. A third attack came when a platoon of British who had come from the Bandon direction was engaged by Christy O'Connell's men who forced the British to withdraw. The fourth assault was dealt with by Tom Kelleher's section at the rear of Crossbarry, where two IRA men were killed. Tom Barry reinforced this section and the men succeeded in shooting an officer, whereupon the remaining British turned and ran.

As Barry rounded up his men, he congratulated them and explained that they would have a twenty-mile march ahead of them. Just as they were about to move out, though, the IRA spotted groups of disorganised British soldiers in the distance. They appeared to be leaderless, as they were standing around in the centre of a small field on the sloping hillside east of Crossbarry. Barry ordered all of his men to line up and prepare to fire. Tom Kelleher remembered that the sound of a hundred IRA rifles firing in three successive moments, and all at the same time, was very effective as 'helter-skelter the English broke in all directions ... The Battle of Crossbarry was over.'[4]

By attacking the British at Crossbarry, the IRA had succeeded in breaking up the enemy's encircling movement, but there were some losses. Jeremiah O'Leary, Con Daly and Peter Monahan (who had joined the IRA after deserting the British Army) were killed during the fight.[5] Ten British soldiers were killed in the fight. The lost chance of capturing Barry's flying column was a big blow to the British who had been very close to achieving a major coup.

The IRA captain, Patrick Coakley, who had divulged the position of the IRA to the British was court martialled by the IRA and sentenced to death but this was commuted and he was exiled from Ireland instead.

SHOOTING OF CHARLIE HURLEY

Not far from Crossbarry, the Third West Cork Brigade O/C, Charlie Hurley, wounded at the Upton Ambush (see Chapter Ten), had been trapped and killed by British forces. He was recuperating in Forde's farm in Ballymurphy, which was Brigade Headquarters, when he was killed by men of the Essex Regiment under Lieutenant General Arthur Percival. Barry recalled that they could hear the gunfire as they lay in wait for the British at Crossbarry and in his memoirs he was effusive in his praise of Hurley.

Lieutenant General Arthur Percival of the Essex Regiment of the British Army.

AMBUSH AT BALLYTURN (BALLYTURIN) GALWAY

Brigid Ryan, a Cumann na mBan member in Galway, reported to the South West Galway Brigade of the IRA that RIC District Inspector Cecil Blake was going to be at a party at John Baggot's Ballyturn House, near Gort, County Galway. Blake had been involved in a raid on a Catholic church during mass, in which shots were fired. He had a reputation for producing his pistol in shops to demand service, and his wife Eliza also carried a gun; she once produced it in a shop in Gort and threatened to shoot the proprietor if anything ever happened to her husband.

The Brigadier of the South West Galway Brigade, Joseph Stafford, and Patrick Glynn, Vice-O/C of the Gort Battalion, together with seven other IRA men took over the gate lodge of Ballyturn House on 15 May 1921. They lay in wait there for seven hours while Blake and other guests enjoyed the party.

At seven o'clock, Blake and his friends drove to the exit, only to find the gate locked. British Army Captain Fiennes Wykeham Mann Cornwallis got out of the car to attend to the gate and the IRA ambushers, who had locked it, shouted, 'Hands up!' Cornwallis dodged out of the way and managed to fire a number of shots. The IRA poured fire on the car. Cornwallis, Lieutenant William McCreery and Eliza Blake and her husband Cecil were all killed.[6] Margaret Gregory, a daughter-in-law of the famous Irish writer Lady Augusta Gregory, was in the car but unharmed; she was brought by the IRA down to Ballyturn House where a note was handed to the Baggots to tell them that if there were reprisals, the house would be burned down.

An RIC man, John Kearney, was shot dead by his comrades when they arrived at the scene of the ambush later. Kearney had been passing information to the IRA, and his fellow officers, suspecting as much, took the opportunity to kill him and blame the IRA. There were wide-scale reprisals in the area, and a number of homes were burned by the Black and Tans and RIC.

THE THOMPSON SUBMACHINE GUN

The Thompson submachine gun was designed by General John T. Thompson in the United States during the First World War but was first produced in 1921. The weapon is also known as the tommy-gun or simply T Gun, but because of its association in the early years with the IRA it also gained the respectful nickname 'Irish Sword'.

Thomas Fortune Ryan, an American tobacco, insurance and transportation magnate, was a Clan na Gael stalwart who realised that this portable weapon might prove useful to the IRA back in Ireland. While the weapon was in the development phase, Ryan made contact with Harry Boland who was in the US with Éamon de Valera. Thompson and Ryan formed a company called Auto-Ordnance Corporation, and Harry Boland ordered the first 250 guns. Although there were prototypes, the first factory-made weapon came off the production line in March 1921 with the serial number 41. The first tommy-guns were brought to Ireland in May 1921 to be shown to the IRA by two US Army men representing the Thompson Corporation, Major James Dineen and Captain Patrick Cronin.[7] Having tested the weapons in tunnels under the Casino at Marino (a folly in north Dublin), Collins and the IRA leaders were impressed. The guns could fire a magazine of twenty rounds but the bulkier circular drums could carry a hundred rounds.[8] A weapon of this magnitude would strike fear into the British in Ireland, and Collins, never one to be cautious, ordered 653, which were priced at $225 each. This made up a total of 903 weapons (if we include those ordered by Boland), an order amounting to over $200,000. Money was not in short supply; weapons were.

The first large shipment of nearly five hundred weapons, mostly with serial numbers obliterated, was loaded on-board the *East-Side* bound for Ireland. However, the ship was raided by the US Customs and Justice Department on 15 June 1921 and the illicit cargo was seized.[9] Coincidentally this was also the day on which one of the sample tommy-guns was used in action by the IRA when a train carrying British troops from the West Kent Regiment was riddled in Drumcondra, Dublin.

RESTRUCTURING OF THE IRA

In May 1921, the IRA was restructured and split into sixteen divisions all around Ireland. Each division was split into brigades, which numbered sixty-seven in total. These sixty-seven brigades were subdivided into battalions and then further divided into companies. This was an effort by GHQ to control the IRA and restructure the chain of command. However, the changes met with little success and, in some cases, active resistance especially from the Southern brigades, most notably Cork and Kerry. In fact, the IRA from the First Kerry Brigade did not attend the meeting to structure the First Southern Division. The changes had little time to make a quantifiable difference, but the resistance to what was seen as 'interference' from the 'pen-pushers' in Dublin is an example of the divide between country and city, which would later contribute to, but was not the cause of, the Civil War.

ELECTIONS, 1921

The Government of Ireland Act (see Chapter Nine) divided Ireland into two separate parliamentary regions. Elections for the new parliaments were held in both regions on 22 May 1921. Of the fifty-two seats in the Northern House of Commons, forty went to Unionist candidates, six went to Sinn Féin and six to Joe Devlin's Nationalist Party, which was formed from the ashes of the Irish Parliamentary Party (Home Rule Party). The Southern House of Commons had 128 seats. There was no election as such, as Sinn Féin was unopposed in every constituency except Dublin University, which returned four unopposed Unionists. Just as in 1918, Labour decided not to contest the election.

The Sinn Féin candidates who were elected considered the elections to be for Dáil Éireann (which was illegal according to the British).

Although invited to attend the Dáil, the four Unionists who had been elected attended the 'official' Southern House of Commons on 28 June 1921, which was the only time the Parliament met. Interestingly, the Parliament met in the Royal College of Science for Ireland, which later became Government Buildings, on Merrion Street.

The Second Dáil, convened on 16 August 1921, was made up of Sinn Féin candidates who had been elected for both the Southern and Northern Houses.

THE BURNING OF THE CUSTOM HOUSE

While the elections were taking place, the war plans continued. A memorial outside the Custom House in Dublin reads:

> In proud memory of Edward Dorrens, Seán Doyle, Daniel Head &
> the brothers Patrick & Stephen O'Reilly who died in the Battle of
> the Custom House 25th May 1921; and of the officers and men of the
> Second Battalion & other units of the Dublin Brigade I.R.A. who gave
> their lives for Irish Freedom. They gave their all: may they rest in peace.

Liz Gillis, an expert on the burning of the Custom House, maintains that at least 270 Volunteers took part in an operation that was meticulously planned for months in advance.[10]

Éamon de Valera, who had returned from the US in time for Christmas 1920, presided over a meeting of the IRA Army Council held early in the New Year of 1921. The meeting was held at 40 Herbert Park, the home of Michael Joseph O'Rahilly who had been shot leading a charge against a British barricade on Moore Street in the final hours of the 1916 Rising. Oscar Trayor, O/C of the Dublin Brigade, recalled those present at the meeting besides himself and de Valera: Cathal Brugha, Minister for Defence; Austin Stack, Minister for Home Affairs; Dick Mulcahy, IRA Chief of Staff; J.J. 'Ginger' O'Connell, Assistant Chief of Staff; Michael Collins, IRA Director of Intelligence; Diarmuid

O'Hegarty, IRA Director of Organisation; Gearóid O'Sullivan, IRA Adjutant General (and a cousin of Michael Collins); Liam Mellows, IRA Director of Purchases; Seán Russell, IRA Director of Munitions; Seán McMahon, IRA Quarter Master General and Piaras Beaslaí, IRA Director of Publicity.[11]

De Valera suggested that a sensational IRA strike in Dublin was necessary in order to bring public opinion abroad to bear on the question of Ireland.

A decision was made to set fire to the Custom House, and Traynor began to draw up plans. Built in 1792 and considered one of architect James Gandon's masterpieces, at three storeys over basement, it was an impressively large target. Although made of Portland stone, the building was packed with wooden presses, which contained numerous bundles of combustible papers and files belonging to the Department of Income Tax.

On the appointed day, 25 May, at 12.55pm, the Dublin Brigade IRA began the task of setting the Custom House on fire. Commandant Tom Ennis of the Second Battalion was in charge of the Volunteers who entered the building. They were joined by members of the Squad under Paddy Daly and the Active Service Unit (ASU). Their job was to hold up the entire staff and assemble them in the main hall and provide protection to the Second Battalion.[12] Outside the building, the First Battalion provided protective cover to those inside. More importantly, the First Battalion and the Third and Fourth Battalions took over local fire stations and ensured that the fire brigade remained in situ. The engineers of the Fifth Battalion were involved in cutting telephone wires in manholes and on high telephone poles. A lorry load of paraffin arrived at the rear of the Custom House, and tins of the flammable oil were carried as surreptitiously as possible inside; the paraffin oil was used to saturate every office in the building thoroughly.

The first casualty was the caretaker Francis Davis who put up a struggle and was shot. He died later in the afternoon.[13] Each floor of the building, or particular parts of the floors, was in charge of company O/C, and the signal for calling off the men was to be two sharp blasts on the battalion O/C's whistle. By coincidence, two company O/Cs' whistles were sounded almost together; some men mistook the signal and started to retire.[14] One IRA officer reported that his men had not finished the job and they were sent back to their floor to finish it. But these few minutes were the difference between a successful retirement and the arrival of British forces at 1.25pm, five minutes after the allotted completion time.

Two Crossley tenders full of Auxiliaries turned onto Eden Quay, passing Liberty Hall into Beresford Place. The Auxiliaries jumped from their lorries and took positions behind the pillars that supported the railway. The First Battalion IRA engaged the enemy, firing from revolvers and throwing a number of grenades at them. Seán Prendergast recalled: 'In a thrice all was excitement as rifles and revolver shots rent the air, and billowing smoke of the burning building and flashes of flames could be distinctly seen mounting.'[15] Daniel Head threw a grenade into a British lorry and was shot five times by the Auxiliaries. A double-turreted armoured car driving around the area sprayed bullets from its Hotchkiss machine gun at the IRA men in the Custom House who returned fire with their revolvers.

Edward Dorrins (his name is incorrectly spelled Dorrens on the memorial) of E Company, Second Battalion, had been kidnapped by the Auxiliaries three months previously and thrown into the River Liffey. On this occasion, he was not so lucky as he was shot in the head during the fighting and died instantly. The Quartermaster of the Second Battalion, Paddy O'Reilly, was wounded badly during the battle and seems to have been shot dead afterwards. Harry Colley recalled seeing his corpse on the night before his funeral: 'There was a small bullet entrance wound in the side of his nose, which plainly showed scorching, indicating that the gun, presumably an automatic, had been placed at his head when fired.'[16] Paddy's brother Stephen, who was Assistant Adjutant of the Second Battalion, was also killed in the battle.

One of architect James Gandon's masterpieces, the Custom House in Dublin, having been set alight by the Dublin Brigade IRA. The building burned for five days.

A party of Black and Tans who were billeted in a hotel on the quays came running towards the Custom House. They came under fire from members of the ASU on Butt Bridge. The Tans took cover behind Guinness barrels where they engaged the IRA who eventually withdrew at 1.50pm when their ammunition was spent.

Inside the Custom House, the order was given that all guns were to be dumped and that all Volunteers were to mingle amongst the staff.[17] However, some of the IRA men made desperate bids to run through the gauntlet of British fire. James Slattery recalled that he and Seán Doyle, whose brother Patrick had been executed by the British on 14 March 1921, felt that they 'wouldn't stand a chance' if they were arrested. Both men charged out of the Custom House and were fired on by the British. They escaped but Doyle was shot in the lung and died five days later in the Mater Hospital.[18] Tom Ennis was one of the last to leave the building and managed to escape despite suffering a horrendous bullet wound in the groin. Soon the Auxiliaries entered the Custom House where they shot a young civilian temporary clerk from the Local Government Board, Mahon Lawless, who died later.[19] Two other civilians also died in the shooting; they were James Connolly and John Byrne. Eventually when people had been cleared out of the building, senior staff members helped the British to separate employees from the IRA. In all, 108 Republicans were captured.

When eventually the fire brigade came on the scene, it became clear to which side the firemen gave their allegiance. Upon entering the building, fireman including Michael Rogers 'spread the fire into parts of it which had not previously been on fire'. In order to help a number of IRA men to escape, Rogers went to Tara Street fire station and brought back four spare uniforms for some Volunteers who were still in the Custom House.[20]

Despite the number of arrests and deaths, Oscar Trayor later described the destruction of the Custom House as an 'outstanding success' because it led directly to the arrangement of the Truce on 11 July 1921.[21] Éamon de Valera, who had been missing for the majority of the War of Independence and had not been associated with a battle since 1916, could claim the attack as his victory because it had been his idea.

Above: The fire brigade arrives at the Custom House, 25 May 1921.
Below: IRA suspects are lined up by Black and Tans close to the Custom House. Over a hundred people were arrested.

THE TRUCE

A number of attempts to bring about a cessation of hostilities had been undertaken. For instance, Patrick Clune, the Archbishop of Perth in Australia, had been in communication with Collins and Griffith on the Irish side in late 1920. He also arranged meetings with the Joint Under-Secretary John Anderson and his assistant Mark Sturgis in Dublin Castle. Archbishop Clune's nephew, Conor Clune, had been murdered in the Castle on Bloody Sunday, so he had a special interest in bringing peace to Ireland. However, when he met with Lloyd George in London, the Prime Minister, influenced by the military and by the Conservatives in his coalition government, insisted that any truce would have to involve a surrender of arms, something that the IRA could not countenance. Clune's negotiations were in vain. British generals 'insisted they could crush the IRA within six weeks', which ensured that the British Cabinet rejected the notion of a compromise.[22] The British preferred to wait and see how the establishment of two Parliaments worked out in May 1921. By April, though, even Hamar Greenwood, the Chief Secretary, wanted the hostilities to end, stating at a Cabinet meeting that British forces had failed 'in breaking the terror' and that 'the Irish question' was not going to be solved by continuing the war.[23] Lloyd George again rejected the notion of a truce before the May elections.

WHY THE BRITISH OFFERED A TRUCE

Besides the destruction of the Custom House there are a number of reasons why the British sought a truce. War weariness is one reason. The British had been at war since 1914 and there was only a brief interlude of a couple of months between peace in Europe and war in Ireland. The financial strain was also taking a toll. Admittedly, the IRA in England had cancelled an attack on the financial district of Liverpool, but they planned to increase their targeting of home addresses of Englishmen fighting in Ireland. The British government knew that the IRA could wreak havoc in England.

Tom Barry believed that the 'startling upheaval in British policy was due, and due only, to the British recognition that they had not defeated and could not reasonably hope to defeat in the measurable future, the armed forces of the Irish nation'.[24] Those in command of the British Army were beginning to realise that although they might quell Republicanism, they could not defeat it. First World War General Douglas Wimberley was Assistant Adjutant of the 2nd Battalion, Cameron Highlanders, stationed at Queenstown (Cobh). He felt certain that 'the discontent would merely have smouldered underground. It would have burst into flames as soon as we withdrew.'[25] The famous Field Marshal Bernard 'Monty' Montgomery was stationed in Ireland in 1920–21 as Brigade-Major of the 17th Infantry, also in Cork. In his memoirs, he wrote that the war in Ireland was 'far worse than the Great War which had ended in 1918. It developed into a murder campaign in which, in the end, the soldiers became very skilful and more than held their own. But such a war is thoroughly bad for officers and men; it tends to lower their standards of decency and chivalry, and I was glad when it was over.'[26] Montgomery also said the British 'could probably have squashed the rebellion as a temporary measure, but it would have broken out again like an ulcer' as soon as troops were removed from Ireland.[27]

Winston Churchill, Secretary of State for the Colonies and Chairman of the Cabinet Committee on Irish Affairs, believed that the only way to win would be to raise a force of one hundred thousand new special troops and police. Churchill wanted a 'tremendous onslaught' against the Irish. His Cabinet colleagues Austen Chamberlain and Lord Birkenhead backed him. The Cabinet made a decision on 24 May that if the Southern Parliament did not meet by 12 July, martial law would be extended to all twenty-six counties.

Jan Smuts, who had fought the British in the Second Boer War and was now the Prime Minister of South Africa, was in touch both with Éamon de Valera and with Lloyd George. Smuts helped to draft the speech given by King George V when he opened the Northern Parliament on 22 June 1921. In his speech, the king appealed 'to all Irishmen to pause, to stretch out the hand of forbearance and conciliation, to forgive and forget, and to join in making for the land they love a new era of peace, contentment and goodwill'. On that day, British forces raided a house in Blackrock, County Dublin, and arrested Éamon de Valera. Alfred Cope, the Assistant Under-Secretary, secured his release twenty-four hours later (much to de Valera's bewilderment). Three days later, de Valera received a letter from David Lloyd George, the British Prime Minister, proposing a conference with a view to peace.

THE TERMS OF THE TRUCE

On 8 July 1921, Éamon de Valera met General Nevil Macready in the Mansion House in Dublin, in order to discuss the terms of a proposed truce between the British and the IRA. The British agreed not to bring any more troops or munitions into Ireland or to undertake military manoeuvres. There would be no provocative display of forces, armed or unarmed. There would be no pursuit of the IRA or their armoury by the British. The British also agreed that their secret agents would cease to operate and that the curfew would end. The Irish agreed to cease their attacks on crown forces and civilians. They too agreed not to have any provocative displays of force. The IRA would not interfere with British government property or indeed with private property. Finally, the IRA agreed not to take any action that might necessitate British military interference. The Truce came into effect at twelve noon on 11 July 1921.

THE EVE OF THE TRUCE

Josephine McGowan was the first Cumann na mBan member to be killed in the aftermath of the Rising, dying from injuries received at a protest against the internment of Republican prisoners (see Chapter Two). She is buried in Glasnevein Cemetery and was the posthumous recipient of a War of Independence Medal. Margaret Keogh, another active member of Cumann na mBan, was fatally wounded when her house in Stella Gardens, Ringsend, Dublin, was raided by British forces on 10 July 1921, the eve of the Truce. Margaret was a member of the Irish Clerical Workers Union and Captain of the Croke Ladies Hurling Club. She died of her wounds on 12 July 1921 and was buried in Glasnevin with full military honours.[28]

Four British soldiers who had been strolling around Bandon whilst off duty and unarmed were arrested by the IRA on the evening before the Truce. Their bodies were found in a field the following day; the men had been blindfolded and executed. They were Sappers Alfred G. Camm and Albert Edward Powell, Private Henry Albert Morris and Lance-Corporal Harold Daker.

AN tÓGLACH, JULY 1921

The organ of the IRA warned Volunteers to be cautious of the Truce but said they should observe the ceasefire for as long as it lasted.

> Nothing has happened yet which should cause the Irish Republican Army to relax its vigilances ... and whenever our own noble old Ireland requires them they will spring to her defence again as ready as ever to resist foreign aggression, whoever the aggressor.
>
> A truce is not a peace; we desire peace as we desire freedom and know that one cannot come without the other.[29]

CHAPTER TWELVE

Irish National Aspirations

The number of casualties in the War of Independence in Ireland up to the time of the Truce is 2,141. After the Truce, a team was sent to London to negotiate the future of the Irish Republic. The negotiations did not go well for the plenipotentiaries who did not succeed in getting the British to recognise an Irish republic. The Treaty that they signed was hotly debated in Dáil Éireann, and the assembly split over the terms. Dublin Castle was handed over to the Provisional Government but the cost was high, with the IRA, Sinn Féin and the Irish nation left divided.

CASUALTIES

In comparison to the wholesale slaughter of the First World War, the death toll for Ireland's War of Independence is relatively small at 2,141.[1] However, for a nation with a population of a little over four million, the loss of life was significant as it was often highly concentrated. For instance, the violence in Belfast between 1920 and mid-1922 resulted in the deaths of 470 people. In Cork, scene of some of the fiercest fighting, 528 people were killed between January 1919 and July 1921.

The RIC, Black and Tans and Auxiliaries suffered a total loss during the War of Independence of 514, whilst the British Army losses numbered 262.

By far the greatest number of RIC and British Army members who died were in the counties of Cork, Tipperary, Limerick, Kerry, Clare and Dublin, which is reflective of the amount of action undertaken by the IRA on a county-by-county basis.

The IRA roll of honour from January 1919 to 11 July 1921 lists nearly 650 names. However, Professor Eunan O'Halpin from Trinity College Dublin suggests that the figure for IRA killed is as low as 467. A figure of 898 civilians is also given by O'Halpin. The historian Pádraig Óg Ó Ruairc says that of those civilian casualties, 198 were spies and alleged spies who were shot by the IRA.

CASUALTIES, JANUARY 1917 TO DECEMBER 1921

RIC/Black & Tans/Auxiliaries/British Army	776
IRA	467
Civilians	898
Total	2,141

IRA prisoners aboard a British battleship, autumn 1921.

TALKS ABOUT TALKS

After some deliberation, Éamon de Valera accepted an invitation from the British Prime Minister to attend a conference in London. This conference was essentially 'talks about talks'. There was much correspondence between de Valera and Lloyd George. De Valera wanted a conference that would recognise the Irish as representatives of a sovereign independent state. However, Lloyd George would not entertain that and wrote to his Irish counterpart saying: 'I told you that we looked to Ireland to own allegiance to the Throne, and to make her future as a member of the British Commonwealth'. Lloyd George again wrote to de Valera with a fresh invitation for Irish delegates to attend a conference, 'with a view to ascertaining how the association of Ireland with the community of nations known as the British Empire may be reconciled with Irish national aspirations'. De Valera replied, quoting that line, and accepting the invitation.

As regards the team that would negotiate the terms of a treaty, de Valera had a few choices amongst the seven men who made up the Irish Cabinet, besides himself: Cathal Brugha, Austin Stack, Michael Collins, Arthur Griffith, Robert Barton and W.T. Cosgrave. Brugha and Stack simply refused to go. Collins did not want to go, arguing that, 'It was an unheard-of thing that a soldier who had fought in the field should be elected to carry out negotiations. It was de Valera's job, not his.'[2] But de Valera was far too Machiavellian to allow his name to be appended to a treaty that he well knew would not please everyone in Ireland. He also knew that the British would be unlikely to give in to the demand for a republic. Thus, although he had attended the 'talks about talks' (and Collins had not), de Valera insisted that Collins should go to England. To the suggestions that de Valera might go to London without attending the negotiations and be there for the team as an advisor, de Valera argued that it was better if he remained in Ireland, as it would give the negotiating team an excuse to refer back to the President, thus buying some breathing space. De Valera also argued that he was the President, the symbolic head of the Irish Republic, and that it would have been incongruous for him or King George to be at the negotiations.

On 14 September 1921, the Dáil approved three of the Cabinet members, Griffith, Collins and Barton, and two others, Éamonn Duggan and George Gavan Duffy, as plenipotentiaries to go to London to negotiate with the British. Plenipotentiaries, by definition, are given the full power of independent action on behalf of their government, typically in a foreign country.

The tragedy is that de Valera did not go to London. After his time in the US, he was well trained in dealing with politicians. Had Michael Collins, who represented violent republicanism, been left in Ireland as the 'Ace Card', someone who needed to be appeased, de Valera could have used the threat of the resumption of hostilities as a bargaining chip. As it transpired, the British themselves used that very threat as their method of pushing the plenipotentiaries to the edge.

IRISH TEAM IN LONDON

The negotiations lasted for under two months, from 11 October to 6 December 1921. Throughout that time, the Irish delegation stayed at 22 Hans Place in Knightsbridge, London. Collins, however, stayed at 15 Cadogan Gardens, with his security team and entourage including Liam Tobin, Emmet Dalton, Tom Cullen, Joe Dolan, Joe Guilfoyle, Ned Broy and Seán MacBride.[3] One obvious reason why Collins was against going to London was that if the negotiations broke down, he might be arrested by the British. Emmet Dalton purchased a Martinsyde bi-plane for £2,600.[4] This was essentially the first 'Irish Air Force' aeroplane. Manned by Charlie Russell and Jack MacSwiney, it was fuelled and ready to fly Collins and the team out of Croydon Airfield in any emergency.[5] The Hans Place delegates included Arthur Griffith,

Plenipotentiaries (excluding Michael Collins) and other members of the Irish team in London for the Treaty negotiations.

Robert Barton, Eamonn Duggan and George Gavan Duffy. Erskine Childers and Fionán Lynch were joint secretaries to the team and Diarmuid O'Hegarty and John Chartres acted as assistant secretaries. They were joined by Cumann na mBan member Lily O'Brennan and two stenographers, Alice and Ellie Lyons, who had been working for Collins at GHQ. Cathleen Napoli McKenna also resided at Hans Place and undertook secretarial duties, mostly for Arthur Griffith. Many other individuals were also part of the entourage with the Irish negotiators, including Desmond FitzGerald, Joseph McGrath, Dan MacCarthy, Michael Knightly, David L. Robinson and Bridget Lynch, who was married to Fionán.

NEGOTIATING A TREATY

The first meeting in Downing Street was very formal and the Irish delegation found itself confronted by trained, devious, professional political giants. Sitting across the table were Prime Minister David Lloyd George whose political prowess had earned him the moniker the 'Welsh Wizard'; Austen Chamberlain, Lord Privy Seal, Leader of the House of Commons and son of Joe Chamberlain who had campaigned against Home Rule for Ireland; Lord Birkenhead, or F.E. Smith, the Lord Chancellor, well-known Conservative loyalist and also the man who had prosecuted Roger Casement in 1916; Laming Worthington-Evans, the Conservative Secretary for War; Hamar Greenwood, the Chief Secretary for Ireland and the IRA's nemesis; Gordon Hewart, the Attorney General; the formidable Secretary of State for the Colonies, Winston Churchill; and two of Britain's finest civil servants – Lionel George Curtis, who wrote *The Commonwealth of Nations* in 1916, and Tom Jones, the Welsh advisor and secretary to Lloyd George. Supporting this formidable team on the outside was one of the finest civil services in the world.

Arthur Griffith was the official chairman of the Irish delegation. However, he confided in Collins that his health was suffering and asked him to assume unofficial leadership of the delegation. Collins wrote in his notes about the pressure of the discussions: 'To go for a drink is one thing. To be driven to it is another.'[6]

Between 11 and 24 October, seven plenary sessions were held. Following the plenary sessions, Griffith and Collins asked to engage in informal discussions with two representatives from each side. In these discussions, Collins and Griffith (as Chairman of the Irish Plenipotentiaries) spoke with Chamberlain and an alternate member of the British team. Gavan Duffy impressed upon de Valera that this policy of dividing the Irish delegation was dangerous. According to Barton, 'from the moment Griffith and Collins met Lloyd George and Chamberlain alone their power to resist weakened. They became almost pro-British in their arguments with us and Duffy and I often felt we had to fight them first and the English afterwards.'[7]

Lloyd George was also in regular meetings with the Ulster Unionist leader Sir James Craig. The British Primer Minister was trying to convince the Northern Ireland Prime Minister that the Northern parliament could come under an All-Ireland parliament. Craig was unimpressed. His alternative was that the Northern and Southern parliaments would have equal powers, flatly refusing the All-Ireland parliamentary ideal. Instead, the British came up with the concept of a boundary commission, which Griffith believed 'would give us most of Tyrone, Fermanagh and part of Armagh, Down etc.'[8] Lloyd George, in a private meeting, convinced Griffith to agree to back the British in a proposal to the Unionist leaders concerning an All-Ireland Parliament, which would give 'Ulster' the right to remove itself within twelve months. Griffith agreed to back this plan and gave his word to Lloyd George that he would not repudiate it, believing that it was only a ruse on the Prime Minister's part to appease the Unionists. Robert Barton recalled how Arthur Griffith used to repeat about the Unionists: 'If they do not come in, they will lose half their territory and they can't stay out.' The Irish delegates were convinced that partition of the island was inevitable but that the Boundary Commission would convince the North of the necessity of unity. As it transpired, the Boundary Commission did not meet until 1924, and achieved nothing, as the Northern Ireland Government refused to cooperate..

It should be remembered that there was regular contact between the plenipotentiaries and Dublin. Every weekend, one or more of the delegates returned home to meet with the other cabinet members. Indeed, Collins met with de Valera on several of these visits. Following a cabinet meeting in Dublin on 25 November, attended by Collins and Griffith, the two men presented to the British a memorandum on 'External Association', which was an idea being worked on by de Valera (see below). The British rejected it outright although Griffith argued that the Irish delegates had no authority to deal with the British on any other basis than the exclusion of the Crown from Irish affairs. Another cabinet meeting in Dublin was summoned for 3 December.

Meanwhile in the Six Counties, Tyrone County Council pledged its allegiance to Dáil Éireann, declaring that the people of Tyrone and Fermanagh would never accept separation from the rest of Ireland. The offices of the council were raided and its books were seized by the RIC. In four days of violence in Belfast, twenty-six people were killed. In the west of Ireland, de Valera, who was reviewing the IRA, said in an address to the Mid-Clare Brigade, 'We know the savagery that can be used against us and we defy it.' The Ennis County Council stated in an address to de Valera that if 'British statesmen are planning another betrayal ... we tell you we are ready ... We will follow you if needs be to the death.'[9]

The British gave the final draft of the Treaty to the Plenipotentiaries on the first day of December. The delegates all sailed for Dublin, and Griffith met de Valera and gave him the document. De Valera told Griffith that he could not accept its terms. A cabinet meeting was convened, which proved to be long, fractious and exhausting. De Valera held firm to what he had said to Griffith. Cathal Brugha, Gavan Duffy, Robert Barton and Erskine Childers were also against signing. Collins believed that further concessions could be obtained on trade and defence and argued that it would be a year before the oath of allegiance would have to be taken. He suggested recommending the Treaty to the electorate but recommending non-acceptance of the oath. At the meeting, de Valera asked the plenipotentiaries to go back to London and make the British understand that the Irish were prepared to face a renewal of the conflict as the alternative to partition of the nation and the oath to the British crown. But on being pressed, de Valera said that if there had to be an oath, it should be in conformity with external association. He made a suggestion to Barton and Childers but it was an informal, hasty discussion and they managed to scribble down only a few of his words. Barton appealed to de Valera to return with the delegation to London, and for a while it appeared as if the President might be considering it. Brugha persuaded Griffith to agree that he would not break on the crown or the oath, that he would not sign the document, and that he would bring it back to the Dáil and, if necessary, the Irish people. The meeting adjourned and it was understood that the delegates were to return to London and tell the British that they would not sign the draft document, that they were ready to face war if necessary.

When the plenipotentiaries returned to London, Gavan Duffy, Robert Barton and Erskine Childers drafted a counterproposal in Hans Place. Collins, Griffith and Duggan, however, refused to present it in that form to Downing Street. Instead, they made certain amendments to the counterproposals, which included substituting the wording of the oath. Griffith then agreed to go with Barton and Gavan Duffy to Downing Street; Collins stayed at Hans Place.

The British reacted badly to the counterproposals. Lloyd George, Chamberlain, Birkenhead and the Chancellor of the Exchequer, Robert Horne, sat with the Irish. As soon as Gavan Duffy said, 'The difficulty is coming into the Empire...', the British, as if prearranged, leapt from their seats and declared that the conference was finished. They said that they were sending word to Craig that negotiations had broken down. The Irish returned to Hans Place.

However, Lloyd George had a plan. He sent word to Griffith and Collins that he would like to meet them the following morning. At that meeting, on 5 December, Lloyd George convinced Collins that the Boundary Commission would save Ireland from partition. Collins and Griffith persuaded the rest of the plenipotentiaries to come to Downing Street that afternoon. Collins, Griffith and Barton held firm on their demand for a statement from Craig that he would accept unity. However, when the meeting resumed after a short break, Lloyd George reminded Griffith of the promise of support he had made some weeks back and Griffith agreed to sign the Treaty. Now Lloyd George pressed home his advantage and spoke solemnly to Barton, saying that any delegate who did not sign now was taking full responsibility for war. He issued an ultimatum:

> I have to communicate with Sir James Craig tonight: here are the alternative letters I have prepared, one enclosing the Articles of Agreement ... the other saying that the Sinn Féin representatives refuse the oath of allegiance and refuse to come within the Empire. If I send this letter it is war — and war in three days! Which letter am I to send?

The Irish returned to Hans Place, where Griffith urged his fellow plenipotentiaries to sign. At 9pm, the final draft of the Treaty arrived by courier. No vital changes had been made. Finally, Collins and Duggan agreed to sign. Barton was reluctant but he too consented. Under duress, Gavan Duffy relented and signed too. After midnight, Collins, Griffith and Barton returned to Downing Street with the signed Treaty.

THE TREATY SIGNATORIES

'Articles of Agreement for a Treaty Between Great Britain and Ireland' or simply 'The Treaty' was signed in the early hours of 6 December 1921, at 2.20am to be precise. The signatories representing the British were David Lloyd George, Austen Chamberlain, Lord Birkenhead, L. Worthington Evans, Hamar Greenwood and Gordon Hewart. The Irish delegation also signed, all in the Irish language; Art Ó Gríobhtha (Arthur Griffith), Micheál Ó Coileáin (Michael Collins), Riobárd Bartún (Robert Barton), Eudhmonn S. Ó Dúgáin (Eamonn Duggan), Seórsa Ghabháin Uí Dhubhthaigh (George Gavan Duffy).

TERMS OF THE TREATY

Under the terms of the Treaty, Ireland could not be called a republic. Rather, Ireland would be called the Irish Free State, which would come into existence one year from the date of the signing of the Treaty. The Irish Free State would have dominion status, like Canada,

New Zealand, Australia and South Africa. The Royal Navy would have access to a number of Irish ports, namely Belfast in the Six Counties, Berehaven and Queenstown in County Cork, and Lough Swilly in County Donegal. The Treaty gave the right for the Six Counties to withdraw from the rest of Ireland. It essentially reinforced the split in Ireland, created by the Government of Ireland Act, 1920, between the six counties of Antrim, Armagh, Down, Fermanagh, Derry and Tyrone, and the remaining twenty-six counties. The British King would be Head of State of the Irish Free State and would be represented by a Governor General.

Article 4 of the Treaty also provided for an oath to be taken by members of the Free State Parliament in the following form:

> I ...... do solemnly swear true faith and allegiance to the Constitution of the Irish Free State as by law established and that I will be faithful to H.M. King George V, his heirs and successors by law, in virtue of the common citizenship of Ireland with Great Britain and her adherence to and membership of the group of nations forming the British Commonwealth of Nations.

EXTERNAL ASSOCIATION OR DOCUMENT NO. 2

While the Plenipotentiaries were in London negotiating the future of their nation, de Valera was working on a 'Plan B' or 'Document No. 2', which concerned an alternative to the notion that Ireland should be part of the British Empire. He called this 'External Association', that is the idea that Ireland would remain a sovereign nation associated with the Commonwealth but not a member. The British monarch might be the head of the association of nations known as the Commonwealth but would not be the head of state of Ireland. De Valera had explained this to Griffith before the plenipotentiaries went to London and, as referred to above, the idea had been raised with the British who had dismissed it.

Nevertheless, after the delegation had presented the signed Treaty to the Dáil, de Valera offered his suggested alternative as Document No. 2. A maths teacher, de Valera used Venn diagrams to illustrate his concept. The terms of Document no. 2 included the idea that 'Ireland shall be associated with the States of the British Commonwealth' and that 'for purposes of the Association, Ireland shall recognise His Britannic Majesty as head of the Association'.

THE TREATY DEBATES

The Cabinet voted four to three in support of the Treaty and it was put to Dáil Éireann. Considered to be the most acrimonious of debates the parliament of Ireland ever witnessed, the Treaty debates involved political invective, name-calling and much loss of tempers. The debates ran from

TDs attending the Treaty debates. Left to right: Kathleen Clarke (widow of Tom Clarke, architect of the Easter Rising); Countess Markievicz; Kate O'Callaghan (widow of Michael O'Callaghan, Mayor of Limerick murdered in 1921 – see Chapter Ten); and Margaret Pearse (whose sons Patrick and Willie were executed in 1916).

14 December to 7 January 1922. The Anglo–Irish Treaty was ratified by Dáil Éireann on 7 January 1922. It passed by a narrow margin of 64 for and 57 against, with three TDs abstaining.

De Valera formally resigned as President on 10 January. A motion to re-elect him was defeated by only two votes. During the last hours of the debates, he said:

> As a protest against the election as President of the Irish Republic of the Chairman of the Delegation, who is bound by the Treaty conditions to set up a State which is to subvert the Republic, and who, in the interim period, instead of using the office as it should be used — to support the Republic — will, of necessity, have to be taking action which will tend to its destruction, I, while this vote is being taken, as one, am going to leave the House.[10]

De Valera got up to leave and his supporters followed him. The exchange that took place gives some idea of the acrimony between the pro-Treaty Collins and two of the TDs who were anti-Treaty:

> Collins: Deserters all! We will now call on the Irish people to rally to us. Deserters all!
>
> David Ceannt: Up the Republic.
>
> Collins: Deserters all to the Irish nation in her hour of trial. We will stand by her.
>
> Countess Markievicz: Oath breakers and cowards.
>
> Collins: Foreigners — Americans — English.
>
> Markievicz: Lloyd Georgites!

The original motion, that Arthur Griffith be appointed President of Dáil Éireann, was then carried unanimously by those remaining in the House. After the vote for Griffith, de Valera and his supporters returned to the Dáil and listened to an appeal by a Labour deputation under Thomas

Johnson, concerning the high rate of unemployment. De Valera then spoke and congratulated Griffith on his election as President of Dáil Éireann. But he warned:

> Whenever he functions, or will function in his other capacity as head of another government, we cannot recognise that government at all. We will have to insist and continue insisting on our attitude that that government is not the legitimate government of this country until the Irish people have disestablished the Republic, and we shall do everything in our power to see they do not disestablish it.

Erskine Childers, the man who had armed the Volunteers in 1914, then aimed a question at Griffith, concerning his dual role as head of the Dáil and soon-to-be head of the Provisional Government. President Griffith replied with some vitriol:

> Before this proceeds any further, I want to say that President de Valera [Griffith still calling him President] made a statement — a generous statement — and I replied. Now (striking the table) I will not reply to any Englishman in this Dáil (applause).

Childers spoke again: 'If he had banged the table before Lloyd George in the way he banged it here, things might have been different (cries of 'Order!' and applause).' Countess Markievicz interjected, 'And Griffith is a Welsh name.' Eventually Griffith, as President, said:

> I think President de Valera is acting fairly; some of the other members are not. We want to get a chance. We have not spoken about ourselves, but for three months past we have been working night and day. We were faced with the task of fighting our English opponents first, and then we had to come and fight our Irish friends, and now we have to take on as big a job as ever men took on (hear, hear). We want a chance. We cannot meet every day here and at the same time try and carry out the things.

If President de Valera — I will still call him President — agrees, I will fix a month hence as the date for the next meeting, and we will meet again on this day month. Give us a chance to do some thing in the meantime. We cannot work as it is.

De Valera, concerned about a potential split in the IRA, replied:

We ought, I think, to take that as reasonable. Everybody ought to regard it as reasonable (applause). The only thing we are really anxious about is the Army and perhaps the Minister of Defence would give us some idea of what he proposes to do. I am anxious myself as an individual who knows the Army. I am anxious to know what the position of the Army will be. I fear that, unless the Army is kept intact as the Army of the Republic, we will not have that confidence — the members of the Army will not have that confidence — which is necessary if we are to keep them as a solid unit.

Richard Mulcahy as Minister for Defence then spoke:

The Army will remain occupying the same position with regard to this Government of the Republic, and occupying the same position with regard to the Minister of Defence, and under the same management, and in the same spirit as we have had up to the present (hear, hear).

De Valera replied, 'I do not want to pin you down any further, so I will take it at that.' He then seconded a motion to thank the hosts of the debates, and it should be noted that the debates did not end on a sour note:

I have great pleasure in seconding that proposal. The University authorities were very kind when, while I was acting as President of the Dáil — President of the Republic — I asked that we might be given accommodation here. Then as Chancellor of the University, I am delighted that this historic meeting — although for many reasons it will be a sad one — was held here (applause).

Richard Mulcahy then spoke again:

> On a point of explanation; what I said apparently has not been under-
> stood, and it has been suggested I avoided saying what could have been
> said very simply. It is suggested I avoided saying the Army will continue
> to be the Army of the Irish Republic. If any assurance is required — the
> Army will remain the Army of the Irish Republic (applause).

THE PROVISIONAL GOVERNMENT

On 14 January, the 'Provisional Government of the Irish Free State'
was formed by sixty pro-Treaty Dáil members in the Mansion House,
Dublin. Interestingly, the four Unionists elected for the Dublin University did attend this session. The 'Southern Parliament' passed a motion
approving the Treaty and elected Michael Collins as Chairman of the
Executive Committee. Richard Mulcahy was in charge of Defence, and
Eoin O'Duffy became Chief of Staff of the National Army.

Members of the Provisional Government of the Irish Free State gather on the steps of
the Mansion House, Dublin.

DUBLIN CASTLE HANDED OVER

The seat of British power and, indeed, the centre of the administration of British rule, Dublin Castle, was symbolically handed over to the Provisional Government of the Irish Free State on 16 January 1922. According to one of the most prolific Irish historians, Tim Pat Coogan, an official at the Castle is reported to have admonished Michael Collins for being tardy: 'You're seven minutes late, Mr. Collins.' Collins is reputed to have replied, 'We've been waiting 700 years, you can have the seven minutes.'[11] Collins hoped that the handing over of British Army barracks to the Irish would be seen as a great victory for Ireland.

ANTI-TREATY AND PRO-TREATY

A significant number of IRA leaders were against the Treaty; these included Rory O'Connor, Liam Lynch, Cathal Brugha and Ernie O'Malley, to name but a few. An Army Convention was held on 26 March, which adopted a resolution confirming that the IRA affirmed its allegiance to the Irish Republic. A new executive was elected and Rory O'Connor, at a press conference, repudiated the Dáil and IRA GHQ. Liam Lynch did his best to reunite the divided IRA and continued to hold discussions with Michael Collins. Both men were IRB Supreme Council members and neither wanted to see an Irish civil war.

The Black and Tans and Auxiliaries began to leave the twenty-six counties, some to join the Specials in the Six Counties and some eventually to join a Palestine gendarmerie. However, the pro-Treaty Provisional Government, instead of relying on the Republican Police, began to recruit for a civic guard and also set up a Criminal Investigations Department (CID) at Oriel House, recruiting from amongst the IRA those of a pro-Treaty stance.

Conclusion

The British Government has rarely cared about the effects its treaties have on the internal affairs of foreign nations. The Treaty of Nanking was a peace treaty that ended the First Opium War (1839–42) between Britain and China. It was the first of what the Chinese later called the 'unequal treaties', because they were not negotiated by nations treating each other as equals but were imposed on China after a war.

The British Empire often left trouble in its wake. The Balfour Declaration, which saw the creation of a Zionist homeland for Jewish people in Palestine, contributed in turn to the creation of an apartheid state in Israel today. The division of India and Pakistan in 1947 certainly stands as a constant reminder of the British Empire's inability to leave peace in the wake of her departure.

Similarly, the Anglo–Irish Treaty, as signed in 1921, was an unfair imposition on Ireland. Lloyd George and Winston Churchill suffered little as a result of the Treaty they so skilfully foisted upon Arthur Griffith and Michael Collins. When Lord Birkenhead proclaimed that he had signed his political death warrant when he signed the Treaty, Michael Collins presciently retorted that he had signed his 'actual death warrant'. The British had forced his hand into signing a document that split the Irish nation and divided the IRA along pro-Treaty and anti-Treaty lines. Initially the split was purely political. But gradually it became violent.

On 14 April 1922, the anti-Treaty IRA under Rory O'Connor, Ernie O'Malley and Oscar Traynor, occupied the Four Courts, a building synonymous with the 1916 Rising, hoping to provoke a war with the British forces, who were still numerous in Dublin. They hoped that if trouble started, both sides of the IRA would unite and recommence the fight against the British, for an Irish Republic.

On 22 June 1922, two London IRA men, Reggie Dunne, O/C London IRA, and IRA Volunteer Joseph O'Sullivan, assassinated Sir Henry Wilson on his doorstep in London. Henry Wilson was an advisor on security to the new Northern State. He had advised stepping up recruitment for the Special Police, and many nationalists held him responsible for the harsh measures and violence directed at Catholics in the Six Counties. Joseph O'Sullivan, having lost a leg in the war, was unable to run from the scene, and was captured by a crowd of people in the area. Dunne attempted to assist his comrade by returning to help but he too was captured.

Sir Henry Wilson was a Field Marshal, the highest rank in the British Army. Two men in England were beside themselves with rage, namely Lloyd George and Winston Churchill. All evidence suggests that the person who ordered the shooting was Michael Collins, who had called Wilson 'a violent Orange partisan'. It should be remembered that Collins had ordered the shooting of Captain Percival Lea-Wilson in 1920, in retaliation for his abuse of Tom Clarke in 1916 (see Chapter Five). It seems clear that in this instance Collins was exacting revenge on Field Marshal Henry Wilson. It was a message of defiance to the British establishment, but also part of the continuing IRA campaign in the Six Counties.

Collins sent his Squad man Joe Dolan over to London to meet Sam Maguire (who had sworn Collins into the IRB), to see if they could affect the rescue of Dunne and O'Sullivan.[1] If the order to shoot Wilson had come from the Four Courts, why did Collins bother attempting to rescue those who had pulled the trigger on behalf of the anti-Treaty IRA? The most logical conclusion would seem to be that Collins gave the order for Wilson to be shot. However, it is not possible to date when that order was made, and it might have been before the Truce. In any case, Reginald Dunne and Joseph O'Sullivan were hanged in Wandsworth Prison, London, on 10 August 1922.

London pointed the finger of blame for the shooting of Wilson at the IRA in the Four Courts. Churchill threatened that unless the Four Courts Garrison were removed, the British would consider the Treaty 'as having been formally violated' and that they 'shall resume full liberty of action'. Essentially Churchill was saying that the British would remove the IRA from the Four Courts. Collins had a choice here. If he chose to let the British take on the Four Courts, that could have two consequences. In an ideal world, the IRA would re-unite against the old enemy, Britain. But in reality, even if Collins himself walked into the Four Courts and joined forces with the IRA, the Provisional Government or Free State troops would join with the British against their old IRA comrades. And that is essentially what happened. Churchill loaned the Free State Army two 18-pounder guns, the same machinery used by the British to bombard the Republicans in the 1916 Rising. General Nevil Macready, head of the British Army in Ireland, was still in Dublin when British artillery, this time in Irish hands, bombarded the IRA, thus starting the Irish Civil War.

It was a brutal civil war, and the violence of 1919–21 paled in comparison. The Free State forces formally executed seventy-seven Republicans. There were also 150 extra-judicial executions carried out by the Free State forces against their former comrades. Erskine Childers, the Englishman who had imported into Howth weapons that were used in the 1916 Rising, was one of those executed by the Free State. Liam Mellows, who had led the Galway men and women during the 1916 Rising, was another. Michael Collins himself was killed in an ambush by the IRA at Béal na mBláth on 22 August 1922. When the Civil War 'ended' in May 1923, the country was divided — physically by the imposition of the border at the Six Counties, and politically by the Civil War itself.

It is easy to hold Éamon de Valera or Michael Collins responsible for the violence that resulted after the War of 1919–21. However, the blame for the Irish Civil War might more fairly be placed on a different pair of culprits: David Lloyd George and Winston Churchill.

Notes

CHAPTER TWO

1. Lawless, Joe, WS 1043, pg.177.
2. Stapleton, Bill, WS 822, pg.15.
3. McCarthy, Joseph, WS 1497, pg.84.
4. Good, Joe, WS 388, pg.26.
5. Robbins, Frank, WS 585, pg.110–111.
6. McCarthy, Cal, *Cumann na mBan and the Irish Revolution*, Cork: The Collins Press, 2014, pg.77.
7. Coogan, Tim Pat, *Michael Collins*, London: Hutchinson, 1990, pg.70.
8. McCabe, Liam, WS 1212, pg.3.
9. O'Mahony, Seán, *The First Hunger Striker – Thomas Ashe 1917*, Dublin: The 1916–1921 Club in association with Elo Publications, 2001, pg.6–7.
10. Nugent, Laurence, WS 907 pg.127; O'Sheil, Kevin, WS 1770, pg.674.
11. CAB/23/6.
12. Stapleton, William, WS 822, pg.22.
13. Gillis, Liz and Mary McAuliffe, *Richmond Barracks 1916*, Dublin: DCC, 2016, pg.101.
14. CAB/23/8.
15. Hopkinson, Michael, *The Irish War of Independence*, Dublin: Gill and Macmillan, 2002, pg.32.
16. Breen, Dan, *My Fight for Irish Freedom,* Dublin: Talbot Press, 1924, pg.32–36.
17. *Nenagh Guardian*, 25 January 1919, pg.2.
18. Robinson, Seamus, WS 1721, pg.30.
19. Breen, Daniel, WS 1739, pg.21–22.
20. Lynch, Michael, WS 511, pg.88.
21. Coogan, Tim Pat, *De Valera*, London: Hutchinson, 1993, pg.124–6.
22. *Derry Journal*, 10 March 1919, pg.3.
23. Hartney, Michael, WS 1415, pg.5.
24. O'Brien, Edmond, WS 597, pg.26.
25. Ibid., pg.31.
26. Robinson, Seamus, WS 1721, pg.42.
27. Ryan, Bridget, WS 1488, pg.8.

CHAPTER THREE

1. Curran, Monsignor M., WS 687, pg.361.
2. Carroll, F.M. (Ed.), *The American Commission on Irish Independence 1919,* Dublin: Mount Salus Press, 1985, pg.6.
3. Macardle, Dorothy, *The Irish Republic*, London: Victor Gollancz, 1937, pg.295–6.
4. McDonnell, Michael, WS 225, pg.2.
5. Noyk, Michael, WS 707, pg.19.
6. Walsh, Richard, WS 400, pg.106.
7. Kennedy, Seán, WS 842, pg.18–19.
8. Slattery, James, WS 445, pg.5.
9. Ó Snodaigh, Pádraig and Arthur Mitchell (eds), *Irish Political Documents 1916–1948*, Dublin: Irish Academic Press, 1985, pg.66.
10. Ryan, Meda, *The Real Chief, Liam Lynch,* Cork: Mercier, 1986, pg.36.
11. Leddy, Con, WS 756, pg.7.
12. O'Callaghan, Leo, WS 978, pg.4.
13. *Freeman's Journal*, 9 September 1919, pg.5.
14. McDonnell, Michael, WS 225, pg.2.
15. Byrne, Vincent, WS 423, pg.17.
16. Daly, Paddy, WS 387, pg.11.
17. Stapleton, William, WS 822, pg.35.
18. Byrne, Vincent, WS 423, pg.33.
19. Connell, Joseph, *Dublin in Rebellion*, Dublin: Lilliput, 2009, pg.81.
20. Dalton, Charles, WS 434, pg.8.
21. Ibid., pg.8.
22. Slattery, James, WS 445, pg.5.
23. Napoli-McKenna, Cathleen, WS 643, pg.1.
24. Brennan, Robert, WS 779, pg.586.
25. Murphy, John J., WS 204, pg.11.
26. Nelligan, David, *The Spy in the Castle*, London: MacGibbon and Key, 1968, pg.50.
27. Slattery, James, WS 445, pg.7.
28. Leonard, Joseph, WS 547, pg.4.
29. Byrne, Vincent, WS 423, pg.13.
30. McDonnell, Michael, WS 225, pg.5.
31. Daly, Paddy, WS 387, pg.19.
32. Breen, *My Fight for Irish Freedom, pg.84.*

CHAPTER FOUR

1. Hopkinson, *The Irish War of Independence,* pg.44.

2. *Fermanagh Herald*, 24 January 1920, pg.6.

3. Thornton, Frank, WS 615, pg.36.

4. Dolan, Joseph, WS 663, pg.1.

5. Daly, Paddy, WS 387, pg.24.

6. Dolan, Joseph, WS 663, pg.2.

7. Leonard, Joseph, WS 547, pg.7.

8. McGahey, John, WS 740, pg.4.

9. Marron, Phillip, WS 657, pg.4.

10. O'Malley, Ernie, *On Another Man's Wound*, Boulder, CL: Roberts Rinehart, reprinted 1999 (first pub. 1936), pg.126.

11. Kehoe, Michael, WS 741, pg.61.

12. Walsh, Richard, WS 400, pg.105.

13. Archer, Liam, WS 819, pg.18–19.

14. Murphy, Michael, WS 1547, pg.13–17.

15. Thornton, Frank, WS 615, pg.40.

16. Dolan, Joseph WS 663, pg.11.

17. McMahon, Paul, *British Spies and Irish Rebels*, Woodbridge, Suffolk: Boydell Press, 2008, pg.30.

18. *Belfast Newsletter*, Monday, 9 April 1920, pg.5.

19. Byrne, Vincent, WS 423, pg.38.

20. Caldwell, Patrick, WS 638, pg.24.

21. Byrne, Vincent, WS 423, pg.38.

22. Ó Ruairc, Pádraig Óg, *Blood on the Banner*, Cork: Mercier, 2009, pg.113.

23. Bratton, Eugene, WS 467, pg.6.

24. British Cabinet Papers, 30 April 1920, CAB/23/21, pg.62.

25. Noyk, Michael, WS 707, pg.27.

26. Dolan, Joseph, WS 663, pg.6.

27. Dwyer, T. Ryle, *The Squad*, Cork: Mercier, 2005, pg.107.

28. Fitzgerald, George, WS 684, pg.20–21.

29. Kennedy, Tadhg, WS 1413, pg.76.

CHAPTER FIVE

1. O'Mullane, Brighid, WS 450, pg.13–14.

2. O'Brien, Annie, WS 805, pg.20.

3. Ní Riain, Eilis, WS 568, pg.39.

4. *Freeman's Journal,* Monday 5 July 1920, pg.6

5. Macardle, *The Irish Republic,* pg.351.

6. Kotsonouris, Mary, 'Revolutionary Justice', *History Ireland,* Issue 3, 1994.

7. Byrne, Vincent, WS 423, pg.42.

8. Daly, Paddy, WS 387, pg.32.

9. Crowley, Tadhg, WS 435, pg.30–32.

10. Toomey, Thomas, *The War of Independence in Limerick,* 2010, pg.329.

11. Crowley, Tadhg, WS 435, pg.33.

12. Kearney, Cornelius, WS 1460, pg.5.

13. Toomey, *The War of Independence in Limerick,* pg.341.

14. Crowley, Tadhg, WS 435, pg.35.

15. Kearney, Cornelius, WS 1460, pg.6.

16. Prendergast, Seán, WS 755, pg.320–321.

17. Fitzgerald, George, WS 684, pg.23.

18. Dolan, Joseph, WS 663, pg.7.

19. Prendergast, Seán, WS 755, pg.323–326.

20. Leahy, Michael, WS 1421, pg.26.

21. Whelan, Patrick, WS 1449, pg.29.

22. Aherne, Joseph, WS 1367, pg.19.

23. Henderson, Frank WS 249, pg.60.

24. Tobin, Liam, WS 1753, pg.7.

25. Balfe, Edward, WS 1373, pg.9.

26. Whelan, Sean, WS 1085, pg.6.

27. Thornton, Frank, WS 615, pg.43.

28. The painting is, at the time of writing, on loan to the National Gallery of Ireland.

29. Mee, Jeremiah, WS 379, pg.8–11.

30. Hawes, Joseph, WS 262, pg.2.

31. *An tÓglach,* July 1920, pg.1.

32. Ryan, *Liam Lynch, The Real Chief,* pg.60–64.

33. Healy, Daniel, WS 1656, pg.11.

34. Culhane, Seán, WS 746, pg.6.

35. Gillis, Liz, *The Hales Brothers,* Cork: Mercier, 2016, pg.62–68.

CHAPTER SIX

1. McGaughey, Jane, *Ulster's Men: Protestant Unionist Masculinities and Militarization in the North of Ireland, 1912–1923*, London: McGill-Queen's University Press, 2012, pg.143.

2. Fox, Thomas, WS 365, pg.3.

3. McCorley, Roger, WS 389, pg.9.

4. Fox, Thomas, WS 365, pg.6.

5. O'Mullane, Brighid, WS 450, pg.13–14.

6. Ó Ruairc, Pádraig Óg, 'The Women Who Died For Ireland', *History Ireland,* September/October, 2018.

7. Ryan, Desmond, *Seán Treacy and The Third Tipperary Brigade*, Tralee: The Kerryman, 1945, pg.144.

8. O'Keefe, John, WS 1168, pg.10.

9. McGrath, Edmond, WS 1393, pg.13.

10. Lynch, Michael, WS 511, pg.144.

11. Rock, Michael, WS 1398, pg.12.

12. *Drogheda Independent*, Saturday, 25 September 1920, pg.3.

13. Ibid., pg.3.

14. Kerin, Patrick, WS 977, pg.10.

15. Malone, Anthony, WS 1076, pg.10.

16. Kerin, Patrick, WS 977, pg.13.

17. Ó Ruairc, *Blood on the Banner*, pg.169.

18. *Cork Examiner*, Saturday, 25 September 1920, pg.5.

19. Malone, Anthony, WS 1076, pg.12.

20. *Irish Independent*, Saturday, 25 September 1920, pg.4.

CHAPTER SEVEN

1. MacCarthy, John, WS 883, Appendix pg.1–2.

2. Toomey, *The War of Independence in Limerick*, pg.375.

3. Breen, Daniel, WS 1763, pg.93.

4. *Rebel Cork's Fighting Story*, Tralee: The Kerryman, 1947, pg.122.

5. Ibid., pg.124.

6. Ibid., pg.125.

7. *The Liberator*, 30 September 1920, pg.1.

8. Breen, *My Fight for Irish Freedom*, pg.149.

9. O'Brien, Edmond, WS 597, pg.40.

10. Breen, *My Fight for Irish Freedom,* pg.141.

11. Ryan, Desmond, *Fight at Fernside, Dublin's Fighting Story,* Tralee: The Kerryman, 1948, pg.266–7.

12. Lawless, Joseph, WS 1043, pg.329.

13. Breen, *My Fight for Irish Freedom,* pg.147.

14. Ryan, Desmond, *Seán Treacy and The Third Tipperary Brigade,* Tralee: The Kerryman, 1945, pg.274.

15. Brunswick, Seán, WS 898, pg.6.

CHAPTER EIGHT

1. Hannigan, Dave, *Terence MacSwiney*, Dublin: O'Brien Press, 2010, pg.10–11.

2. *Cork Weekly Examiner*, 6 November 1920, pg.5.

3. Power, P.J., 'Mick Fitzgerald, Gallant Soldier of Fermoy', *Rebel Cork's Fighting Story*, Tralee: The Kerryman, 1947, pg.119.

4. Hynes, Frank, WS 446, pg.67–9.

5. 'The Sack of Tralee', *Kerry's Fighting Story*, Tralee: The Kerryman, 1947, pg.228.

6. Fitzgerald, Patrick, WS 1079, pg.10.

7. *Irish Independent*, Tuesday, 9 November 1920, pg.5.

8. *Evening Herald*, Thursday, 11 November 1920, pg.1

9. McCann, John, 'Torture and Execution of Kevin Barry', *Dublin's Fighting Story,* Tralee: The Kerryman, 1948, pg.281.

10. Barry-Moloney, Katherine, WS 731, pg.33–34.

11. O'Neill, Seán, WS 1154, pg.20.

12. Sexton, Seán, WS 396, pg.5.

13. MacEoin, Seán, WS 1716, p108.

14. McKeon, James, WS 436, pg.7.

15. Sexton, Seán, WS 396, pg.8.

16. MacEoin, Seán, WS 1716, pg.118.

17. McDermott, Jim, *Northern Divisions*, Belfast: Beyond the Pale, 2001, pg.202.

18. Béaslaí, Piaras, 'Fourteen British Officers and Agents Executed in Dublin on Bloody Sunday', *With The IRA In The Fight For Freedom*, Tralee: The Kerryman (no date) pg.219.

19. *Evening Herald*, Dublin, Monday, 22 November 1920, pg.1.

20. Connell, *Dublin in Rebellion,* pg.180.

21. O'Brien, Annie, WS 805, pg.20–21.

22. Foley, Michael, *The Bloodied Field*, Dublin: O'Brien Press, 2014, pg.155–58.

23. Taylor, Rex, *Michael Collins*, London: Hutchinson, 1958, pg.134.

24. *Weekly Irish Times*, Saturday, 27 November 1920, pg.1.

25. *Evening Herald*, Monday, 22 November 1920, pg.1.

26. Connell, *Dublin in Rebellion*, pg.201.

27. Lynch, Michael, WS 511, pg.63.

28. Foley, Michael, *The Bloodied Field*, Dublin: O'Brien Press, 2014, pg.216.

29. Hansard, 22 November 1920, vol. 135, cc.38–43.

30. Hansard, 20 October 1920, vol. 133, cc 1022–23.

31. Moylett, Patrick, WS 767, pg.50.

32. British Cabinet Papers, 30 April 1920, CAB/23/21 pg.59.

33. O'Duffy, Francis, WS 665, pg.20.

34. Ibid., pg.18.

35. Ó Duibhir, Liam, *Prisoners of War*, Cork: Mercier, 2003, pg.208–210.

36. *Evening Herald*, Dublin, Monday, 22 November 1920.

37. McNamara, Conor, *War and Revolution in the West of Ireland*, Newbridge, County Kildare: Irish Academic Press, 2018, pg.152.

CHAPTER NINE

1. Barry, Tom, *Guerilla Days in Ireland*, Cork: Mercier Press, 1955, pg.36–37.

2. Ibid., pg.40–41.

3. Ryan, Meda, *Tom Barry, IRA Freedom Fighter*, Cork: Mercier Press, 2003, pg.36.

4. *Cork Weekly Examiner*, Saturday, 11 December 1920, pg.6.

5. Power, P.J., 'A Night of Murder and Arson in Fermoy', *Rebel Cork's Fighting Story*, Tralee: The Kerryman, 1947, pg.210.

6. Coss, James, WS 1065, pg.9.

7. *Cork Weekly News*, Saturday, 18 December 1920, pg.1.

8. Ibid.

9. White, Gerry and Brendan O'Shea, *The Burning of Cork*, Cork: Mercier Press, 2006, pg.106.

10. O'Donoghue, F., 'The Sacking of Cork', *Rebel Cork's Fighting Story*, Tralee: The Kerryman, 1947, pg.95–97.

11. White and O'Shea, *The Burning of Cork*, pg.165.

12. Ó Ruairc, *Blood on the Banner*, pg.212–213.

13. Toomey, *The War of Independence in Limerick*, pg.485–496.

14. 'Seamus', 'The Engagement at Caherguillamore, Bruff', *Limerick's Fighting Story*, Tralee: The Kerryman, 1948, pg.199.

15. Macardle, *The Irish Republic*, pg.420.

CHAPTER TEN

1. Dalton, Charles, WS 434, pg.21.

2. Moylett, Patrick, WS 767, pg.49.

3. Dalton, Charles, WS 434, pg.23.

4. Stapleton, William, WS 822, pg.72.

5. Newell, Thomas (Sweeney), WS 698, pg.7.

6. Stapleton, William, WS 822, pg.74.

7. Dalton, Charles, WS 434, pg.27.

8. Dwyer, Denis, WS 712, pg.6.

9. Ibid., pg.9.

10. Manning, John, WS 1720, pg.24.

11. O'Donoghue, Michael, WS 1741, p145.

12. Macready, Nevil, *Annals of an Active Life, Vol. 2,* New York: Doran and Company, 1925, pg.543.

13. O'Donoghue, Michael, WS 1741, pg.145.

14. Horgan, Edward, WS 1644, pg.12.

15. Barry, *Guerrilla Days in Ireland,* pg.116.

16. Ryan, Thomas, WS 783, pg.101.

17. Doody, Daniel, WS 796, pg.7.

18. O'Connell, Richard, WS 656, pg.20.

19. Meade, Seán, WS 737, pg.9.

20. O'Connell, Richard, WS 656, pg.21.

21. Meade, Maurice, WS 891, pg.26.

22. Ibid., pg.27–28.

23. Donnelly, Simon in *The Complete Book of Irish Jailbreaks 1918–1921,* Tralee, County Kerry: Anvil Books, 1971, pg.115.

24. Price, Dominic, *We Bled Together,* Cork: The Collins Press, 2017, pg.207.

25. Kennedy, Patrick, WS 499, pg.8.

26. Daly, Jeremiah, WS 1015, pg.6.

27. O'Sullivan, John, WS 1376 pg.9

28. Daly, Jeremiah, WS 1015, pg.6.

29. Willis, Richard and John Bolster, WS 808, pg.12–13.

30. Neville, Frank, WS 443, pg.12.

31. O'Leary, Diarmuid, WS 1589, pg.9.

32. Finn, Seamus, WS 858, pg.10–11.

33. Berkeley, George, WS 994, pg.121.

34. *Rebel Cork's Fighting Story,* Tralee: The Kerryman, 1947, pg.235.

35. O'Leary, Diarmuid, WS 1589, pg.6.

36. *Rebel Cork's Fighting Story*, pg.238.

37. Higgins, Patrick, WS 1467, pg.6.

38. Buckley, William, WS 1009, pg.17.

39. O'Donoghue, Michael, WS 1741, pg.146.

40. Ibid., pg.148.

41. Berkeley, George, WS 994, pg.123.

42. James Maloney, WS 1525, pg.23.

43. Seamus Fitzgerald, WS 1737, pg.31.

44. Clancy, Máire, WS 806, pg.6–17.

45. *An tÓglach*, March 1921, pg.1.

46. A member of the Black and Tans by the name of William Mitchell was hanged the same day as Foley and Maher. Mitchell, possibly innocent, was charged in connection with burglary and the murder of Robert Dixon, a magistrate in Wicklow.

47. Price, Dominic, *The Flame and the Candle*, Cork: The Collins Press, 2012, pg.135–139.

CHAPTER ELEVEN

1. Begley, Florence, WS 1771, pg.1.

2. Kelleher, Tom, 'Rout of the British at Crossbarry', *Rebel Cork's Fighting Story*, pg.156.

3. O'Driscoll, Michael, WS 1297, pg.6.

4. Kelleher, 'Rout of the British at Crossbarry', *Rebel Cork's Fighting Story*, pg.161.

5. Calnan, Cornelius, WS 1317, pg.7.

6. McNamara, *War and Revolution in the West of Ireland*, pg.132–133.

7. The serial numbers on the guns were 46, 50 and 51.

8. They used .45 ACPs (Automatic Colt Pistol rounds).

9. Other shipments of tommy-guns did reach Ireland. Fifty were landed just before the Truce and on 29 July a further fifteen arrived. Over the course of the next few months, about a hundred arrived in various small batches and were used by both sides during the Civil War.

10. Gillis, Liz, *Burning of the Custom House*, Dublin: Kilmainham Tales, 2017, pg.82.

11. Traynor, Oscar, WS 340, pg.68.

12. Gillis, *Burning of the Custom House*, pg.84.

13. Ibid., pg.107–8.

14. Colley, Harry, WS 1687, pg.81.

15. Prendergast, Seán, WS 755, pg.519.

16. Colley, Harry, WS 1687, pg.84.

17. Harpur, James, WS 536, pg.14.

18. Slattery, James, WS 445, pg.16–17.

19. Gillis, *Burning of the Custom House*, pg.124.

20. Fallon, Las, *Dublin Fire Brigade and the Irish Revolution*, Dublin: South Dublin Libraries, 2012, pg.78.

21. Traynor, Oscar, WS 340, pg.67.

22. Ó Ruairc, Pádraig Óg, *Truce*, Cork: Mercier Press, 2016, pg.36.

23. Ibid., pg.39.

24. Barry, *Guerilla Days in Ireland*, pg.224.

25. Ó Ruairc, *Truce*, pg.54.

26. Montgomery, Bernard, *The Memoirs of Field-Marshal Montgomery*, Barnsley: Pen and Sword Books, 2005, pg.39–40.

27. Ó Ruairc, *Truce*, pg.54.

28. Ó Ruairc, Pádraig Óg, 'The Women Who Died For Ireland', *History Ireland*, September/October 2018, pg.37.

29. *An tÓglach*, 22 July 1921, pg.1.

CHAPTER TWELVE

1. O'Halpin, Eunan, 'Counting Terror' in David Fitzpatrick (ed.), *Terror in Ireland*, Dublin: Lilliput, 2012, pg.152.

2. Coogan, *Michael Collins*, pg.228.

3. Connell, Joseph E.A., *Michael Collins, Dublin 1916–22*, Dublin: Wordwell, 2017, pg.393.

4. Dalton, Emmet, WS 641, pg.2–5.

5. Connell, *Michael Collins, Dublin 1916–22*, pg.394.

6. Coogan, *Michael Collins*, pg.242.

7. Ibid., pg.243.

8. Macardle, *The Irish Republic*, pg.557.

9. Ibid., pg.575–576.

10. See oireachtas.ie for full debate.

11. Coogan, *Michael Collins*, pg.310.

CONCLUSION

1. See Joe Dolan's Witness Statement number 900 with the Bureau of Military Archives. Dolan was a Free State supporter and had nothing to gain by laying the blame for the assassination with Michael Collins, his comrade.

Index

J

M